WEAVING IT TOGETHER

4

Milada Broukal

Glendale Community College

Heinle & Heinle Publishers
A Division of International
Thomson Publishing, Inc.
Boston, Massachusetts 02116 U.S.A.

I T P

The publication of *Weaving It Together 4* was directed by members of the Newbury House Publishing Team at Heinle & Heinle:

Erik Gundersen, **Editorial Director**
John McHugh, **Market Development Director**
Kristin Thalheimer, **Production Services Coordinator**

Also participating in the publication of this program were:

Publisher: Stanley J. Galek
Director of Production: Elizabeth Holthaus
Project Manager: Hockett Editorial Service
Manufacturing Coordinator: Mary Beth Hennebury
Photo Coordinator: Martha Leibs-Heckly
Senior Assistant Editor: Ken Pratt
Interior Designer: Winston • Ford Visual Communications
Illustrator: James Edwards
Photo/video specialist: Jonathan Stark
Cover Illustrator: Lisa Houck
Cover Designer: Judy Ziegler, Gina Petti

Photo Credits (page numbers are given in boldface):
Art Resource—**2, 3, 4**; Annie Leibovitz—**14**; Robert Rathe, Stock, Boston—**44** (top); Alan Becker, The Image Bank (bottom)—**44**; Jean-Claude Le Jeune, Stock, Boston—**87** (Amish); Nita Winter, The Image Works—**87** (Boy Scouts); Barbara Alper, Stock, Boston—**87** (Red Cross); Comstock—**114** (left), **208**; Melanie Carr, Zephyr Pictures—**114** (right), **143** (man at computer); Beringer/Dratch, The Image Works—**143** (man with pipe); Denise DeLuise, Zephyr Pictures— **143** (woman in hat), **155** (right); W. Hill, The Image Works—**143** (woman with briefcase); Jonathan Stark—**143** (woman with glasses); Charles Kennard, Stock, Boston—**155** (left); Frank Siteman, Stock, Boston—**189**; James Keyser, Time Magazine—**220**.

•••

Heinle & Heinle Publishers is a division of International Thomson Publishing, Inc.

Manufactured in the United States of America

Library of Congress Cataloging-in-Publication Data
Broukal, Milada.
      Weaving it together / Milada Broukal.
         p.   cm.
      ISBN 0–8384–6594–3
      1. English language—Textbooks for foreign speakers.   I. Title.
PE1128.B7149   1995
428.2'4—dc20
                                                              95–48835
                                                              CIP

10 9 8 7 6 5 4 3 2

CONTENTS

To the Teacher xi

To the Student xv

Part I: Reading and Writing 1

① Chapter 1: Artists 2

Pre-reading Questions. 2

Reading 1: Frida Kahlo 4

Vocabulary 7

Themes. 9
  Famous 9
  Deadly 10

Comprehension 11

Discussion 13

Reading 2: Christo 14

Vocabulary 16

Themes 17
  Strange and Inexplicable 17
  Transitory/Brief. 18

Comprehension 19

Discussion 21

Writing: Summary, Paraphrasing. 21

Organizing: The Essay 22
  The Introduction 23
  The Body Paragraphs 27
  Developing Body Paragraphs 27
  The Conclusion. 30

② Chapter 2: Language 32

Pre-reading Questions 32

Reading 1: Spell It in English 33

Vocabulary 37

Themes 39
  Combine 39
  The Start 40

Comprehension 40

Discussion 43

Reading 2: Coconut and Satellite 44

Vocabulary 46

Themes 47
  To Bring Back 47
  Fly 48

Comprehension 49

Discussion 51

Writing: Summary, Paraphrasing, Research 51

Student Essay: The Chinese Art of Writing 52

Student Essay Follow-Up 53

Organizing: The Process Analysis 53
  Thesis Statement for the Process Essay 54
  Organizing the Process Analysis Essay 55
  Time Expressions 55

Writing Practice 57

3 **Chapter 3: Hygiene** **59**

Pre-reading Questions 59

Reading 1: Cleanliness 60

Vocabulary 63

Themes 65
  To Please 65
  To Control 66

Comprehension 66

Discussion 69

Reading 2: Cleaner Fish 70

Vocabulary 73

Themes 74
  Judge 74
  Important 75

Comprehension 76

Discussion 78

Writing: Summary, Paraphrasing, Research 79

Student Essay: Cleanliness 80

Student Essay Follow-Up 81

Organizing: Definition: Literal and Extended 81
    Introduction to the Definition Essay 84
Writing Practice... 85

4   Chapter 4: Groups, Organizations, and Societies   87

Pre-reading Questions 87
Reading 1: The Camorra 89
Vocabulary... 92
Themes 94
    Organize 94
    Guilty People... 95
Comprehension 98
Reading 2: Stranglers in a Strange Land 99
Vocabulary.. 101
Themes 103
    Dangerous 103
    Suggest.. 104
Comprehension... 105
Discussion 106
Writing: Summary, Paraphrasing, Research.................... 106
Student Essay: Rastafarians 107
Student Essay Follow-Up 108
Organizing: Description.. 109
    The Dominant Impression 109
    Figures of Speech 109
    Metaphor... 111
Writing Practice... 112

5   Chapter 5: Psychology   114

Pre-reading Questions 114
Reading 1: Body Language..................................... 115
Vocabulary.. 117
Themes 119
    Having Little Fat 119
    Having Much Fat... 120
    Temper.. 120
Comprehension.. 120

Discussion 123

Reading 2: Extroversion and Introversion 124

Vocabulary 126

Themes 128
   Show 128
   Prefixes 129

Comprehension 130

Discussion 132

Writing: Summary, Paraphrasing, Research 133

Student Essay: Classifying Personalities by Way of Astrology . . 133

Student Essay Follow-Up 135

Organizing: Classification 135
   The Principle of Classification 135
   Introduction in the Classification Essay 138
   Transitions in the Classification Essay 138

Writing Practice 140

6 Chapter 6: Fashion in History — 142

Pre-reading Questions 142

Reading 1: The Toe of the Shoe 144

Vocabulary 147

Themes 149
   Time Periods 149
   Compound Adjectives 151

Comprehension 152

Discussion 154

Reading 2: Trousers and Skirts 155

Vocabulary 158

Themes 158
   Rough and Not Rough 159
   Foreign Words and Phrases 162

Comprehension 163

Discussion 165

Writing: Summary, Paraphrasing, Research 166

Student Essay: Short Skirts of the Twenties and Sixties 167

Student Essay Follow-Up 168

Organizing: Comparison and Contrast...........................169
   Finding Two Comparable Items................................169
   Basis of Comparison..170
   Thesis Statement...170

Organizing a Comparison and Contrast Essay.................171
   Block Organization Outline...................................171
   Point-by-Point Organization Outline.....................172

Comparison and Contrast Indicators...........................172
   Comparison Indicator Words................................173
   Contrast Indicator Words....................................173

Writing Practice...175

7 Chapter 7: Nutrition — 177

Pre-reading Questions 177

Reading 1: The Story on Food Additives.......................179

Vocabulary..182

Themes...189
   To Eat..184
   To Make Impure 185

Comprehension...185

Discussion 188

Reading 2: BGH: The Debate Goes On.........................189

Vocabulary..192

Themes...193
   To Get in the Way..193

Comprehension...194

Discussion 196

Writing: Summary, Paraphrasing, Research...................197

Student Essay: The Negative Sides of Fast Food 198

Student Essay Follow-Up..199

Organizing: Cause and Effect Essay 199
   The Cause Analysis Essay 200
   The Effect Analysis Essay...................................201
   The Causal Chain 204

Writing Practice...206

8 Chapter 8: Technology — 208

Pre-reading Questions 208

Reading 1: The World of Virtual Reality 210

Vocabulary 213

Themes 215
  Helpful 215
  Examine 216

Comprehension 217

Discussion 219

Reading 2: Crippled by Computers 220

Vocabulary 224

Themes 225
  Damage 225
  Legal Action 226

Comprehension 227

Discussion 230

Writing: Summary, Paraphrasing Research 230

Student Essay: Traps of the Information Revolution 231

Student Essay Follow-Up 233

Organizing: Argument Essay 233
  Using Specific Evidence 235

Organizing Your Argument 236
  The Introduction 236
  Body Paragraphs 236
  The Conclusion 238

Writing Practice 239

Part II: How to Write — 241

1 How to Get Ideas, Draft, Revise, and Edit — 242

A. Getting Ideas 242
  Brainstorming 242
  Clustering 242
  Freewriting 244

B. Drafting 245

C. Revising 245
  Revision Checklist 246

D. Editing...247
  Editing Checklist for Sentences and Paragraphs..........247
  Editing Symbols for Words and Punctuation..............248

2 **How to Do Library Research**   **248**

A. The Catalog..249
  Finding the Listing....................................249
  Reading the Card or Display............................250
  What to Look For.......................................251
  Getting the Book.......................................252

B. Reference Books.......................................253
  Going Online..253

C. Periodical Indexes 253

3 **How to Quote**   **255**

A. Omitting Words and Adding Words.......................255

B. Reporting Words.......................................256

4 **How to Paraphrase**   **257**

Steps for Paraphrasing...................................262

5 **How to Summarize**   **263**

  Summary Checklist.....................................267

6 **How to Construct Sentences**   **268**

A. Avoid Fragments.......................................268

B. Avoid Run-on Sentences................................272

C. Avoid Faulty Shift in Person..........................277

D. Avoid Faulty Subject and Verb Agreement...............280
  Subjects Taking a Singular Verb.......................280
  Subjects Taking a Plural Verb.........................281
  Subjects Taking Either a Singular or a Plural Verb.....281

E. Avoid Faulty Parallel Construction....................284

F. Avoid Shifts in Time..................................288

7 **Punctuation**   **291**

A. Capital Letters.......................................291

B. Quotation Marks.......................................295

C. Commas: Rules 1, 2, and 3.............................299

D. Commas: Rules 4, 5, and 6 303
E. Other Punctuation 307
   Period 307
   Question Mark 307
   Exclamation Mark 308
   Semicolon 308
   Colon 308
   Dash 308

8 Spelling   **311**
A. Confusing Word Pairs 312
B. Useful Spelling Rules 320
   The Final y 320
   The i *before* e 322
   Doubling Consonants 322
   Words with a Silent e 325
   Plurals 327

TO THE TEACHER

Rationale

Weaving It Together, Book 4, is the fourth in a four-book series that integrates reading and writing skills for students of English as a second or foreign language. The complete program includes the following:

Book 1 . . . Beginning level

Book 2 . . . High beginning level

Book 3 . . . Intermediate level

Book 4 . . . High intermediate level

The central premise of *Weaving It Together* is that reading and writing are interwoven and inextricable skills. Good readers write well; good writers read well. With this premise in mind, *Weaving It Together* has been developed to meet the following objectives:

1. To combine reading and writing through a comprehensive, systematic, and engaging process designed to effectively integrate the two.

2. To provide academically bound students with serious and engaging multicultural content.

3. To promote individualized and cooperative learning within the moderate- to large-sized class.

Over the past few years, a number of noted researchers in the field of second language acquisition have written about the serious need to effectively integrate reading and writing instruction in both classroom practice and materials development. *Weaving It Together* is, in many ways, a response to this need.

Barbara Kroll, for example, talks of teaching students to read like writers and write like readers (1993). She notes: "It is only when a writer is able to cast himself or herself in the role of a reader of the text under preparation that he or she is able to anticipate the reader's needs by writing into the text what he or she expects or wants the reader to take out from the text." Through its systematic approach to integrating reading and writing, *Weaving It Together* teaches ESL and EFL students to understand the kinds of interconnections between reading and writing that they need to make in order to achieve academic success.

Linda Lonon Blanton's research focuses on the need for second language students to develop authority, conviction, and certainty in their writing. She believes that students develop strong writing skills in concert with good reading skills. Blanton writes: "My experience tells me that empowerment, or achieving this certainty and authority, can be achieved only through performance — through the act of speaking and writing about texts, through developing individual responses to texts." (1992)

For Blanton, as for Kroll and others, both reading and writing must be treated as composing processes. Effective writing instruction must be integrally linked with effective reading instruction. This notion is at the heart of *Weaving It Together*.

Organization of the Text

Weaving It Together, Book 4, consists of two parts. The first part contains eight thematically organized units, each of which includes two reading passages, and a different aspect of essay organization. The second part, How to Write, is a practical reference guide presenting common sentence structure problems, troublesome points of usage, punctuation, and techniques for writing and essay development, together with practice exercises.

Each chapter contains the following sequence of activities:

1. **Pre-reading questions and activity:** Each chapter is introduced with visuals accompanied by a set of discussion questions. This is followed by a pre-reading activity related to the theme of the chapter. The purpose of the pre-reading questions and activity is to prepare students for the reading by activating their background knowledge and encouraging them to call on and share their experiences.

2. **Readings:** Each chapter contains two high-interest, nonfiction passages related to the theme of the chapter. The second reading is a passage selected from a book or magazine article. Each reading is followed by vocabulary activities, comprehension exercises, and discussion.

3. **Vocabulary Practice:** Vocabulary words are practiced in a multiple-choice format exercise. This is followed by a more in-depth exercise under the heading **Themes.** Here one or two words from the vocabulary are selected, and their difference in usage with regard to other words with similar meanings is examined.

4. **Comprehension:** There are three types of comprehension exercises. The first, *Looking for the Main Ideas*, concentrates on a general understanding of the reading. This exercise may be done after a first reading or used as pre-reading questions. The second comprehension exercise, *Looking for Details*, concentrates on developing skimming and scanning skills. This exercise may also be given as a pre-reading assignment. The third comprehension exercise, *Making Inferences and Drawing Conclusions*, develops the skill of inferring meaning from what is not directly stated in the passage.

5. **Discussion:** Students may work in small or large groups and interact with each other to discuss questions that arise from the reading. These questions ask students to relate their experiences to what they have learned from the reading.

6. **Writing: Writing a Summary, Paraphrasing, and Research** These optional writing activities are cross-referenced to the How to Write section where students may practice specific composition-related skills that are hard to master for many second-language writers.

7. **Model essay:** The essay in each chapter is written by an international student whose writing skills are slightly more advanced than those of the writers who will use *Weaving It Together, Book 4*. The essay follows the general rhetorical form of North American academic prose, and provides a natural preparation for the more discrete points taught in the organizing section. Follow-up work and questions about the student essay reinforce essay organization techniques.

8. **Organizing:** In each of the eight chapters, a different aspect of essay organization is developed. These aspects include essay organization, structure, transitions, and rhetorical devices the student will use to develop his/her own essay. Exercises following the points taught reinforce the organizational techniques introduced.

9. **Pre-writing:** Using brainstorming, freewriting, and clustering techniques presented in the How to Write section, students are encouraged to begin conceptualizing their work before outlining their essay.

10. **Developing an outline:** Using the ideas they have generated in the pre-writing section, students put together an outline for their essay. This outline acts as a framework for the work ahead.

11. **Writing a rough draft:** A rough draft of the essay is written. *Weaving It Together* encourages students to write several rough drafts, since writing is an ongoing recursive process.

12. **Revising your rough draft using the checklist:** Students can work on their own or with a partner to check their essays and make any necessary alterations in content. Teachers are encouraged to add to the checklist provided any further points they consider important.

13. **Editing the essay:** In this section, students are encouraged to work with a partner or their teacher to correct spelling, punctuation, vocabulary, and grammar.

14. **Writing the final copy:** Students prepare the final version of the essay.

Journal Writing

In addition to the projects and exercises in the book, I strongly recommend that students be instructed to keep a journal in which they correspond with you. The purpose of this journal is for them to tell you how they feel about the class each day. It gives them an opportunity to tell you what they like, what they dislike, what they understand, and what they don't understand. By having students explain what they have learned in the class, you can discover whether or not they understand the concepts taught.

Journal writing is effective for two major reasons. First, since this type of writing focuses on fluency and personal expression, students always have something to write about. Second, journal writing can also be used to identify language concerns and troublespots that need further review. In its finest form, journal writing can become an active dialogue between teacher and student that permits you both to learn more about your students' lives and to individualize their language instruction.

References

Blanton, Linda Lonon (1992). "Reading, Writing, and Authority: Issues in Developmental ESL." *College ESL*, 2, 11-19.

Kroll, Barbara (1993). "Teaching Writing *Is* Teaching Reading: Training the New Teacher of ESL Composition," in *Reading in the Composition Classroom* (Heinle & Heinle Publisher, Boston), 61-81.

TO THE STUDENT

This book will teach you to read and write in English. You will study readings on selected themes and learn strategies for writing a good essay on those themes. In the process, you will be exposed to the writings and ideas of others, as well as to ways of expressing your own ideas so that you can work toward writing an effective essay in English.

As you know, writing well in English may be quite different from writing well in your native language. Good Chinese or Arabic writing is different from good English writing. Not only are the styles different, but the organization is different too. Good organization in an essay written for a professor in South America is different from good organization for a professor in North America.

The processes of reading and writing are closely interconnected. Therefore, in this text we are weaving reading and writing together. I hope that the readings in this text will stimulate your interest in writing, and that Weaving It Together will make writing in English much easier for you.

Milada Broukal

Weaving It Together: **Book 4**

ACKNOWLEDGMENTS

I would like to express my gratitude to the following individuals who reviewed *Weaving It Together* at various stages of its development and who offered many ideas and suggestions:

- Cheryl Benz, Miami-Dude Community College
- Barbara Rigby-Acosta, El Paso Community College
- Greg Conner, Orange Coast College (CA)
- P. Charles Brown, Concordia University, Montreal
- Marilyn Spaventa, Santa Barbara City College
- Bettye Wheeler, El Paso Community College
- Colleen Weldele, Palomar College (CA)
- Sheri Wickham, Brookhaven College (TX)

I would also like to thank all my students at Glendale College who contributed their essays to this text. Last, but not least, my very special thanks to my editor Erik Gundersen for his insights and encouragement throughout this work.

PART I

Reading
and Writing

Chapter 1: Artists

PRE-READING QUESTIONS

Discuss these questions with your classmates or teacher.

1 Most of Frida Kahlo's works are portraits of herself. What do you think this tells us about her?

2 Which other famous artists painted self-portraits? What do the portraits say about their lives and feelings?

3 Describe the life of an artist that you know. Do you think it is difficult to be an artist? Are there hardships they have to face that other working people don't?

Match each artist named in the box below with the facts about his or her life. Then say which artist is your favorite and why.

Salvador Dali   Vincent van Gogh   Claude Monet
Georgia O'Keeffe   Paul Gauguin

1. X studied art in Chicago and New York and then became a teacher. He/she went back to becoming a painter in 1918. X married a photographer in 1924. He/she loved the New Mexico desert so much that he/she went to live there in 1929. X painted dramatic abstract landscapes, flowers, and other objects of nature. X was known for his/her independent lifestyle.

2. X was born in Paris and studied art there. While in Paris he/she met other future impressionists like himself/herself. After a period of poverty in the 1870s, he/she became more financially secure. He/she then moved to a town in France called Giverny and painted works in series such as *Rouen Cathedral* and *Waterlilies*.

3. X is considered a tragic painter because he/she never achieved recognition in his/her lifetime. In 1888 he/she moved from Paris to Arles in the south of France. Gauguin visited him/her there and the two had violent disagreements, providing X's first mental seizure. He/she started to express his/her emotional state in his/her work. In 1890 X moved north to Auver-sur-Oise where he/she committed suicide.

4. X is one of the most famous surrealist artists. X was only six when he/she sold his/her first painting. By the time X reached the age of seventy-five, he/she was so famous that a letter would reach him/her addressed only with the word *España* (Spain, which is his/her native country) and the sketch of a moustache. His/her works are highly realistic in style and have a strange dreamlike imagery.

5. In 1883 he/she gave up his/her job as a stockbroker and became a full-time painter. He/she left his/her spouse and children and emigrated from Paris to Tahiti. He/she was attracted to Polynesia because he/she believed primitive art and life was superior to so-called civilization. He/she painted the life of the people of the islands. Although X became less happy with life in Tahiti, he/she remained there until his/her death.

Reading 1: Frida Kahlo

Independence, rebelliousness, self-assurance—these are traits shared by many famous people. It seems particularly true of artists, and is certainly true of Frida Kahlo, who belonged to the first generation of famous North American women artists.

Even as a child, Mexico's best-known woman painter exhibited an independent, rebellious spirit and lack of restraint that often got her into trouble. She preferred to run, jump, and skip instead of walk, and she found it difficult to control herself even in church, where she giggled and teased her younger sister.

At the age of six, however, Frida's life changed dramatically. She got polio and was confined to her bed for nine months. The disease left Frida's right leg shorter and thinner than her left, and when she had recovered enough to return to school, she walked with a limp. She was often teased by her playmates, and although that was emotionally painful for her, she compensated by being outgoing and gained a reputation as a "character." Her father encouraged her to play sports to strengthen her leg, and eventually she was able to walk quite well. Frida's father, Guillermo, a professional photographer and amateur painter, was a great influence in her life.

In 1922, at the age of fifteen, Frida was enrolled at the National Preparatory School in Mexico City, which was near her hometown of Coyoacan. This was the beginning of the postrevolutionary period in Mexico and the country was experiencing a time of cultural rebirth as well as reform. There was a strong spirit of nationalism and pride in Mexico's heritage. Frida identified with the revolution intellectually, emotionally, and spiritually.

After a few months at the school, Frida adopted a radical[1] new look. Although her father, whom she adored, was European, Frida rejected her European clothes in favor of overalls.[2] She cut her thick, black hair short like a boy's, and rode around Coyoacan on a bicycle—shocking everyone. She even changed her birthdate from 1907 to 1910 to show her sympathy with the Mexican Revolution and to identify herself with the beginnings of modern Mexico.

Frida thrived on[3] the intellectual, social, and cultural stimulation at school. She made friends easily, and quickly became part of the notorious Cachuchas, a group of seven boys and two girls—intelligent yet rebellious students who named themselves after the caps worn at the school. Their keen[4] minds were matched only by their contempt for authority and capacity for trouble. Kahlo's natural independence and mischievous[5] nature fit right in. She cut classes and joined in their escapades.[6]

One day the Cachuchas let a donkey loose in a classroom. Another time one of the Cachuchas set off fireworks next to a dog, who ran wildly through the school creating chaos. Frida was even expelled from school once but managed to regain entrance by boldly appealing to the minister of education.

Meanwhile Frida was developing a strong sense of self-assurance and belief in herself. She showed an aptitude for science and intended to go on to medical school and become a doctor. Although she didn't become a physician, her studies in biology and physiology later influenced her work. In many of her paintings, hearts, glands, and other organs are displayed, both inside and outside the body.

A turning point[7] occurred in Kahlo's life in September 1925, when she was involved in a near-fatal accident. The bus in which she was riding home after school collided with a trolley car. The impact caused a metal rail to break loose, piercing Frida's entire body with the steel rod. The Red Cross

---

[1] radical = completely different.
[2] overalls = loose pants fastened over the shoulders, usually worn by workers over other clothes.
[3] thrived on = grew, developed.
[4] keen = sharp, quick at understanding.
[5] mischievous = bad behavior that causes trouble, especially of children.
[6] escapades = wild, exciting acts usually causing trouble.
[7] turning point = a time of important change in one's life.

doctors who arrived and examined the victims separated the injured from the dying, giving the injured first priority. They took one look at Frida and put her with the hopeless cases.

The doctors eventually treated Frida and miraculously she survived. She suffered a broken spine, collarbone, pelvis, and two broken ribs. Her right leg was broken in eleven places, and her right foot crushed. Her left shoulder was dislocated. From that point on, Frida Kahlo would never live a day without pain.

Although Frida recovered enough to lead a fairly normal life, the accident had severe psychological and physical consequences. She had to abandon her plans to become a doctor, and she had to recognize that she would be a near-invalid for the rest of her life. Her slowly healing body kept her in bed for months, and it was during this time that Kahlo began to paint. She read every book on art she could get her hands on and, exactly one year after her accident, produced her first painting, a self-portrait dedicated[8] to her school boyfriend, the leader of the Cachuchas.

Some artists look to nature or society for their inspiration, but Frida Kahlo looked inward. After her crippling accident, Kahlo depicted her pain in haunting,[9] dreamlike self-portraits. Most of her two-hundred paintings explore her vision of herself. In *The Broken Column* (1944), her body is open to reveal a cracked column in place of her spine. In *The Wounded Deer* (1946), a small deer with Frida's head and a body pierced with arrows, runs through the woods.

In 1929, Kahlo married the famous Mexican artist Diego Rivera. It would be an emotionally turbulent marriage, however, with a divorce in 1939 and remarriage in 1940. Rivera made no secret of his infidelities and caused Kahlo much pain, although his devotion and admiration for her as an artist never diminished. Rivera's betrayal of Kahlo's devotion inflicted great injury on her, as is revealed in a series of paintings depicting their relationship. "I have suffered two accidents in my life," she wrote, "One in which a streetcar ran over me. The other is Diego."

Kahlo's condition required many operations to try to straighten her spine and repair her foot, but with each one, her condition seemed to worsen. Often she painted in bed with an easel[10] her mother had designed for her. Her health seriously declined in her forties but Kahlo always kept

---

[8] dedicated = gave as a tribute to a person.

[9] haunting = not easily forgotten, remaining in the mind.

[10] easel = a wooden frame that holds a canvas while it is being painted.

her lively spirit. By then she was internationally known. When a Mexican gallery wanted to have a major exhibition of her work, she arranged to have her elaborately decorated, four-poster bed[11] carried into the gallery so that she could receive people.

Frida died in July 1954, in the same room of the bright blue house in which she had been born. She left her work as her legacy,[12] to be sure. But equally inspirational is her life story and the fact that by transforming pain into brilliant art, Kahlo triumphed[13] over misfortune.

---

[11] four-poster bed = a bed with four corner posts designed to support curtains.
[12] legacy = what she left behind after her death.
[13] triumphed = was victorious or successful.

VOCABULARY

Select the letter of the answer that is closest in meaning to the italicized word or phrase.

1. Independence, rebelliousness, *self-assurance*—these are traits shared by many famous people.
    a. optimism
    b. confidence
    c. strength
    d. moodiness

2. Kahlo showed an energetic lack of *restraint* that often got her into trouble.
    a. stress
    b. force
    c. self-control
    d. laziness

3. In church she giggled and *teased* her sister.
    a. made fun of
    b. encouraged
    c. punched
    d. punished

4. Although her playmates often teased her, and this was emotionally painful for her, she *compensated* by being outgoing.

  a. rewarded

  b. repayed

  c. forgave

  d. attacked

5. Kahlo became part of the *notorious* Cachuchas, a group of seven boys and two girls—intelligent yet rebellious students who named themselves after the caps worn at school.

  a. unpopular

  b. fearless

  c. disreputable

  d. unequaled

6. The Cachuchas' keen minds were matched only by their *contempt* for authority and capacity for trouble.

  a. doubt

  b. devotion

  c. envy

  d. hatred

7. The *impact* of the bus colliding with the trolley car caused a metal rail to break loose.

  a. crash

  b. disaster

  c. conflict

  d. bump

8. In September 1925, Kahlo was involved in a near-*fatal* accident.

  a. dangerous

  b. alarming

  c. unavoidable

  d. deadly

9. After her accident Kahlo *depicted* her pain in self-portraits.

    a. advertised

    b. taught

    c. portrayed

    d. determined

10. Kahlo's marriage to Diego Rivera was emotionally *turbulent*.

    a. stormy

    b. romantic

    c. strong

    d. delicate

Themes

Famous

notable/celebrated/eminent/
acclaimed/illustrious/renowned/notorious

The words above all mean *famous*. They differ in meaning as follows:

notable = a person or event that is worth noticing for a particular reason.

Example:

Among other things, San Francisco is notable for its Victorian architecture.

Task: What is the city in which you live notable for?

celebrated = well-known by the public. The word is usually used in speaking of intellectual or esthetic things.

Example:

The O.J. Simpson case is one of the most celebrated court cases of this century.

Task: Name a place celebrated for its beauty.

eminent = famous for outstanding qualities, usually in public life or in the academic field.

Example:

Ireland produced some eminent writers at the turn of the century.

Task: Name an eminent person and explain why he or she is famous.

illustrious = famous for noble qualities, learning, great deeds, or wealth.

Example:

The book is about the illustrious conquests of our heroes.

Task: Name an illustrious person or persons.

renowned = famous for a particular quality.

Example:

Shakespeare is renowned for his plays.

Task: Name a person who is renowned and what that person is
renowned for.

acclaimed = recognized by the public, strongly approved and praised.

Example:

The hospital was acclaimed for its heart transplant surgery.

Task: Name an organization or group of people acclaimed for something.

notorious = famous for bad things.

Example:

The artist was notorious for his shocking behavior.

Task: Name three notorious people. What were they notorious for?

Deadly

fatal/deadly/lethal/mortal

The words above all mean *bringing death*. Put each of the words in the
box below under the correct heading. You may use the same word more
than once.

disease virus	accident blow	danger injuries	poison weapon	drug mistake

fatal	lethal	deadly	mortal

A. Looking for the Main Ideas

Write complete answers to the following questions.

1. What is the main idea of paragraph 3?

2. What is paragraph 9 mostly about?

3. Which line states the main idea of paragraph 11?

4. Which sentences contain the main idea in paragraph 12?

B. Skimming and Scanning for Details

Scan the passage quickly to find the answers to these questions.
Circle the letter of the best answer.

1. As a young girl, Frida Kahlo was _____ .

    a. sweet-natured

    b. studious

    c. lazy

    d. rebellious

2. Polio left Frida with a limp, and as a result she became _____ .

    a. shy and withdrawn

    b. outgoing and unconventional

    c. polite and graceful

    d. unfriendly and mean

3. Frida's father was a _____ .

    a. photographer

    b. politician

    c. psychologist

    d. professor

4. At school, Frida joined _____ .

    a. the revolution

    b. the debating team

    c. a rebellious group of students

    d. an art club

5. When Frida was in school, her goal was to become _____ .

    a. an artist

    b. a scientist

    c. a doctor

    d. a revolutionary soldier

6. Which area of study eventually influenced Kahlo's painting?

    a. Math

    b. Physiology

    c. History

    d. Literature

7. Kahlo began to paint _____ .

    a. while she was a member of the Cachuchas

    b. after an accident left her bedridden

    c. during the Mexican Revolution

    d. when she was still a child

8. Which of the following does *not* describe Kahlo's artwork?

    a. She painted many beautiful landscapes.

    b. She often used herself as a subject for her work.

    c. She painted pictures showing pain and suffering.

    d. She painted even when she was very ill.

9. Kahlo considered her marriage to Diego Rivera _____ .

    a. a convenient arrangement

    b. one of the best things that ever happened to her

    c. essential to the advancement of her career

    d. a painful episode in her life

10. At the time of her death, Kahlo was _____ .

    a. still an unknown artist

    b. not accepted as an accomplished artist

    c. sorry she had ever taken up art

    d. a famous North American woman artist

C. Making Inferences and Drawing Conclusions

Some of the following statements can be inferred from the passage and others cannot. Circle the number of each statement that can be inferred.

1. Shy, withdrawn people are not as likely to achieve fame as bold, confident people.

2. Sometimes tragic incidents can turn out to be positive influences in our lives.

3. Frida Kahlo was influenced by events that occurred both inside and outside her own life.

4. Frida Kahlo was easily intimidated by those in positions of authority.

5. Several instances in Kahlo's life prove that she had a weak character.

6. If it were not for the bus accident in which Kahlo was involved, she probably would never have become a famous artist.

7. Frida used her art as a means to express her personal feelings.

8. Frida Kahlo's painting can be described as cheerful and optimistic.

9. Kahlo's marriage to Diego Rivera influenced her art.

10. Frida's physical disabilities would have eventually led her to withdraw from society.

DISCUSSION

Discuss these questions with your classmates.

1. How do you think that painting helped Frida Kahlo with her problems?

2. Many of Kahlo's paintings express pain and tragedy. Do you like to see that in a work of art? If so, why? If not, what would you like to see?

3. Many people judge a work of art by how realistic it is and by the technical skill of the artist. They may look at a piece of modern art and say, "Anyone can do that." Is evidence of an original mind also important? Discuss.

Reading 2: Christo

The following passage is taken from *Living with Art*, 3rd edition, an art text for college students written by Rita Gilbert, published by McGraw-Hill, New York, 1992 (reproduced with permission).

Who *is* that wrapped man?

The photographer poses a figure outdoors in New York City, all trussed up[1] like a mummy.[2] Is this human package the artist who once wrapped a wall in Rome, a girl in London, a walkway in Kansas City, a tree in Holland, a monument in Milan, a floor in Chicago? The artist who once wrapped a whole section of the Australian coast (cliffs and all) in plastic sheeting? The artist who wrapped a historic bridge in Paris with 10 acres of silky champagne-colored fabric? The artist who plans to wrap the Whitney Museum in New York and a government building in Berlin (but hasn't yet)? Has the wrapper been wrapped? If so, then this is the artist who calls himself, simply, Christo.

Despite the very public nature of his work, the man himself is something of a mystery. Christo Javecheff was born in 1935 in Bulgaria, a country of eastern Europe. He studied at the Fine Arts Academy in Sofia, his nation's capital, then traveled by way of Prague and Vienna to Paris, cross-

---

[1] trussed up = tightly wrapped or tied up.
[2] mummy = a body treated for burial with preservatives in the manner of the ancient Egyptians.

ing the border from the then-communist bloc into the West by a method he calls "a long story." It was in Paris, in 1958, that Christo began wrapping things, at first on a modest scale. As he tells it, he began with small objects, the objects he found in his studio, such as chairs and tables and bottles. In Paris, too, Christo met Jeanne-Claude de Guillebon, who became his wife and later his business manager and partner. Their son Cyril was born in 1960.

The first of the large-scale wrapped projects was made in Cologne, Germany, in 1961, when Christo allowed his own art exhibition to spill outside[3] a gallery beside the Rhine harbor onto the docks. A stack[4] of oil barrels and other harbor paraphernalia, plus rolls and rolls of industrial paper piled on the dock, soon became the *Dockside Packages*. Other ambitious wrappings followed. In 1964 Christo moved his base to New York City, but his projects keep him traveling constantly, often to far points of the globe.

For Christo, projects may have a beginning, but they don't really have an end. Even though the physical structure—the wrapping or other construction—is invariably taken away after a few days or weeks, the project remains active. Projects whose physical form has been realized, including the *Running Fence* and the *Surrounded Islands*, live in the sketches and films and photographs and recounting of their history.

Christo's most recent project was *The Umbrellas*, which called for planting 1,340 blue umbrellas at a site in Japan and 1,760 yellow umbrellas in California. Installed in November 1991, *The Umbrellas* took an unpredictable and tragic turn when one of the 485-pound yellow ones came loose in a freak accident and killed a passerby. The shocked artist had the entire installation dismantled immediately.

Some observers have criticized the artist for the transitory nature of his works. But Christo has a ready reply: "I am an artist, and I have to have courage . . . Do you know that I don't have any artworks that exist? They all go away when they're finished. Only the sketches are left, giving my works an almost legendary character. I think it takes much greater courage to create things to be gone than to create things that will remain."

---

[3] to spill outside = to go beyond a shape's borders.

[4] a stack = an orderly pile, one on top of the other.

Look at the reading on Christo to help you choose the best answer to each of the following questions.

1. Which of these words is similar in meaning to *poses* as it is used in paragraph 1?

   a. tries to control

   b. makes a choice

   c. puts in position

   d. attempts to explain

2. What is another word for *modest* in paragraph 2?

   a. large

   b. limited

   c. useful

3. Which word in paragraph 3 means "articles of various kinds"?

4. Which definition of *ambitious* is correct?

   a. deserving much praise

   b. requiring great effort

5. In paragraph 4, *invariably* means _____ .

   a. always

   b. sometimes

   c. often

   d. never

6. The best substitute for the word *realized* in paragraph 4 is _____ .

   a. accomplished

   b. repeated

7. Choose the word most similar in meaning to *installed* as used in paragraph 5.

   a. taken away

   b. formed

   c. cut off

   d. put in place

8. Which word in paragraph 5 means unusual?

9. Another way of expressing *dismantled* as it is used in the passage would be _____ .

    a. attached

    b. fixed up

    c. changed

    d. taken apart

10. Which of these statements is true?

    a. *Transitory* means long-lasting.

    b. Something that is *transitory* is different or unique.

    c. *Temporary* is similar in meaning to *transitory*.

Themes

Strange and Inexplicable

freak/weird/eerie/inscrutable

The adjectives *freak*, *weird*, *eerie*, and *inscrutable* all mean strange and inexplicable. They differ as follows:

freak = unnatural. It is usually used to describe an occurrence, such as an accident.

weird = very strange, may be supernatural or even frightening.

eerie = very strange, causing fear and uneasiness.

inscrutable = cannot be understood, mysterious. It is used to describe people or their actions.

Put the following words under the correct headings. You may use a word or words more than once.

a story	a person	a sound	a sensation
a secret	a fish	a stare	a circumstance
a place	weather conditions		a walk in a dark forest

freak	weird	eerie	inscrutable

Transitory/Brief

Transitory, or *transient,* and *brief* all mean "lasting only for a short time." They differ as follows:

transitory or **transient** = not permanent.

Example:
Life is transitory.
Life is transient.
When *transient* is used of people, it means "staying only for a short time."

brief = of a short duration.

Example:
He took a brief look at the letter.

Put the following words under the correct heading. You may use the same word more than once.

happiness	a letter	visitors	a meeting
a talk	happening	example	a story
a note	wealth	an encounter	

transitory	transient	brief

COMPREHENSION

A. Looking for Main Ideas

Some of the following statements from the Christo reading are main ideas and some are supporting statements. Find the statements in the passage. Write M in the blank in front of each main idea. Write S in the blank in front of each supporting statement.

____ 1. The artist who plans to wrap the Whitney Museum in New York and a government building in Berlin (but hasn't yet).

____ 2. If so, then this is the artist who calls himself, simply, Christo.

____ 3. Despite the very public nature of his work, the man himself is something of a mystery.

____ 4. Christo Javecheff was born in 1935 in Bulgaria, a country of eastern Europe.

____ 5. He studied at the Fine Arts Academy in Sofia, his nation's capital, then traveled by way of Prague and Vienna to Paris, crossing the border from the then-communist bloc into the West by a method he calls "a long story."

____ 6. For Christo, projects may have a beginning, but they don't really have an end.

____ 7. Even though the physical structure—the wrapping or other construction—is invariably taken away after a few days or weeks, the project remains active.

____ 8. Projects whose physical form has been realized, including the *Running Fence* and the *Surrounded Islands*, live in the sketches and films and photographs and recounting of their history.

B. Skimming and Scanning for Details

Scan the passage quickly to complete the following sentences.
Fill in the blanks.

1. Christo once wrapped a section of the _____ coast.

2. Ten acres of silky fabric were used to cover _____ .

3. Christo began wrapping things in _____ in 19___ .

4. Christo began by wrapping small objects such as _____ and _____ and _____ .

5. Jeanne-Claude de Guillebon became Christo's _____ and _____ .

6. Christo's first large-scale project was named _____ and took place in 1961 in Cologne, Germany.

7. The Cologne project involved wrapping _____ .

8. In 1964, Christo moved his base to _____ , although he continues to travel the globe.

9. Some people have criticized Christo because _____ .

10. All that is left of Christo's projects are _____ .

C. Making Inferences and Drawing Conclusions

Some of the following statements are facts from the reading. Other statements can be inferred from it. Write F in the blank in front of each factual statement. Write I in the blank in front of each inference.

___ 1. Christo is an unusual kind of artist.

___ 2. Christo's projects started out small and got bigger and bigger.

___ 3. Christo has wrapped everything from bridges to himself.

___ 4. Christo doesn't create his art to satisfy his critics.

___ 5. Christo sees value in the most common objects.

___ 6. Christo was upset when one of his umbrellas killed a passerby.

___ 7. Christo does a lot of traveling to accomplish his work.

___ 8. Christo is an international artist.

___ 9. Christo doesn't like to talk about his escape from Eastern Europe.

___10. Christo is a sensitive and courageous artist.

DISCUSSION

Discuss these questions with your classmates.

1. What do you think about the fact that Christo's art is only temporary? Do you think his work should really be considered art?

2. Why do you think Christo put his art in natural settings? Do you think it is important for artwork to be visible to the public? Discuss your reasons.

3. What is the function and status of artists in our society?

WRITING

Writing a Summary

Write a one-paragraph summary of Reading I. Check your summary with the summary checklist on page 265.

How To **Write**

HOW TO SUMMARIZE
PAGE 263

Paraphrasing

Paraphrase paragraph 4 (For Christo...) in Reading II.
Begin paraphrasing with
According to Gilbert...
Based on Gilbert's book...

How To **Write**

HOW TO PARAPHRASE
PAGE 257

The Essay

An essay consists of several paragraphs that develop one topic. An essay has three parts:

1. The Introduction

   This is generally one paragraph that introduces the topic and tells the reader what will follow in the subsequent body paragraphs. The introduction contains the **thesis statement**, which is the central idea of the essay. The thesis statement usually comes at the end of the introduction.

2. The Body Paragraphs

   The number of body paragraphs depends on the number of main points you want to discuss. The body paragraphs support the thesis statement in the introduction.

3. The Conclusion

   This paragraph ends the essay. It sums up the main points or restates the thesis statement. It also leaves the reader with a final thought or comment on the topic.

The number of paragraphs that an essay should have depends on the depth of the writer's examination of the topic. For this level, essays written in class contain from two to four paragraphs, as well as an introduction and a conclusion.

Essay Form

Introduction		
General Statements		
Thesis Statement		
Body Paragraphs		
Each body paragraph supports the thesis.		
Body Paragraph A:	Develops a single point related to the thesis.	
Body Paragraph B:	Develops a second point related to the thesis.	
Body Paragraph C:	Develops another point related to the thesis.	
Conclusion		
The conclusion restates the thesis or summarizes the main points and gives a final comment.		

▶ The Introduction

The function of an introduction in an essay is to introduce the topic and present the thesis. An introduction should also be interesting enough to make the reader want to continue on to find out what you have to say.

There are several strategies that can help make your introduction more interesting to the reader. Here are some suggestions:

Start with a strong opinion. Starting with a strong opinion can catch the reader's attention because the reader may not have thought of this point of view before.

> There are no creatures on earth less practical than humans. And nothing shows our frivolity better than fashion. From women's hoop skirts to men's high hats, fashion victims through the ages have endured the ridiculous, the uncomfortable, and the absolutely dangerous in their desire to be fashionable. Even our feet, which are normally planted firmly on the ground, have suffered the pains of keeping up with the latest craze.

Start with a question. Starting with a question is a way of breaking into a subject, using the rest of the essay, including the thesis statement, to answer the question.

> Cleanliness is considered a virtue, but just what does it mean to be clean? As most of us have had the unpleasant occasion to discover, one person's definition can be quite different from another's. From Istanbul to Indianapolis, people have their own ways of keeping clean and their own reasons for doing so.

Start with a quotation. Starting with a quotation can make your introduction lively. The quotation should be directly linked to the main idea of the essay. It can be a well-known saying, a remark from a well-known person, or a line from a song or poem.

> "Let me have men about me that are fat," says Shakespeare's Julius Caesar to Marcus Antonius. In his opinion, fat people are more trustworthy than thin ones, that is, those with a "lean and hungry look," who "are dangerous."

Start with an anecdote. Starting with an anecdote or story makes an abstract idea more real to the reader. The anecdote should be related to the thesis.

> Imagine walking on the surface of Mars. You follow the channels where water is believed to have once flowed, hike across the flat plains covered with rocks of all sizes, and jump the basin called

Hellas, measuring more than 930 miles across. After you explore the polar caps, you climb the huge volcano Olympus Mons, which is twice as high as Earth's highest peak. Seem impossible? It may be in the real world, but not in virtual reality.

An introduction has two parts:

    1. General statements

    2. Thesis statement

1. General Statements

The first sentence in an introductory paragraph should be a general statement about the topic. Its purpose is to get the reader's attention (see the above introductions) and to give background information on the topic. Each statement that follows the general statement should be more specific than the one before it, usually ending with the thesis statement. Your introduction, therefore, will have a funnel shape as seen in the diagram below.

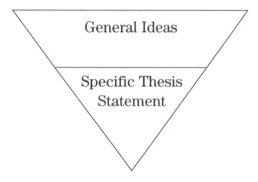

2. Thesis Statement

The thesis statement is usually the last sentence in the introduction. It is also the most important sentence in the introduction. A thesis statement gives the specific topic and central idea of the whole essay. It states the writer's approach to (method of organization) or attitude to the central idea, and may list the subtopics that will be discussed in the body paragraphs. Each of the topic sentences in the body paragraphs should relate to the thesis statement.

Remember these points about a thesis statement:

    1. It states the main topic.

    2. It may list subdivisions of the topic.

    3. It may indicate the method of organization.

The thesis statement should also:

- be expressed in a complete sentence.

- express an opinion, an idea, or a belief. It should not be a plain fact.

Example:

Not a thesis statement:
Diet colas contain artificial sweeteners.

Thesis statement:
Artificial sweeteners in diet colas may be dangerous to one's health.

- express only one idea about a topic. If it expresses more than one, the essay will lack unity.

Example:

Not a thesis statement:
Advertising on American television is becoming more sophisticated and there are some interesting movies.

Thesis statement:
Advertising on American television is becoming more sophisticated.

- not just announce a topic.

Example:

Not a thesis statement:
I am going to write about traffic problems in Thailand.

Thesis statement:
Traffic problems in Thailand disrupt people's lives.

| Exercise 1 |

Read the following sentences. Some are thesis statements and some are not. Put a check mark next to each thesis statement.

____ 1. Art has played a vital role in society since the earliest cave dwellers painted scenes on cave walls.

____ 2. Art today is more varied than at any other time in history, and art is one way to help people with emotional problems.

____ 3. Art is a form of human expression, and thus a means of fulfilling an important human need.

____ 4. I am going to write about the function of art during the Renaissance.

____ 5. We can enrich our lives by developing a more active appreciation of the art we live with.

_____ 6. For children, painting and drawing are play activities.

_____ 7. Folk art is a term applied to works made by individuals with no academic training in art.

_____ 8. Folk art is a spontaneous, personal, and appealing form of art.

_____ 9. Modern artists enjoy much greater freedom than artists of even a few generations ago, and photography is now considered an art form of its own.

_____10. The social role of artists has changed over time.

_____11. A patron is a person who buys or orders works of art.

_____12. Without patrons, artists could not prosper.

Exercise 2

Read the following introductory paragraphs and answer the questions that follow.

There is a difference between being an onlooker and being a true observer of art. Onlookers just walk by a work of art, letting their eyes record it while their minds are elsewhere. They have no true appreciation of art. Observers, on the other hand, are informed and appreciative. They have spent the time and energy to educate themselves so that art will be meaningful. They don't just exist side by side with art, they live with it and are aware of its existence in even the smallest part of their daily lives.

1. What is the topic?
2. What is the thesis statement?
3. What device is used to catch the reader's interest?

What is art? People in the past always thought they knew what art was. Today, however, art is harder to define. Art in this century is far more complex, for several different reasons. People are exposed to the art of many times and cultures. Much of modern art is difficult to classify. And to further complicate things, we now have works of art created in media undreamed of a few decades ago, including electronic images that may disappear within moments of their creation. It's no wonder that people are asking what exactly art is and isn't, and how we can tell the difference.

4. What is the topic?
5. What is the thesis statement?
6. What device is used to catch the reader's interest?

"The only difference between me and a madman is that I am not mad," said Salvador Dali, probably the most famous Surrealist artist. Like many other modern artists, such an Vincent van Gogh, Edvard Munch, and Jean Dubuffet, Dali was interested in the relationship between madness and creativity. Certainly the works of these artists, with their swirling lines, strange scenes and fantastic dreamlike quality, appear to be the products of unstable minds. Van Gogh produced a whole body of work while in an asylum, so the question of whether madness contributed to his work, and might even have been the force behind it, is a valid one. Where does creativity end and madness begin? Is the line that separates them so thin as to be unrecognizable? These are questions that must be explored in any study of the relationship between madness and creativity in the world of art.

7. What is the topic?

8. What is the thesis statement?

9. What device is used to catch the reader's interest?

▶ The Body Paragraphs

The number of paragraphs in the body of an essay written for this class may range from two to four. Their function is to explain or prove the thesis statement.

Remember the following points about body paragraphs:

1. *The main idea of the body paragraph should support the thesis statement.* If the thesis statement is about the advantages of exercise—"Regular exercise is beneficial to health."—then the topic sentence of each body paragraph should be about *how* regular exercise is beneficial for health.

2. *Each body paragraph should discuss one aspect of the thesis.* If you are writing about the benefits of exercise, then each body paragraph would discuss one benefit of exercise for health.

3. *The body paragraphs should follow an order.* The order of the paragraphs is determined by the type of organization you are using. Each body paragraph should follow the other smoothly through the use of transitions.

▶ Developing Body Paragraphs

Once you have written a thesis statement, you can develop the topics for the body paragraphs in several ways, depending on your thesis statement. You can break it into reasons, steps in a process, advantages and disadvantages, causes, effects, examples, points of comparison and contrast.

A simple way of developing body paragraphs is to look at the central idea of the thesis statement and turn it into a question. The answers to the question will help you decide on the body paragraphs.

Example:
Thesis statement:
Regular exercise is beneficial to health.
Question:
In what way is regular exercise beneficial to health?
Answers:
Exercise is good for blood circulation.
It burns up extra calories.
It keeps the body and muscles flexible.

The central idea of the thesis statement is *beneficial to health*. Asking the question "in what way?" provides the answers above. Each body paragraph would focus on a different benefit of exercise.

Example:
Thesis statement:
Hawaii and Alaska have some similarities.
Question:
What similarities?
Answers:
Both are not connected to the forty-eight contiguous states.
Both have a large population of native peoples.
Both are expensive states in which to live.

Here the body paragraphs break down by looking at the points of similarity.

Exercise 3

Look at the following thesis statements and the two supporting topic sentences that follow the question that is being asked and write the last topic sentence.

1. Thesis: There are advantages to having a small family.

Topic sentences:

I. Parents can afford more things.

II. Family decisions are easier.

III. _____.

2. *Thesis: Watching television has harmful effects on society.*

Topic sentences:

I. Families no longer talk to each other.

II. People lose interest in their community.

III. _____.

3. *Thesis: New York and Los Angeles have many contrasts.*

Topic sentences:

I. There are climatic differences.

II. There are differences in cultural life.

III. _____.

4. *Computers have benefitted society in different ways.*

Topic sentences:

I. Operations are made faster.

II. Fewer workers are needed, saving money for employers.

III. _____.

5. *Thesis: There are advantages to stopping smoking.*

Topic sentences:

I. You can have a better social life.

II. You can get back your self-esteem.

III. _____.

➡️ The Conclusion

The final paragraph, or conclusion, should make the reader feel that you have completed what you set out to do in your thesis statement. The conclusion is often introduced or signaled for the reader by a transition, such as "in conclusion," "to sum up," or "thus."

What you say in the conclusion depends on what you developed in your essay. However, here are some points to consider in writing a standard conclusion.

A conclusion consists of:

- a restatement of the thesis in different words.

or

- a restatement of the main points of the essay and a final comment on the subject, based on what you have written. Do not, however, bring up a new topic in the conclusion.

Read the following introduction and the sample concluding paragraph.

There is a difference between being an onlooker and being a true observer of art. Onlookers just walk by a work of art, letting their eyes record it while their minds are elsewhere. They have no true appreciation of art. Observers, on the other hand, are informed and appreciative. They have spent the time and energy to educate themselves so that art will be meaningful. They don't just exist side by side with art, they live with it and are aware of its existence in even the smallest part of their daily lives.

In conclusion, onlookers are unaware and unappreciative of the art surrounding them in their daily lives. Observers, having educated themselves, are able to admire, enjoy, and appreciate art at any level, from a bold and imaginative magazine advertisement to an architecturally classic public building to an Impressionist painting in an art museum. Rather than allow the rich visual world to slip by them, observers pause to let their eyes and minds absorb artistic images of all kinds. Their deep appreciation of artistic expression stretches their intellectual and emotional experiences, thus opening up new areas of enjoyment.

Read the following introductions and write your own concluding paragraphs.

1. What is art? People in the past always thought they knew what art was. Today, however, art is harder to define. Art in this century is far more complex, for several different reasons. People are exposed to the art of many times and cultures. Much of modern art is difficult to classify. And to further complicate things, we now have works of art created in media undreamed of a few decades ago, including electronic images that may disappear within moments of their creation. It's no wonder that people are asking what exactly art is and isn't, and how we can tell the difference.

2. "The only difference between me and a madman is that I am not mad," said Salvador Dali, probably the most famous Surrealist artist. Like many other modern artists, such as Vincent van Gogh, Edvard Munch, and Jean Dubuffet, Dali was interested in the relationship between madness and creativity. Certainly the works of these artists, with their swirling lines, strange scenes and fantastic dreamlike quality, appear to be the products of unstable minds. Van Gogh produced a whole body of work while in an asylum, so the question of whether madness contributed to his work, and might even have been the force behind it, is a valid one. Where does creativity end and madness begin? Is the line separating them so thin as to be unrecognizable? These are questions that must be explored in any study of the relationship between madness and creativity in the world of art.

Chapter 2: Language

Heere bigynneth the Knyghtes Tale.

Whilom, as olde stories
  tellen us,
Ther was a duc that highte
  Theseus;
Of Atthenes he was lord
  and governour,
And in his tyme swich
  a conquerour
That gretter was ther noon
  under the sonne.

Once, as old stories tell,
  there was a prince
Named Theseus that in
  Athens ruled long since,
A conqueror in his time;
  for rich lands won
There was no greater
  underneath the sun.

PRE-READING QUESTIONS

Discuss these questions with your classmates or teacher.

1 Look at the photograph of the Old English manuscript and the modern translation. Which words are spelled differently today?

2 Which letters of the alphabet are written differently?

3 There were no spelling rules when Old English was spoken. What problems do you think people had as a result of this?

4 Do you think spelling rules are important? Why or why not?

5 What spelling rules do you know in English?

Six words in the list below are spelled wrong. Find the misspelled words and correct them. Use a dictionary to check your answers.

1. pronunciation (the way you say a word)

2. batchelor (unmarried male)

3. superintendant (manager)

4. exerpt (selected passage from a book or film)

5. absorption (process of being absorbed)

6. tarrif (import fee)

7. occurence (happening)

8. newstand (place where you buy newspapers and magazines)

9. separate (to move apart)

10. nighttime (at night)

Reading 1: Spell It in English

English spelling is confusing and chaotic, as any student of English knows all too well. "How can the letters *ough* spell so many different sounding words," they ask, "like *dough, bough, rough,* and *through?*" And what about a word like *colonel* that clearly contains no *r,* yet pretends it does, and *ache* with its *k* sound, instead of the *chuh* sound of *arch?* And why does *four* have a *u* while *forty* doesn't? There are no simple rules for English spelling, but there is an explanation behind its complexity. We have only to look back in history.

The British Isles

Over the centuries, the English language has been like a magnet, attracting words from numerous other languages. It all started with the Britons, an ancient people living in a part of western Europe that eventually became the British Isles.[1] They spoke a language called Celtic, which was a combi-

---

[1] The British Isles = Great Britain (England, Scotland, Wales) and Ireland.

nation of the early forms of Irish,[2] Scottish,[3] and Welsh.[4] When the Britons were conquered by the Romans and later the Germanic tribes, their language was also invaded. The merging of the languages gave birth to Old English (an early form of the Modern English we know), and a Latin alphabet replaced, with a few exceptions, the ancient Germanic alphabet. In the ninth century, the conquering Norsemen from Scandinavia added their pinch of language spice,[5] as did the French in the eleventh century.

By the fourteenth century, English, with its mix of at least five languages, had evolved into what is called Middle English and had become Britain's official language. At that time, however, its spellings were far from consistent or rational. Many dialects had developed over the centuries and sometimes people adopted the spelling used in one part of the country and the pronunciation used in another. For instance, today we use the western English spellings for *busy* and *bury*, but give the first the London pronunciation *bizzy* and the second the Kentish[6] pronunciation *berry*. Of course, this all happened when English was primarily a spoken language, and only scholars knew how to read and write. Even they appear to have been quite indifferent to matters of consistency in spelling, and were known to spell the same word several different ways in a single sentence.

Even after William Caxton set up England's first printing press in the late fifteenth century, and the written word became available to everyone, standard spelling wasn't considered very important. As a matter of fact, the typesetters in the 1500s made things even worse by being very careless about spelling. If a blank space needed to be filled or a line was too long, they simply changed the spellings of words to make them fit. Moreover, many of the early printers in England were from Germany or Holland and didn't know English very well. If they didn't know the spelling of a word, they made up one! Different printers each had their favorite spellings, so that one word might be spelled five or six different ways, depending on who printed the passage.

Throughout this period, names and words appear in many different forms. For instance, *where* can be found as *wher, whair, wair, wheare, were,* and so on. People were even very liberal about their names. More than eighty spellings of Shakespeare's name have been found, among

---

[2] Irish = the language of Ireland.

[3] Scottish = the language of Scotland.

[4] Welsh = the language of Wales.

[5] a pinch of language spice = a little bit of variety in the language.

[6] Kentish = of Kent, a county in Southeast England.

them *Shagspeare, Shakspeare,* and even *Shakestaffe.* Shakespeare himself didn't spell his name the same way in any two of his six known signatures—he even spelled his name two different ways in his will.

By the late sixteenth century and early seventeenth centuries, some progress had been made in standardizing spelling due to the work of various scholars. By then, however, English spelling was far from a simple phonetic system. For one thing, word pronunciations had changed too rapidly for a truly phonetic spelling to keep up. Also, English had borrowed from many languages and ended up having far too many sounds (more than forty) for the twenty-six letters in its Roman alphabet. By the time printing houses finally began to agree on standard spellings, many of these written forms were only a shadow of their spoken selves. In other words, spelling and pronunciation sometimes had little in common.

Finally in 1775, Samuel Johnson gave English its first great dictionary. His choice of spellings may not have always been the best or the easiest, but the book helped to make the spellings of most English words uniform. Eventually, people became aware of the need for "correct" spelling. Meanwhile, on the other side of the Atlantic, Noah Webster was standardizing American English in his *American Dictionary of the English Language* and *American Spelling Book.* Although the British had been complaining about the messiness of English spelling for some time, it was the Americans with their fanaticism for efficiency who screamed the loudest. Webster not only favored a simplified, more phonetic spelling system, but also tried to persuade Congress to pass a law making the use of nonstandard spelling a punishable offense.

Mark Twain[7] was of the same mind—but laziness figured into his opinion. He wasn't concerned so much with the difficulty of spelling words as he was with the trouble in writing them. He became a fan of the "phonographic alphabet," created by Isaac Pitman, the inventor of shorthand—a system in which symbols represent words, phrases, and letters. "To write the word 'laugh,'" Twain wrote in *A Simplified Alphabet,* "the pen has to make fourteen strokes—no labor is saved to penman." But to write the same word in the phonographic alphabet, Twain continued, the pen had to make just three strokes. As much as Twain would have loved it, Pitman's phonographic alphabet never caught on.

---

[7] Mark Twain = A famous American author (1835–1910) who wrote many books including *The Adventures of Tom Sawyer* and *The Adventures of Huckleberry Finn.*

Interest in reforming English spelling continued to gain momentum on both sides of the Atlantic. For a while, it seemed as if every famous writer and scholar had jumped on the spelling bandwagon.[8] Spelling reform associations began to pop up everywhere. In 1876, the American Philological Association called for the "urgent" adoption of eleven new spellings: *liv, tho, thru, wisht, catalog, definit, gard, giv, hav, infinit,* and *ar.* In the same year, the Spelling Reform Association was formed, followed three years later by a British version.

In 1906, the philanthropist Andrew Carnegie gave $250,000 to help establish the Simplified Spelling Board. The board quickly issued a list of 300 words that were commonly spelled two ways, such as *ax* and *axe,* and called for the simplest of the two. The board helped to gain acceptance for quite a few American spellings, including *catalog, demagog,* and *program.*

Eventually the Simplified Spelling Board got carried away with its work, calling for such spellings as *tuff, def, troble,* and *yu.* The call for simplified spelling quickly went out of fashion, particularly with the onset of World War I and the death of Andrew Carnegie. The movement never died out completely, however. Spelling reform continued to be an ongoing, if less dramatic, process, as it had been for centuries. Without the benefit of large donations or outside agencies, many words have shed useless letters. *Deposite* has lost its *e,* as has *fossile* and *secretariate. Musick* and *physick* have dropped their needless *k*'s, and *catalogue* and *dialogue* have shed their last two vowels.

As long as the world goes around, language will continue to change. New words will be added; spellings will be altered. But because people are most comfortable with the familiar, it's not likely that we'll ever see a major change in the way most words are spelled. Anyway, what would we do without the challenge of English spelling?

---

[8] jump on the bandwagon = join the majority.

Select the letter of the answer that is closest in meaning to the italicized word or phrase.

1. The *merging* of the different languages gave birth to Old English.

    a. crossing

    b. confusion

    c. blending

    d. complication

2. By the fourteenth century, English with its mix of languages *evolved* into what is called Middle English.

    a. improved

    b. appeared

    c. spread

    d. developed

3. Even scholars were quite *indifferent* to matters of consistency in spelling, and were known to spell the same word in different ways in a single sentence.

    a. uncaring

    b. superior

    c. unsocial

    d. confused

4. People were even *liberal* about the spellings of their names, using different spellings on the same page.

    a. receptive

    b. interested

    c. understanding

    d. free

5. Americans with their *fanaticism* for efficiency complained the most about the messiness of English spelling.

    a. spirit

    b. obsession

    c. excitement

    d. fascination

6. Interest in reforming English spelling continued to *gain momentum* on both sides of the Atlantic.

    a. be temporary

    b. become stable

    c. grow stronger

    d. get weak

7. The *philanthropist* Andrew Carnegie gave $250,000 to help establish the Simplified Spelling Board.

    a. person who is an expert in language

    b. kindhearted person who actively helps others

    c. person who is famous for his or her written work

    d. person known for his or her wealth

8. The Spelling Board outlived its usefulness when it *got carried away* with its work.

    a. became over-enthusiastic

    b. was removed

    c. got to continue

    d. became successful

9. The call for simplified spelling went out of fashion with the *onset* of World War I.

    a. outcome

    b. tragedy

    c. end

    d. start

10. Many words *shed* useless letters.

    a. changed

    b. kept

    c. dropped

    d. added

Combine

· ·

mix/blend/merge/mingle

The words above all mean *to combine*. They differ in meaning as follows:

mix = to combine to make a whole, so that parts cannot be separated from each other.

blend = to combine into a whole, looking harmonious together.

merge = to become part of something else, or part of something larger.

mingle = to mix with another thing or with people so as to become an undivided whole, yet retain individual characteristics.

Fill in the blanks with one or more of the combining verbs above. Use the correct tense.

1. *They _____ different varieties of coffee for this taste.*

2. *The artist _____ yellow and blue to get the green color he wanted.*

3. *The prince left the palace at night _____ with the people in the streets.*

4. *They _____ the two companies for greater power.*

5. *The color of the painting _____ well with the colors of the room.*

6. *To make this cake you must _____ all the ingredients together well before you bake it.*

7. *The new student didn't _____ well with the others in her class.*

8. *Don't forget to _____ with the other guests at the party.*

beginning/onset

Both the *beginning* and the *onset* mean the *start*. However, they differ as follows:

beginning = the starting point.

onset = the beginning of something bad, or the first attack of something bad, something that you don't want.

Some of the words in the box below go with *onset*, some go with *beginning*, and some relate to both. Put each of the words under the correct heading.

a disease	a war	a performance	a bad cold
summer	winter	a dispute	a trip
vacation	quarrel	ceremony	a good friendship

beginning	onset

COMPREHENSION

A. Looking for the Main Ideas

Circle the letter of the best answer.

1. The main idea of paragraph 3 is
   a. by the time English had become a written language, the influence of several languages and dialects had made spelling and pronunciation very inconsistent.
   b. scholars didn't help the problem of spelling inconsistency because they often spelled words several different ways.

c. in Britain, English words had different spellings and pronunciations in different parts of the country.

d. by the fourteenth century, English had evolved into Middle English and was Britain's official language.

2. Paragraph 6 is mostly about

a. how progress was made in standardizing spelling by the seventeenth century.

b. why English spelling and pronunciation were often very different.

c. how English had many more sounds than it had letters in its alphabet.

d. why printing houses played a role in standardizing spelling.

3. Paragraph 12 is mainly concerned with

a. the work of the Simplified Spelling Board.

b. why the call for simplified spelling went out of fashion.

c. the many words that have been shortened by dropping useless letters.

d. the ongoing changes in English spelling.

B. Skimming and Scanning for Details

Scan the passage quickly to find the answers to the following questions. Write complete answers.

1. According to the passage, what combination of languages formed the Celtic language?

2. Name four conquering peoples whose languages affected the development of the English language.

3. Before the invention of the printing press, English was mostly what kind of language?

4. Why were the typesetters of the 1500s not very helpful when it came to making spelling standard?

5. Who was responsible for giving English its first great dictionary?

6. What kind of spelling system did Noah Webster favor?

7. What is shorthand and who invented it?

8. What purpose did spelling reform associations serve?

9. In the last sentence of paragraph 11, to what does the last *their* refer?

10. Why are we not likely to see major changes in the way words are spelled?

C. Making Inferences and Drawing Conclusions

The answers to these questions are not directly stated in the passage. Circle the letter of the best answer.

1. The passage implies that

    a. conquering tribes forced the Britons to speak their languages.

    b. English was a "pure" language before the fourteenth century.

    c. the influence of other languages made English a rich but complicated language.

    d. when Britain made English its official language, it stopped foreign words from entering the language and making English even more complicated.

2. From the passage, it can be concluded that

    a. scholars weren't much more educated than the masses.

    b. until the first dictionaries were written, even educated people weren't overly concerned with the spelling of words.

    c. the invention of the printing press didn't have a significant influence on the English language.

    d. there was no real need for an English dictionary before Johnson wrote his in 1755.

3. It can be inferred from the passage that

    a. if it weren't for Mark Twain, many English words would now be spelled differently.

    b. Andrew Carnegie never played a significant role in the area of American spelling.

  c. spelling reform associations had less influence on English spelling changes than the natural course of language changes today.

  d. thanks to many concerned people, spelling is simpler now than it was 200 years ago.

4. The author's tone is

  a. informal.

  b. sentimental.

  c. insincere.

  d. argumentative.

DISCUSSION

Discuss these questions with your classmates.

1. How would you simplify English spelling?

2. Why do you think proposals to reform English spelling have not won support?

3. If a spelling system based on pronunciation were devised in English, on whose pronunciation would you base it?

Reading 2: Coconut and Satellite

The following extracts are taken from the book *Great Expressions* by Marvin Vanoni, published by William Morrow & Co., New York, 1992. They illustrate the historical development of the words *coconut* and *satellite*.

Coconut

Portuguese parents of the six-teenth century threatened their children with the bogeyman[1] if they didn't behave. They called the bogeyman *coco*, from a Latin expression meaning "skull."[2] No child had ever actually seen a *coco*, but they knew it had an ugly face.

The Portuguese traders who first arrived at the Pacific Islands found a variety of palm trees that bore a large brown nut about the same size as a man's head. They were shocked to see three black marks on the nut—two eyes and a mouth. It resembled a bogeyman so much that they called it *coconut*. The word was soon adopted by the English and is still with us today.

---

[1] bogeyman = an imaginary monster used to threaten children.

[2] skull = the bone of the head.

Satellite

No other city, ancient or modern, can be compared with Rome in terms of world domination. For a period of more than a thousand years the metropolis was the hub of Western civilization. Eventually, however, the very life of the Empire was threatened by economic unrest and a series of rapid changes in government.

Matters reached such a state that no person of importance dared to walk the streets of the capital without an escort. Many notables were literally surrounded by armed bodyguards; members of such a guard were known as satellites, from an old name for an "attendant."

Despite their satellites, one aristocrat after another was murdered. External difficulties multiplied, the Empire crashed, and classical Latin ceased to be the language of commerce and science. But learned men revived the ancient tongue ten centuries later and used it for most formal speech. Among the resurrected terms was *satellite*, which medieval rulers[3] applied to their personal guards.

Johannes Kepler[4] (1571–1630) thought of the king's satellites when he heard about the strange bodies revolving about Jupiter. Discovered by Galileo,[5] the secondary planets hovered about the planet like guards and courtiers[6] encircling a prince. So in 1611 Kepler named them *satellites;* soon the term was applied to all heavenly bodies[7] that revolve about primary masses.[8]

---

[3] medieval rulers = rulers in the period of history between 1100 and 1500.

[4] Johannes Kepler = A German astronomer who discovered the shape of the planets' orbits around the sun.

[5] Galileo = (1564–1642) An Italian astronomer who was the first to use a telescope. He made several important discoveries, including the orbiting planets of Jupiter.

[6] courtiers = officers or attendants of a king or queen.

[7] heavenly bodies = planets, stars, satellites, etc.

[8] primary masses = planets.

Look at the "Satellite" passage to answer the following questions.

1. Which word is most similar in meaning to *domination* as it is used in paragraph 1?

    a. government

    b. balance

    c. power

    d. courage

2. Which word in paragraph 1 means "capital city"?

3. Which of these words is closest in meaning to *hub* as used in the passage?

    a. mystery

    b. center

    c. spectacle

    d. origin

4. Which word in paragraph 1 means *dissatisfaction*?

5. What is an *escort*, as used in paragraph 2?

    a. a weapon used for protection

    b. a person who guards another

6. Which of these statements is true?

    a. Notables are famous or important people.

    b. Notables are people who worked for the government.

7. Which of the following is closest in meaning to the phrase "literally surrounded" in paragraph 2?

    a. actually surrounded

    b. surrounded by educated people

    c. surrounded according to writings

8. What would be another way of expressing the word *ceased* as used in the passage?

    a. was terminated

    b. completed

    c. stopped

    d. concluded

9. What word in paragraph 3 is similar in meaning to *resurrected*?

10. What does *hovered about* in paragraph 4 mean?

      a. moved around in the air

      b. moved cautiously about

      c. stayed in the air in one place

      d. stayed in a line in the air

Themes

To Bring Back

revive/restore

Both *revive* and *restore* mean to bring back into use or existence. The difference in meaning is as follows:

revive = to bring back into existence (life) or to take place again.

restore = to bring back to the original state or bring back into use.

The words in the box below belong either with *revive* or *restore*. Put them under the correct headings.

furniture	old customs	an old building	to health
a work of art	a person	a plant	a ruined temple
old feelings of anger		peace	

revive	restore

Look up the verbs *resurrect* and *resuscitate*.

> Which of the following can be used with *resuscitate?*
> a custom   a hope   a dying person   a fashion

Fly

fly/hover/glide/soar/swoop

fly = to move through the air or cause to move through the air.

hover = to stay in the air in one place, usually used in speaking of birds and certain kinds of aircraft.

glide = to move in the air in a smooth, easy, and silent way without using energy.

soar = to fly fast or high. Also used when speaking of rising prices and temperature.

swoop = to fly down quickly, especially in attack.

Complete the sentences with one [or more] of the verbs above. Use the correct verb tense.

1. A cloud of dust _____ over the city.

2. The bag _____ across the room and hit me on the head.

3. Few people could afford to buy a new car when prices _____ with the new tax.

4. I often wonder how the eagle can _____ effortlessly in the sky without moving its wings.

5. The rocket _____ up into the sky.

6. When she threw the seeds, the birds _____ down to eat them.

7. The helicopter _____ above the man in trouble on the mountain.

8. The boat seemed to _____ over the lake.

A. Looking for the Main Ideas

Some of the following statements from the two excerpts are main ideas and some are supporting statements. Find the statements in the reading. Write M in the blank in front of each main idea. Write S in the blank in front of each supporting statement.

___ 1. Portuguese parents of the sixteenth century threatened their children with the bogeyman if they didn't behave.

___ 2. No child had ever actually seen a *coco*, but they knew it had an ugly face.

___ 3. No other city, ancient or modern, can be compared with Rome in terms of world domination.

___ 4. For a period of more than a thousand years the metropolis was the hub of Western civilization.

___ 5. Johannes Kepler (1571–1630) thought of the king's satellites when he heard about the strange bodies revolving about Jupiter.

___ 6. Discovered by Galileo, the secondary planets hovered about the planet like guards and courtiers encircling a prince.

___ 7. So in 1611 Kepler named them satellites; soon the term was applied to all heavenly bodies that revolve around primary masses.

B. Skimming and Scanning for Details

Scan the passage quickly to complete the following sentences.

1. *The Portuguese word for bogeyman was _____, a word taken from a Latin expression meaning _____.*

2. *The Portuguese traders thought the three black marks on the palm nut looked like _____.*

3. *The Portuguese traders called the palm nut a _____ because they thought it looked like _____.*

4. *The Roman empire was threatened by* _____ *and rapid changes in* _____.

5. *Life became so dangerous for aristocrats that they dared not* _____.

6. *Important people began to surround themselves with* _____, *who became known as satellites.*

7. *The word* satellite *came from an old word for* _____.

8. *When the Roman empire was destroyed, the Latin language stopped being used for* _____ *and* _____.

9. *When the Latin language was revived after centuries, medieval rulers used the word* satellite *to refer to their* _____.

10. _____ *gave the name satellite to the heavenly bodies revolving around* _____.

C. Making Inferences and Drawing Conclusions

Some of the following statements are facts taken from the reading. Other statements can be inferred from the reading. Write F in the blank in front of each inference.

____ 1. Sixteenth century Portuguese parents tried to frighten their children into behaving.

____ 2. Latin has been one of the most influential languages in the world.

____ 3. Childhood experiences influence our behavior throughout our lives.

____ 4. The Portuguese traders saw a resemblance between the palm nut and the dreaded coco of their childhood.

____ 5. The Portuguese traders had vivid imaginations.

____ 6. Latin influenced English and other languages many years after Latin was no longer spoken.

___ 7. Throughout history, no other city has had the power of Rome.

___ 8. Even the greatest civilization can fall into ruin.

___ 9. Rome was destroyed by both internal and external forces.

___10. As time goes on, sometimes words can become more generalized in their meaning.

DISCUSSION

Discuss these questions with your classmates.

1. Certain English words are formed by combining parts of two other words, usually the first part of one and the last part of another. An example of this is *smog*, which is a combination of *smoke* and *fog*. Other examples include *brunch* and *motel*. Words formed with this technique are called portmanteau words. Create five new portmanteau words.

2. Describe the process you would use in learning a new language.

3. Imagine that four of you are together in a deserted part of the world. None of you speaks the same language. Describe the process of creating a language to communicate with each other.

WRITING

Writing a Summary

Write a one-paragraph summary of Reading 1.
Check your summary with the Summary Checklist on page 265.

How To **Write**

HOW TO SUMMARIZE
PAGE 263

Paraphrasing

Paraphrase paragraph 1 of "Satellite" in Reading 2. Begin paraphrasing with According to Vanoni, . . .
or
Based on Vanoni's work, . . .

How To **Write**

HOW TO PARAPHRASE
PAGE 257

Research

You may use your research later to write a process analysis essay.

Choose a process, procedure, or event leading to a change over a period of time.

How To **Write**

HOW TO DO LIBRARY RESEARCH
PAGE 248

*Consult appropriate sources in the library and/or use your own expe-
rience or that of friends to gather information.*

The following are suggested topics:

How the education system works (in the United States or your country).
How the digestive system works.
How a holiday is celebrated (in the United States or your country).
How babies learn to talk.
How to learn to use a computer.
How you get a divorce.
How a volcano explodes.

Read the following essay written by a student.

The Chinese Art of Writing

Chinese is one of the most remarkable pieces of art in language
that humankind has ever made. In elementary school, Chinese teachers ask their students to write not only correctly but beautifully by
printing a picture for each character. Chinese is different from western languages such as German, French, or English because it has no
alphabet. Instead it contains 50,000 characters. If a person knows
5,000 of the most commonly used characters, they can read a newspaper. The more characters a person knows indicates how intellectual
that person is. Chinese is one of the world's oldest languages and its
written form as in most languages developed from the pictograph.

Five thousand years ago, Thi Chi was credited with the invention
of the written Chinese language. He created the first Chinese characters by imitating the shapes of living things in the world. The sign for
sun was a circle with a wavy line through it to show heat (⊙). The
sign for mountain had three peaks (Ⱳ). The sign for a child was a
child reaching for mother (ⴄ). The sign for man looked like a man
(ⴗ). These signs or pictographs could be easily understood because
they looked like real things.

Then, after a few centuries the Chinese made these pictographs
easier to draw. The signs were called characters and are used to this
day. These are some of the examples of the changes: the character for
sun became (日); the character for mountain became (山), and the
character for child became (子). Two lines open at one hundred and
twenty degrees (人) now represents man.

Later, it became necessary to express more ideas, so strokes were
added to the characters, or characters were combined. With extra

strokes a character had a new meaning. For example, a man with expanded arms at one hundred and eighty degrees (大) represents big, and two dots on each side of a man (小) means small. Characters were combined to make new words as in the example of the character to bark (口犬) which is made up of the combination of (口) mouth and (犬) dog. Another example of this kind is the character for good (好) which is made up of a woman and child because in China as well as everywhere a mother with her child is a good thing. Sometimes a character is repeated to make a different word as in the character for forest (林) which is the repetition of tree (木).

From the first character that Thi Chi created, Chinese words have expanded to more than ten thousand. The Chinese language also had an influence on other Asian languages such as Japanese and Korean which somehow contain some Chinese characteristics. Chinese is not only a tool for people to communicate with but it is also an important subject for Chinese artists to study. Chinese fine handwriting or calligraphy was considered a branch of painting and calligraphy was often combined with painting in a work of art. Chinese can be considered as one of the most beautiful languages in the world without question.

Chun Che
Taiwan

STUDENT ESSAY FOLLOW-UP

1. What is the writer trying to do in this essay?

2. Underline the thesis statement.

3. Are time signals used through each phase of the process?

4. Underline the topic sentences in each of the body paragraphs. Are the topic sentences supported?

5. Is the process of the development clear?

ORGANIZING

The Process Essay

In Reading 1, "Spell It in English," we saw how English spelling developed over time to what it is today. In Reading 2, we saw how the words *coconut* and *satellite* originated and how they came to mean what they mean today. Both these readings use a chronological (time) order.

A process essay can describe events in the order they occurred over a period of time, such as in a history or a biography. It can also describe events over a period of time such as a morning, a day, childhood, during the war, in the order the events occur.

Another type of process essay can describe a technical process such as how a computer works or how hair is transplanted or how chocolate is made. (This type of essay contains many verbs in the passive form.)

Yet another type of process essay is the "how to" essay in which you tell someone how to do or make something. This type includes topics such as how to prepare a special dish, or how to get a driver's license.

The essential component in all process essays is time order, and the use of time expressions and transition signals indicate the time sequences clearly.

▶ Thesis Statement for the Process Essay

- The thesis statement for a process that is historical should name the process and indicate chronological order through words like *developed* or *evolved*.

Student Essay Thesis:
>   Chinese is one of the world's oldest languages and its written form as in most languages *developed* from the pictograph.

- The thesis statement for a technical process should name the process and indicate that it involves a series of steps.
>   Hair transplantation is a fairly simple process.

- It may also name the main steps in the process:
>   The main steps in the process of hair transplantation are removal of the desired number of hair transplants, removal of small plugs in the bald area, and the insertion of the hair transplants.

- The thesis statement of a "how to" essay is the same as the one for the technical process. It should name the process or item and indicate that it involves a number of steps.
>   Baking your own bread can be quite easy if you follow these steps.
>   Rescue breathing for a person who is unconscious involves a sequence of steps that must be followed carefully.

▶ Organizing the Process Analysis Essay

Deciding how to divide a process essay into paragraphs can be tricky. If you are writing a historical or narrative type of chronological process, divide your paragraphs by major time periods as in the student essay. However, if you are writing about how to do something, the following guidelines will help you:

- *Introduction*

    Introduce the topic and explain why the process is performed, by whom it is performed, and in what situation it is performed. You may list the main steps of the process in the order in which they are performed.

- *Body Paragraphs*

    Start to describe the process, introducing the first step in a topic sentence. You may at this point state the equipment and supplies needed for the process. Divide the process into three or four major steps. Each major step would be a body paragraph. For example, if you were describing a wedding ceremony in your country, the first major step would explain the preparations, the next would describe the ceremony, and the last would describe the reception or banquet.

- *Conclusion*

    Summarize by restating the main steps and describing the result. The type of conclusion will depend on the type of process you are describing (see the student essay).

▶ Time Expressions

Time may be indicated by a preposition with a date or historical period: *in 1920, by the 16th century, over the next ten years*, or other time expressions. We will look at some prepositions commonly used with time.

During indicates the duration of the activity from beginning to end, usually without stating the length of time.

For indicates the length of time or an appointed time.

Since indicates a period of time from its beginning to the present.
    He has been living there *since* 1920. (He is still there.)
    During her first year at college, she performed remarkably.
    I waited *for* an hour. My appointment was *for* three o'clock.

Other prepositions of time indicate when or how long: *as, in, on, to, till, up to, upon, as early as, as soon as, as late as.*

The process should be completed *in* three hours.
He worked *till* ten o'clock.
She spends *up to* three hours every day rehearsing.
The class will have a test *on* Friday.
She woke up *as soon as* it was daylight.
Cook the beans *from* twenty-five to thirty-five minutes.
Leave to thaw for an hour *upon* taking it out of the freezer.

Dependent clauses can be introduced by prepositions used as adverbs (*after, before, until*) or by adverbs (*when, while*):

After (or *when*) you have made a rough draft, start revising your work.
Before starting on the second draft, make sure that your details support your topic sentences.
Don't forget to look up the spelling of words you are unsure of *when* you are editing.
Do not be distracted *while* you are editing each sentence.

Other useful words that indicate a sequence in a process are ordinal numbers: *first, second, third;* and interrupters: *next, then, later, simultaneously, eventually.* These expressions place an action in the past: *previous to, prior to, just before.*

Prior to writing your research, make sure you have all the information at hand.
Next, revise your draft.

Task: Look back at Reading 1 and underline all the words that indicate time or sequence.

Exercise 1

Fill in the blanks using the following time words. Each choice can be used only once.

	while	still	for	1561	when	in 1637
until	during	after	in 1499	later	then	in 1542

The first European to discover the Amazon River was Spanish explorer Vicente Pinzon _____. He had been on Columbus's first voyage seven years earlier and was _____ determined to find a route to the Orient. _____ he sailed into the mouth of the Amazon and looked at the mighty river ahead of him, he thought he had gone around the world and hit the Ganges River in India. He stopped at some islands in the mouth of the river and _____ sailed on.

Thirty-three years _____, _____, Francisco de Orellana became the first European to travel the entire river, although that was not what he set out to do at all. _____ a Spanish expedition became stranded in the jungles of Eastern Peru, Orellana was sent down the Napo River to find food. But starvation, sickness, and Indian attacks took place, and Orellana couldn't get back upriver. Instead, he followed tributaries to the Amazon and _____ sixteen months of incredible hardships, he and what was left of his party made it all the way to the sea.

In _____, the notorious Lope de Aguirre traveled the Amazon _____ on the run from Spanish troops. He left a trail of death and destruction throughout the Amazon all the way to the sea.

No one traveled the entire river _____ another 76 years, _____ a Portuguese captain, Pedro Texeira, became the first to complete an upriver "ascent" _____.

WRITING PRACTICE

Choose one of the following topics.

1 Use one of the topics you researched in this chapter to write a process essay using chronological order or steps.

2 Write a process essay on how you recovered from an illness or accident.

3 Write a process essay on learning a foreign language.

4 Write a process essay on a ceremony in your country (for example, a wedding). Indicate the sequence of steps clearly.

1. Pre-writing

Work alone, with a partner, or in a group.

1. Brainstorm the topic. Choose the pre-writing technique you prefer.

2. Brainstorm how to divide your process essay into three or four parts.

3. Work on a thesis statement.

How To Write

BRAINSTORMING
PAGE 242

2. Outlining

A. Organize your ideas.

Step 1: Write your thesis statement.

Step 2: Divide your steps into three or four paragraphs.

Step 3: Provide details of each step in the paragraphs.

B. Make a more detailed outline. The essay outline on page 22 will help you.

3. Write a Rough Draft.

4. Revise Your Rough Draft. Use the checklist on page 246.

How To Write

DRAFTING
PAGE 245

5. Edit Your Essay. Use editing symbols on pages 247—248.

How To Write

EDITING
PAGE 247

6. Write Your Final Copy.

Chapter 3: Hygiene

PRE-READING QUESTIONS

Discuss these questions with your classmates or teacher.

1 Do you think of some cultures as being neater or cleaner than others? Why?

2 What religious rituals do you know of that are cleansing?

3 What is your opinion of public baths? Why do you think they are important in some cultures?

ACTIVITY

Take the following quiz, circling T for true and F for false. Then compare your answers with those of your classmates. When you have finished, check the answers on page 86.

1. The ancient Romans did not place much emphasis on personal cleanliness.   T   F

2. Up until the 1870s in Europe and America, doctors washed their hands only after surgery—not before.   T   F

3. Shrimps clean other fish in the sea.   T   F

4. In colonial Pennsylvania and Virginia, there were laws that forced people to bathe at least once a month.   T   F

5. During the Middle Ages in Europe, people bathed when they were baptized and seldom after that.   T   F

6. For thousands of years people have been aware that germs cause disease.   T   F

Reading 1: Cleanliness

Cleanliness is considered a virtue, but just what does it mean to be clean? As most of us have had the unpleasant occasion to discover, one person's definition can be quite different from another's. From Istanbul to Indianapolis, people have their own ways of coming clean and their own reasons for doing so.

Cleanliness has had a long and varied history with mixed reviews. Sometimes it's popular; sometimes it's not. Throughout the ages, personal cleanliness has been greatly influenced by religion, culture, and technology. Moreover, bathing has served many functions in addition to hygiene. Baths are also places for social gathering, mental and physical relaxation, and medicinal treatment. Archaeological evidence suggests that bathing is as old as the first civilizations. Soaplike material has been found in clay jars of Babylonian origin, dating back to about 2800 B.C. One of the first known bathtubs came from Minoan Crete, and a pretty sophisticated plumbing system of clay pipes is known to have existed in the great palace of King Minos, built in 1700 B.C. The ancient Egyptians didn't have such plumbing expertise, but are known to have had a positive attitude toward hygiene. They washed with soapy material made of animal and vegetable oils and salts, and sat in a shallow kind of bath while attendants poured water over them.

The Greeks prized cleanliness, although they didn't use soap. Instead they rubbed oil and ashes on their bodies, scrubbed with blocks of rock or sand, and scraped themselves clean with a curved metal instrument. A dip in the water and anointment with olive oil followed. They were no doubt clean, but how would they smell if we followed them down the street today?

There were public Grecian baths as well as private ones, but they didn't serve the social purpose of the Roman baths. It seems that no one in history has indulged in bathing the way the Romans did. Nearly a dozen large and magnificent public bathhouses dotted the city, and many hundreds of private baths were found in homes. Emperor Caracalla's bath could accommodate 1,600 bathers at a time. Emperor Diocletian entertained crowds of more then 3,000 in the marble splendor of his bath, finished in A.D. 305. Apparently the Romans had lots of time on their hands because bathing was not just an exercise; it was an event. First a bather entered a warm room to sweat and to engage in lengthy conversations. Fine oils and sand were used to cleanse the body. Next came a hot room where the bather would be treated to even more sweating, splashing with water, more oils and scraping, and yet more talk. Finally the Roman concluded the process by plunging into a cool and refreshing pool. In the early years of the baths, men and women had separate areas, but eventually the sexes mixed and the baths lost their virtuous purpose.

So corrupt was Roman society and its baths that the fathers of the early Christian church discouraged bathing. The hygienic practices of the Greeks and Romans were repressed to such an extent that Europe during the Middle Ages has been said to have gone a thousand years without a bath. Queen Isabella of Castille boasted that she had bathed only twice in her life—at birth and before her marriage. Religion wasn't the only reason why Europeans didn't bathe. Although the royal and wealthy sometimes indulged, commoners found bathing virtually[1] impossible. With no running water, polluted rivers, and soap taxed as a luxury item, the ordinary citizen had little opportunity to bathe. As a result, people lived in filth,[2] clothing was infested with vermin,[3] and disease was rampant.

---

[1] virtually = almost.

[2] filth = very bad dirt.

[3] vermin = insects that live on the body of humans or animals.

Early Americans, being of European origin, brought their dirty habits with them. By the 1800s, however, both Europeans and Americans were reforming their ways. As it became known that filth led to disease, governments began to improve sanitation standards. Wash houses were built and bathing became a good thing again. In the U.S., tubs, water heaters, and good indoor plumbing put bathing within the reach of ordinary citizens. They like it so much that today the average American claims to shower or bathe more than seven times a week.

In America, clean means not only free of dirt, but free of odor as well, or rather, human odors only, because millions of dollars are spent each year on powders and perfumes that cover up any natural smells that might slip by. As any deodorant ad will tell you, to have body odor (B.O.) is a grave social offense.

European countries such as France do not have this obsession with body odor. Many men in particular do not use deodorants. They think washing the armpits daily is clean enough. In many European countries where people live in older houses that don't have showers, tub bathing is done once or twice a week. Hair is also washed much more infrequently than in America, and it is common and perfectly acceptable for the hair of European women to have a faintly dirty odor.

In many Middle Eastern countries, cleanliness has religious overtones that link spiritual and physical purification. The Jewish people have many religious laws relating to hygiene, both personal and in the preparation of food. Muslims, too, live by some very strict rules related to cleanliness. For example, they are required to wash certain parts of their bodies, such as their feet and hands, before they pray. Since the time of Mohammed, sweat baths, or *hammams*, have been recommended and serve not only as places for cleansing but also as retreats and opportunities for socializing. As a matter of fact, the Crusaders, who enjoyed hammams, brought the idea of the public bath back to Europe with them and introduced the use of thermal baths as therapy for a variety of ills.

For many Middle Easterners, baths are a sort of ritual, a major affair that takes longer than an hour. Bathing begins with a steam, followed by rubbing the body with a hard towel, then soaping and rinsing. People usually want to lie down after a bath. Since it takes so long and is so exhausting, they indulge in baths once a week. Another reason why they prefer to bathe less frequently than Americans is because they believe daily washing dries out the skin and hair, which is actually quite true. Americans, however, make up for that by using vast amounts of hair conditioners and skin lotions.

Asian cultures are very strict and ritualistic about their cleanliness. The Japanese in particular are known for their personal hygiene, which extends from the removal of their shoes and wearing of special slippers before entering any house or building, to extensive washing before meals.

It is logical to conclude that cleanliness has many different meanings and is judged by a variety of standards. Clean means pure, in a religious sense, as well as clean of body. For some it means being "squeaky clean"[4] and smelling like roses. For others, a more "natural" state is acceptable. Whether it means washing one's hands and face, or a head-to-toe scrubbing, cleanliness is a cultural practice, with enough stories and emotions behind it to make a real soap opera.

---

[4] squeaky clean = extremely clean.

VOCABULARY

Select the letter of the answer that is closest in meaning to the italicized word or phrase.

1. A dip in the water and *anointment* with olive oil followed.

    a. rub

    b. application

    c. soak

    d. wash

2. No one in history *indulged in* bathing the way the Romans did.

    a. pleased themselves in

    b. made rules against

    c. talked and wrote about

    d. had the patience for

3. The baths lost their *virtuous* purpose.

    a. practical

    b. natural

    c. small

    d. good

4. The hygienic practices of the Greeks and Romans were *repressed*.

    a. encouraged

    b. defined

    c. held back

    d. debated

5. Queen Isabella *boasted* that she had bathed only twice in her life.

    a. said proudly

    b. argued often

    c. expressed quickly

    d. denied strongly

6. The clothing of commoners was often *infested with* vermin.

    a. free of

    b. decorated with

    c. made by

    d. full of

7. Disease was *rampant.*

    a. not commonly found

    b. easily controlled

    c. avoided at all cost

    d. spread everywhere

8. In America, body odor is a *grave* social offense.

    a. serious

    b. harmful

    c. rare

    d. frequent

9. In many Middle Eastern countries, cleanliness has religious *overtones.*

    a. rituals

    b. meanings

    c. controls

    d. results

10. Sweat baths also served as *retreats.*

    a. locations for parties

    b. opportunities to get work accomplished

    c. places to get away and rest

    d. areas in which to exercise

To Please

••

indulge/spoil/pamper

To *indulge*, *spoil*, and *pamper* all mean to please oneself or please others. They differ as follows:

To indulge = to gratify one's desires or those of others usually out of weakness.

To spoil = to treat others very well or too well to the point of doing unnecessary things for them.

To pamper = to treat yourself or others too well to the point of being ridiculous.

Use pamper, spoil, *or* indulge *in the blanks below.*

1. *When under stress, Mary _____ in a box of chocolates, even though she is on a diet.*

2. *I love my dog but I don't _____ it like Susan does. She even buys her dog expensive caviar every week.*

3. *After his heart surgery, he is on a strict diet but he _____ when he goes to a good restaurant.*

4. *They _____ their seventeen-year-old daughter by buying her everything she wants. Last month they bought her the most expensive foreign sports car.*

5. *He _____ his new wife by doing everything she says.*

1. What do you indulge in sometimes?
2. Give an example of how you can spoil a person.
3. How would you like to be pampered?

repress/control

To repress and to control both have similar meanings. However, repress is stronger than control because it means to control to the point where freedom of speech or action is taken away.

Put each of the following words or phrases under the correct headings. In some cases they may belong under both headings.

one's laughter	political opposition	one's temper	
the air pressure	all freedom	a crowd	free speech
creative talent	true feelings	one's weight	
the number of immigrants crossing the border			
the number of calories you eat			

repress	control

COMPREHENSION

A. Looking for the Main Idea

Circle the letter of the best answer.

1. The main idea of paragraph 2 is

   a. bathing has many different functions in society besides that of cleansing the body.

   b. indoor plumbing was achieved by the Minoans in Crete almost 4,000 years ago, although their technology didn't immediately spread to other parts of the world.

c. the Egyptians made up for their lack of sophisticated plumbing by using servants to pour water over them while they bathed.

d. cleansing of the body has been taking place for thousands of years in many different ways and for many different reasons.

2. Paragraph 4 is mostly about

a. the size of the Roman public bathhouses and the emperors who built them.

b. the social purposes of the Roman baths and their eventually corrupting influence.

c. the extent, purpose, and rituals involving the Roman baths.

d. the differences between Roman baths and Greek baths.

3. Paragraph 8 is mainly concerned with

a. European attitudes and habits with respect to cleanliness.

b. the difference between Americans and Europeans in terms of hair grooming.

c. the reasons why people who live in older European houses bathe less often than those who have modern conveniences.

d. the fact that body and hair odor are acceptable in other parts of the world.

B. Skimming and Scanning for Details

Scan the passage quickly to find the answers to these questions. Write complete answers.

1. According to the passage, what three things have influenced the bathing habits of people over the centuries?

2. According to the passage, how were the Greeks different from the Egyptians in their bathing habits?

3. In the last sentence of paragraph 3, to what does the word *them* refer?

4. What bathing rituals were involved during the three stages of bathing in the Roman baths?

5. Why did the leaders of the Christian church discourage bathing in Europe during the Middle Ages?

6. What three problems prevented commoners from taking daily baths in Europe?

7. What finally prompted Europeans and Americans to change their cleanliness habits?

8. What Muslim tradition influenced the introduction of therapeutic thermal baths in Europe?

9. To what does the word *people* in paragraph 10, sentence 3, refer?

10. What are two hygienic habits of the Japanese?

C. Making Inferences and Drawing Conclusions

The answers to these questions are not directly stated in the passage. Circle the letter of the best answer.

1. The passage implies that
   a. only the most advanced societies recognized the importance of cleanliness.
   b. cleanliness can mean only one thing; a body free from dirt and odors.
   c. soap and bathtubs have not always been necessary for cleanliness.
   d. little evidence exists regarding the cleanliness habits of early civilizations.

2. From the passage, it can be concluded that
   a. religion has always had a detrimental effect on society's need for personal cleanliness.
   b. over the ages, some societies have valued personal cleanliness more than others.
   c. during the Middle Ages, Europeans had no need to be concerned with personal cleanliness.
   d. technology has had little effect on Americans' bathing habits.

3. It can be inferred from the passage that

    a. Middle Eastern traditions have had no influence on Western habits of cleanliness.

    b. overwashing can be hazardous to a person's health.

    c. Asian cultures are only concerned with the appearance of being clean.

    d. bathing is a ritualistic and meaningful activity that can be viewed in a cultural context.

4. The author's purpose is to

    a. amuse.

    b. inform.

    c. convince.

    d. dispute.

DISCUSSION

Discuss these questions with your classmates.

1. What is the typical cleaning ritual in your country?

2. How is body odor regarded in your country or other counties?

3. What is your own definition of being clean?

Reading 2: Cleaner Fish

The following passage is from the book *Symbiosis* by Nicolette Perry, published by Blandford Press, Dorsett, Poole, England, 1983. It describes the cleaning habits of fish.

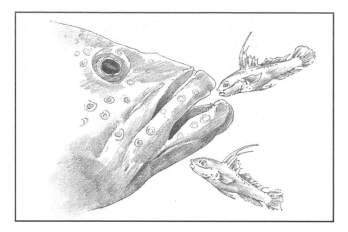

Figure 1   There are at least 45 species of fish that are known cleaners (engage in cleaning symbiosis with other fish). One example is the goby, which cleans the Nassau Grouper. The Black Surgeon fish goes from black to blue while being cleaned by the *Labroides dimidiatus.*

Cleaning symbioses[1] are found in the sea, in freshwater, on land and in the air, but the greatest number of examples concern marine species. It is essential for all creatures to have some method of keeping themselves clean and free from parasites. If they do not, they will probably fall ill from infected wounds or the effects of disease and blood loss from parasites. For those species that are unable to clean themselves it is obviously vital to find some other animal to perform this cleaning function. This chapter is concerned with describing some typical examples of cleaning symbioses as well as the more extraordinary ones.

The vast majority of cleaners are fish; at least 45 species are known cleaners and there may well be many more. Fish that are habitually cleaned often have to modify their usual behavior to allow the cleaners to do their work. It is not normal for aggressive species like shark, barracuda and moray eels to allow small fish to swim safely near them. With known cleaner species, however, these and other fish change their attitude completely and allow the cleaners all over their bodies without displaying any ferocity[2] towards them. The clients will slow down or stop completely

---

[1] symbiosis = the living or working together of two different organisms in a mutually beneficial relationship.

[2] ferocity = fierceness, violence.

(unusual behavior for most fish, as they usually move all the time), open and close their mouths and gill[3] covers and assume awkward-looking postures to help the cleaners. It is quite possible that some species have become extinct because of an inability to establish a cleaning symbiosis. So many individuals could have fallen foul of ectoparasites,[4] fungi and bacteria that the population was made inviable.

Some fishes change color while being cleaned. Black Surgeon Fish go from black to blue when they are being cleaned by *Labroides dimidiatus*. The Goatfish changes from pale brown to pink while the same cleaner picks it over for parasites.

Fishes being groomed guard their cleaners against danger by warning them of the approach of predators. The Nassau Grouper when cleaned by gobies[5] warns its cleaner by suddenly closing its mouth, leaving only a small gap to allow the goby to escape. Even if the grouper is in imminent danger itself it takes time to warn the goby. This shows the regard that the client feels for its cleaner and the service that it performs.

Several species of cleaner set up cleaning stations in one particular place. The local fish soon realize where the cleaner is located and will visit it whenever they require cleaning. Quite astonishing numbers of fish are cleaned in this way: not only territorial species that would normally be found in the area but also migratory ones which have gone out of their way to visit these stations. Client fish will patiently wait their turn to be cleaned, and even form orderly queues.

Quite a considerable amount of observational and experimental work has been done on these cleaning stations. Limbaugh, for example, discovered that over three hundred fish can be cleaned by a single Senorita Fish in a six-hour period. These fish go back to the same cleaner every few days for another session and this enables them to remain in peak condition.

Limbaugh also did some experiments in waters off the Bahamas. He removed all the cleaner fish from one locality and observed the effects on the species normally found there. Within two days the numbers of fish were severely reduced and within two weeks almost all the territorial fish had disappeared. Those that remained had developed the fuzzy marks that are an indication of fungal infection. It had been shown in previous experi-

---

[3] gill = the organ through which a fish breathes.

[4] ectoparasites = parasites that live on the exterior of the host.

[5] gobies = a kind of cleaner fish.

ments that the introduction of cleaners into an aquarium infected by fungi can restore its inhabitants to health.

From the above the value of cleaning symbioses in the marine habitat can easily been seen. Without the work of all the cleaners of the ocean, the effects of parasites, fungi and injury would kill many more species than they do already. The Senorita Fish is an example of a typical cleaner. It is of the wrasse family and lives off the coast of California. It is an active, small, cigar-shaped fish that the local people call the senorita because of its cleaning habits. Its client fishes include the Topsmelt, Black Sea Bass, Opaleye, Blacksmith Fish and many more. These fish are almost all much larger than the cleaner and would normally prey on wrasses of the Senorita's size. They do not attack the senorita, however, but wait patiently until it is their turn to be cleaned, hold themselves still and often in the most peculiar postures while being attended to. The fish in the area of the coast that the Senorita Fish inhabits are especially troubled by fungal infection, and removal of the white growths caused by the fungi is the cleaner's most important function. The cleaning phenomenon has been observed for many years to the extent that one species is popularly called the Cleaner Fish or Wrasse. It is a small, slim fish with cyan-colored[6] body, striped with darker blue or black. The cleaner fish goes on stage further than the senorita in that it actively attracts clients by "dancing." It swims in a vertical position, head downwards, and undulates its body from side to side. This is a most unusual posture for fish, as they usually swim horizontally to the sea bed. This "dancing" makes the cleaner noticeable to even the most myopic fish, and it has become the cleaner's trade mark.

Clients line up, as for the senorita, until it is their turn to be cleaned, and also allow the little fish to enter their mouths and gill cavities unharmed. The contents of various species' stomachs have been examined to assess the quantity of cleaner fish that are eaten, both by fish that are known clients and others. It has been found that very few cleaners are consumed by any species, although fish of similar size make up the bulk of the diet. So few cleaner fish are eaten that it seems probable that the small number that are are taken accidentally by absent-minded clients than actively predated upon.

---

[6] cyan-colored = greenish-blue color.

Look at the reading on cleaner fish to answer the questions.

1. Which of the following words could be substituted for "fallen foul of" in paragraph 2?

    a. been the cause of

    b. been eliminated by

    c. eaten enough of

    d. been harmed by

2. Which of the following is closest in meaning to the word *inviable* as used in paragraph 2?

    a. unable to communicate

    b. unable to survive

    c. unable to move

3. Which word in paragraph 4 means "attended to or cared for"?

4. In paragraph 4, what does *imminent* mean?

    a. immediate

    b. constant

    c. great

    d. frequent

5. Which of these words is closest in meaning to *peak* as it is used in paragraph 6?

    a. top

    b. average

    c. inferior

    d. artificial

6. Which of these statements is true?

    a. Something "fuzzy" is hard and clear.

    b. Something "fuzzy" is covered with fluffy particles.

7. In paragraph 8, what does *undulates* mean?

    a. looks right to left as it passes

    b. advances in stops and starts

    c. moves back and forth in a wavy form

    d. swims quickly in a straight line

8. What is the meaning of *myopic* in paragraph 8?

    a. unable to see faraway objects clearly

    b. having sharp eyes and good hearing

9. Which of these words is closest in meaning to *assess* as used in paragraph 9?

    a. judge

    b. compare

    c. calculate

10. Which word in paragraph 9 is similar in meaning to "the greater part of"?

Themes

Judge

. . . .

assess/estimate/value/rate

To *assess*, *estimate*, *value*, and *rate* are all ways of judging something. They differ as follows:

assess = to judge the quality or worth of something by precise analysis.

estimate = to approximate or guess the quality or worth of something.

value = to judge the quality or worth of something in a positive way.

rate = to judge the quality or worth of something by placing it in a certain rank or number scale.

Put each of the following words or phrases under the correct heading. You may place the same words or phrase under more than one heading.

a person's character	a person's ability	damages
a person's friendship	a person's advice	a person's I.Q.
a house and its contents	a person's losses	a T.V. show

assess	estimate	value	rate

Important
....

vital/crucial/fundamental

The adjectives *vital*, *crucial*, and *fundamental* all mean very important.
They differ in meaning as follows:

vital = of great importance and necessary for life.

crucial = very important, often used for a crisis situation where a
decision has to be made.

fundamental = forming the basis of something.

Choose the correct word in the following sentences.

1 The party wanted to make (vital/fundamental) changes in the law.

2. Some (crucial/vital) evidence regarding the murder case
was revealed.

3. A knowledge of grammar is (crucial/fundamental) for learning
a language.

4. It is (vital/fundamental) that you call an ambulance right now.

5. Timing is (crucial/fundamental) for the success of this operation.

6. Their decision is (crucial/fundamental) for the future of the
elephant population.

A. Looking for the Main Ideas

Some of the following statements from the reading are main ideas and some are supporting statements. Find the statements in the reading. Write M in the blank in front of each main idea. Write S in the blank in front of each supporting statement.

_____ 1. If they do not, they will probably fall ill from infected wounds or the effects of disease and blood loss from parasites.

_____ 2. Fish that are habitually cleaned often have to modify their usual behavior to allow the cleaners to do their work.

_____ 3. With known cleaner species, however, these and other fish change their attitude completely and allow the cleaners all over their bodies without displaying any ferocity towards them.

_____ 4. The clients will slow down or stop completely (unusual behavior for most fish, as they usually move all the time), open and close their mouths and gill covers and assume awkward-looking postures to help the cleaners.

_____ 5. Some fishes change color while being cleaned.

_____ 6. Fishes being groomed guard their cleaners against danger by warning them of the approach of predators.

_____ 7. Even if the grouper is in imminent danger itself it takes time to warn the goby.

_____ 8. Several species of cleaner set up cleaning stations in one particular place.

_____ 9. These fish go back to the same cleaner every few days for another session and this enables them to remain in peak condition.

_____10. Within two days the numbers of fish were severely reduced and within two weeks almost all the territorial fish had disappeared.

B. Skimming and Scanning for Details

Scan the passage quickly to complete the following sentences.

1. Even normally aggressive species like _____ , _____ , and _____ allow small cleaner fish to swim near them.

2. Some species have become extinct because of an inability to _____ .

3. The Goatfish will change from _____ to _____ while being cleaned by cleaner fish.

4. The Nassau Grouper warns its cleaner fish that predators are in the area by _____ .

5. Many larger fish will not wait for the cleaner fish to come to them. Instead they _____ .

6. In a _____-hour period, a single _____ fish can clean over 300 fish.

7. If cleaner fish are taken out of an area they usually inhabit, the client fish that remain after the others have left the area will _____ .

8. If cleaner fish are put in an aquarium with fish infected by _____ , the cleaner fish can _____ .

9. The Cleaner Fish, or Wrasse, attracts clients by doing a dance that involves _____ .

10. In appearance, the Senorita Fish is _____ and _____-shaped.

C. Making Inferences and Drawing Conclusions

Some of the following statements are facts from the article. Other statements can be inferred from the article. Write F in the blank in front of each factual statement. Write I in the blank in front of each inference.

___ 1. Parasites are dangerous to the health of all creatures.

___ 2. If a living creature can't clean itself, then some other animal has to do the job.

___ 3. In a symbiotic relationship, both creatures benefit.

___ 4. Even the simplest animals can adapt to situations when their lives depend on it.

___ 5. Most of the animals whose job it is to clean others are fish.

___ 6. Some fish actually change color while they are being cleaned.

___ 7. A client fish will even go so far as to protect its cleaner fish, even when the client fish is put in danger.

___ 8. Without cleaner fish, all fish would probably become extinct.

___ 9. Even normally aggressive client fish will wait patiently for their turn with a cleaner fish.

___10. A fish's survival instinct is stronger than its desire to eat the smaller cleaner fish.

DISCUSSION

Discuss these questions with your classmates.

1. Discuss the cleanliness habits of the other animals.

2. Discuss the relationship between cleanliness and health in humans and animals.

3. Discuss five ways in which our environment could be cleaned up.

WRITING

Writing a Summary

Write a one-paragraph summary of Reading 1.
Check your summary against the Summary Checklist on page 265.

How To Write

HOW TO SUMMARIZE
PAGE 263

Paraphrasing

Paraphrase paragraph 2 in Reading 2.
Begin with either:
According to Perry, . . .
or
Based on Perry's article, . . .

How To Write

HOW TO PARAPHRASE
PAGE 257

Research

You may use your research later to write your definition essay. The extended definition is discussed on pages 81-82.

How To Write

HOW TO DO LIBRARY RESEARCH
PAGE 248

Choose a particular concept (an abstract word) and define it in two or three ways in an extended definition such as the one in Reading 1. To gather information, you should consult a dictionary, look at related sources in the library, and/or draw on your own experience or that of your friends.

The following are some suggested concepts:

Democracy	Love	Prejudice	Freedom
Patriotism	Fanaticism	Trust	Natural
Beauty	Education	Peace	Intelligence

Read the following essay written by a student.

Cleanliness

According to Webster's dictionary the word *cleanliness* means "habitually kept clean." In fact, the quality, state, or condition of cleanliness is often determined by people's own culture, religion, occupation, or lifestyle. To comprehend the sense of cleanliness each individual or culture has to be considered. In my country, Japan, our basic sense of cleanliness may be more clearly defined when we look at the basic aspects of our lives such as our buildings, our food, and hygiene.

Traditionally it is the custom in Japan to keep our homes clean since a clean house is a reflection of one's self. One way in which we keep our homes clean from outside dirt and germs is by taking off our shoes when entering our homes or even some public places such as schools, local hospitals, and some restaurants. Upon entering a home, shoes are taken off and slippers are worn. Since shoes are taken off when entering someone's home, it is crucial that our socks are clean and have no holes in them. In the home, certain areas or rooms such as the bathroom or the yard require changing into different slippers which are used for that area. Also, our bathrooms are separate from our toilets since the latter is considered to be a dirty place and therefore, must be separate from the clean tub area. Needless to say, our floors are immaculately clean, and must be scrubbed at least once a week.

When eating, there are other aspects of cleanliness that we consider. When eating out in a restaurant, clean chopsticks are provided just as clean silverware is provided in western restaurants. However, it is difficult for a wooden chopstick to be kept really clean, so the Japanese discovered the disposable chopstick. Like most people, we wash our hands before eating, but in addition to this most restaurants provide diners with hot, steamed towels to clean their hands with before a meal. In the home, members of a family each have their individual chopsticks, rice bowl and tea cup.

Being clean and hygienic is important to the Japanese. Westerners visiting Japan may see people wearing white gauze masks, like the ones used by surgeons, when they walk or bike through the city. People wear these because they may have hayfever or they may have a cold and not wish to spread their germs to others or they may be afraid of air pollution. Also, when we have a cold we use paper tissues which we throw away after use. We do not use a handkerchief to blow our noses with. Handkerchiefs are used for drying hands after washing or for wiping our mouths. It is considered good manners to always carry paper tissues with us wherever we go. Another custom we have when we come home from the outside is to wash our hands with soap and water and rinse our mouths with water.

In conclusion, although the quality, state or condition of cleanliness is determined by each individual, culture also plays a significant role. In Japan, there are general cultural norms with regard to cleanliness that most people follow in their daily lives. The main objective in every culture with regard to cleanliness is to keep people healthy.

Noriko
Japan

STUDENT ESSAY FOLLOW-UP

1. Underline the thesis statement.

2. In which three aspects of life in Japan is the writer defining cleanliness?

3. Are all three aspects of life developed in the body paragraphs?

4. Examine paragraph 2. Do all the ideas support and illustrate the topic sentence?

5. Do you like the writer's definition of cleanliness? Explain your answer.

ORGANIZING

Definition: Literal and Extended

Sometimes a definition may appear in an essay to clarify a word. The definition may be expressed in a sentence or a paragraph or may even be the entire essay. The reason for this is that there are two kinds of definitions.

The first kind gives the literal, or dictionary, meaning.

Example
Cleanliness is the state of being free from dirt.

A literal definition is usually expressed in one sentence. However, when you want to give a personal interpretation of a word, you use an extended definition. The extended definition may differ from the literal meaning because it is defined in a particular or personal way. The meaning of an abstract word or concept such as "cleanliness" is often given in an extended definition because such a word can be interpreted in different ways.

Example

> In America, cleanliness not only means to be free of dirt, but free of odor as well.

The extended definition involves the use of various kinds of supporting ideas. Looking back to Reading 1, we see how the word *cleanliness* was defined in the past by the Romans, the Greeks, and then in the Middle Ages. We are then given examples of similarities and differences in ideas of cleanliness among different cultures today.

In Reading 2, Cleaner Fish, cleanliness is seen through the world of fish. We are given examples of various species of cleaner fish and their clients going about their process of "cleaning," and we are told of the importance of "cleanliness" to fish, without which most species would die.

Exercise 1

It is important to make your literal definitions accurate. Look at the definitions below. Which are accurate? Which are not? Rewrite the definitions that are not accurate.

1. Art is a mirror of the human soul.
2. Thermostats are devices that regulate heaters and cooling machines, turning them on and off so they maintain the required temperature.
3. Wind means destruction from devastating storms, or benefits from harnessing energy with windmills.
4. Powered flight is the realization of man's fondest dream over thousands of years.
5. A keynote address is an opening address that outlines the issues to be considered.
6. A mammal is a vertebrate animal with self-regulating body temperature and the capability for milk production in the female.
7. Mountain sickness is a sickness people get when they are in the mountains.
8. Separation anxiety is a negative emotional state that occurs in small children when they are parted from their parents.
9. Good sense is something everyone should hope to have.
10. Education is the key to prosperity.

Exercise 2

Work with a partner, a group, or alone. Look up the following words in a dictionary and write down their literal meanings. Then write three or four ways in which the definitions might be extended either personally, socially, or culturally.

Example

Touch	Literal Meaning:	to bring a bodily part in contact with something.
	Extended Meaning:	
		Different functions in society: a. professional/functional b. social/polite c. friendship, warmth d. love, intimacy
	or	In different cultures: a. in North America b. in Latin America c. in Asia
	or	Necessity for growth and development of certain animals: a. monkeys b. cats c. dogs

1. Space   Literal Meaning: _____

   Extended Meaning: _____

   _____

2. Time   Literal Meaning: _____

   Extended Meaning: _____

   _____

3. Smell   Literal Meaning: _____

   Extended Meaning: _____

   _____

4. Aggressiveness   Literal Meaning: _____

   Extended Meaning: _____

   _____

5. Modesty   Literal Meaning: _____

                    Extended Meaning: _____

                    _____

6. Respect   Literal Meaning: _____

                    Extended Meaning: _____

                    _____

▶ Introduction to the Definition Essay

In the introduction, state the term you are going to define. Then either define it yourself or use a dictionary definition, naming the dictionary and quoting from it. In your thesis statement, restate the term you are going to define and in which way or how you are going to define it, giving two or three aspects with which you will illustrate your definition. Look back at the thesis statement of the student essay to see the three aspects of daily life the student used.

Using etymologies

In your introduction, you may want to look at the word's origin or etymology. Sometimes the original meaning of the word is quite different from its present meaning, and you may want

HOW TO SUMMARIZE
PAGE 263

to show this. The *Oxford English Dictionary* and many other unabridged dictionaries give detailed histories of the origin and development of words. For example, in *Webster's New Collegiate Dictionary*, we see that the word *boycott* comes from Charles Boycott, a land agent in Ireland who was ostracized for refusing to reduce rents; the word prejudice comes from the Latin *praejudicium*, which is made up of *prae*, meaning "before" and *judicium*, which means "judgement."

Using a clear definition

Many times a form of the word or the word itself is used as part of the dictionary definition, which does not make the meaning clear. For example, avoid defining cleanliness as "the state of being clean." It would be clearer if you said, "Cleanliness is the state of being free from dirt."

The following terms have been defined using a form of the term itself.
Rewrite each definition without repeating the term being defined.
Make sure the meaning of the word is clear.

Term	Definition
1. fanaticism:	fanatic outlook or behavior.
2. loyalty:	the quality or state of being loyal.
3. education:	the action or process of being educated.
4. happiness:	the state of being happy.
5. creativity:	the quality of being creative.
6. friendship:	the state of being friends.
7. independence:	the quality or state of being independent.
8. leadership:	the quality of a leader.

Points to Remember for Organization:

- Each body paragraph in your essay should illustrate an aspect of your definition that you stated in your thesis.

- Support each aspect with clear examples. (Look back at the student essay.)

- The conclusion should summarize your personal definition and give a final comment on the term.

WRITING PRACTICE

Choose one of the following topics.

1 Use one of the concepts you researched to write a definition essay using three or four examples.

2 Write a definition essay on the concept of friendship. Use three or four ways to illustrate your definition.

3 Write a definition essay on alcoholism.

4 Write a definition essay on respect, providing illustrations.

1. Pre-writing.

Work alone, with a partner, or in a group.

How To **Write**

BRAINSTORMING
PAGE 242

1 Brainstorm the topic. Write down any mental associations you make with the word to be defined.

2 Brainstorm for examples that can illustrate the word.

3 Work on a thesis statement.

2. Outlining

A. Organize your ideas.

Step 1: Write your thesis statement.

Step 2: Select at least three examples that can best illustrate the term.

Step 3: Read your examples over again to make sure that they all define the term.

B. Make a more detailed outline. The essay outline on page 22 will help you.

3. Write a Rough Draft.

How To **Write**

DRAFTING
PAGE 245

4. Revise Your Rough Draft. Use the revision check-list on page 246.

5. Edit Your Essay. Use the editing symbols on pages 247—248.

How To **Write**

EDITING
PAGE 247

6. Write Your Final Copy.

Answers to Activity on page 60.

1. __F__   2. __T__   3. __T__

4. F   (In Pennsylvania and Virginia, there were laws against bathing, and in Philadelphia, anyone who bathed more than once a month faced jail.)

5. T   (The Christian Church thought bathing was sinful because the body was exposed.)

6. F   (Until Louis Pasteur in the 1850s proved that germs cause disease, people believed that God caused disease to punish people.)

Chapter 4: Groups, Organizations, and Societies

PRE-READING QUESTIONS

Discuss these questions with your classmates or teacher.

1 What groups or organizations can you name? Do you belong to any of them?

2 What are some organizations that are dedicated to doing good in the world?

3 Can you name some organizations that are harmful to society?

GROUPS, ORGANIZATIONS, AND SOCIETIES
WHAT'S ITS NAME?

Read the following descriptions of some groups, organizations, and societies. Then find their name from the selection in the box.

1. This organization teaches young people to be good citizens and trains them to become leaders. Members are taught to do their duty to God, to their country, and to other people. Their motto is *Be Prepared*, and *Learn by Doing*. The organization was started in Great Britain in 1907 by Robert Baden-Powell. Today over five million Americans belong to this organization.

2. This group originated in Switzerland but is now centered in the U.S. and Canada. The largest communities are found in Ohio, Pennsylvania, Indiana, Iowa, and Illinois. This group believes in separation from the world. Members are forbidden to go to war, swear oaths, or hold public office. Their doctrine requires them to farm and to hold a simple way of life. The use of electricity and telephones is forbidden. They limit education to the eighth grade.

3. This international organization calls attention to the environmental dangers of such actions as oil drilling, nuclear bomb testing, and the dumping of radioactive wastes. The group also opposes whaling, the spread of nuclear weapons, and the inhumane killing of animals. Members use direct action and nonviolent methods of protest. They go where an activity that the group considers harmful is occurring. Without using force, they try to stop the activity. The organization was founded in 1969 by a group of Canadians.

4. The men and women who belong to this organization devote their lives to helping people in need and spreading the Christian faith. The organization is supported by gifts of money from people who admire its work. This group is organized like an army. Some of their projects include medical care for the poor, inexpensive lodging for the homeless, and employment agencies to help people find jobs.

5. This is one of the oldest and largest fraternal organizations in the world. It is dedicated to the ideals of charity, equality, morality, and service to God. Members of this organization donate millions of dollars each year to charitable projects. The organization has millions of members worldwide, including three million in the

United States. Membership in this organization is for males only. Recently a similar organization for women was started. This is a secret organization, therefore members will not publicly say they belong to it.

Quakers	Red Cross	Salvation Army	Scouts
The Amish	Masons	Mormons	Greenpeace
Scientology	Big Brother		

Reading 1: The Camorra

It might be hard for a tourist in Italy to believe that the lovely seaside town of Naples was once the home of a powerful criminal group. But it is true that the Camorra once claimed Naples as its own. The Camorra had been a secret society until 1820 when it became publicly known. Since its origins in the 1400s, its heart had always been in Naples but it also flourished in prisons throughout Italy where young felons[1] were taught the techniques of robbery, blackmail, and murder. The strength and prestige of the Camorra escalated through the years, and by the turn of the twentieth century, the insidious society had almost all of southern Italy under its control.

Italy

In the early years of its existence, the Camorra was a Neopolitan[2] prison society. As prisoners served their terms and were released, however, they brought their criminal club to the city, where members worked the streets in gangs. They had secret signs and special methods of communicating with each other. They mewed[3] like cats if the police were near and crowed[4] like cocks when a possible victim approached. A long sigh gave warning that a victim was not alone; a sneeze meant he was not worth the trouble. They were sly as foxes and deadly as poisonous snakes.

---

[1] felons = criminals.

[2] Neopolitan = of Naples.

[3] mewed = made the crying sound of a cat.

[4] crowed = made the loud, high cry of a cock or rooster.

The society grew like mold[5] on cheese, rapidly extending its power and operations. After a while, the Camorra leadership wasn't satisfied with petty street robbery, thievery, and thuggery,[6] and stepped up the society's activities to the more criminally prestigious smuggling, blackmail, and political assassination. The Camorra's influence grew, and eventually the smugglers were in league with princes, who shared their profits. Statesmen, dignitaries,[7] even members of the church were involved in the society's criminal activities.

The power of the Camorra became so widespread that by the mid-nineteenth century the society no longer recruited from the class of the low-born and traditional criminals of Naples, but from the best families in the city. The corrupt young men of wealthy families considered membership in the Camorra an honor. They were attracted to the society's power and took pride in passing the initiation rites and learning the methods of ritual murder[8]—death by stiletto, a small, sharp dagger; and strangulation by garotte, a method of execution borrowed from the Spanish in which the neck is broken with an iron collar.

A central committee made up of the most powerful leaders throughout the country concerned itself with political control of the provinces. The wishes of the committee members were carried out by the society's bands of thugs in every major city. Anyone, from storekeepers to politicians to priests, who refused to obey the committee's directives or who reported Camorra members or activities to the police were murdered.

In Naples, the capital of the Camorra, city officials, the police force, and business owners were held tightly under the society's ironfisted rule. Officers were paid to ignore Camorra thugs who tore apart the shops of owners who refused to pay a weekly fee to the local Camorra chief. Neopolitan politics was dominated by the society and with few exceptions all political candidates were Camorristas.

The Camorra was divided into classes. There were the top-ranking Camorristas who dressed to the nines[9] and mixed with, and extorted money from, people of the highest levels of society. There was a lower level of blackmailers who took advantage of shopkeepers, restaurant owners,

---

[5] mold = soft, greenish growth forming on cheese and other foods.

[6] thuggery = violent crime.

[7] dignitaries = persons of high positions.

[8] ritual murder = ceremonial murder repeated in the same form.

[9] dressed to the nines = dressed perfectly and elegantly.

boat owners, and others. There were political Camorristas and there were murdering Camorristas. There were the lowest-level new recruits and the highest-level older leaders. Each class served the one above it and their local bosses. All served their top man in Naples.

Whatever their eventual ranks in Camorra society, all new recruits were required to serve a one-year apprenticeship to a Camorrista and after that time to give proof of courage and loyalty through the initiation ceremony. In early times the initiation had been quite severe, but it later entailed a pretend duel in which only the arm of the novice was wounded. The Camorristas and the novice stood around a coin that had been laid on the ground. When the signal was given, the novice had to pick up the coin, an apparently simple task except that the Camorristas also had to thrust at the coin—with their knives. Needless to say, things usually got a little sticky for the novice, who was generally pierced through in several places. The reward for this strange form of bravery was three years as the lowest-grade member and service to the Camorrista who was assigned to him as master.

After the initiation, there was a ceremony to receive the novice into the society. This ceremony included cutting one of the novice's veins, then having him take a blood oath to keep the society's secrets and to obey orders. Several other symbolic gestures involving a dagger, a loaded pistol, and a poisoned glass of water showed his readiness to die for the society.

By the turn of the century, the Camorra controlled almost all southern Italy and in many provinces its members were the top political representatives. The only organization that dared try to loosen the Camorra's hold on the country was the state police, the *carabinieri*, whose elite and dedicated officers were chosen from the best families in Italy. In 1900 the carabinieri launched a determined effort to break the power of the Camorra by going after its supreme leader. He managed to escape to the United States, but was captured and returned to Italy where he was imprisoned for thirty years.

In 1907, Italy's King Victor Emmanuel II declared war against the society and sent thousands of police and armed troops into the areas most strongly held by the Camorra. They arrested more than 3,000 top members and the society's leading assassins. They filled the prisons with Camorra members who promptly took control of the facilities. In retaliation for the jailings, numerous high-ranking officials were murdered.

By 1910, the confrontation between the government and the Camorra nearly had reached the level of a civil war, as armies of government soldiers attacked Camorra headquarters and areas under their control. Slowly the government gained the upper hand as hundreds of Camorristas were tried and convicted. Long prison sentences were given to the leaders but many later escaped to the U.S., where they set up operations in major cities such as New York, Chicago, New Orleans, and St. Louis.

For a time, the Camorra competed with the Mafia for supremacy in America, even openly fought for power in street gunfights. The Mafia was better organized than the Camorra, whose power in the U.S. was broken by 1920. Though defeated and far less powerful than they had once been, the Camorra continued to exist in both Italy and America, and maintain their society to this day.

VOCABULARY

Select the letter of the answer that is closest in meaning to the italicized word or phrase.

1. By the turn of the twentieth century, the *insidious* society had almost all southern Italy in its power.
    a. openly widespread
    b. secretly harmful
    c. universally appealing
    d. commonly accepted

2. The Camorra leadership wasn't satisfied with *petty* road robbery.
    a. frequent
    b. usual
    c. minor
    d. precise

3. Eventually, princes were *in league* with the smugglers.
    a. refusing to obey
    b. being greatly concerned
    c. not agreeing
    d. closely cooperating

4. Young men took pride in passing the *initiation rites.*
    a. written tests
    b. ceremonies of admittance
    c. special elections to choose leaders
    d. military training

5. The top-ranking Camorristas *extorted* from people of the highest levels of society.

    a. pleaded

    b. obtained money by force

    c. asked for social acceptance

    d. treated with disrespect

6. The initiation *entailed* a pretend duel.

    a. involved

    b. approved of

    c. caused

    d. described

7. The arm of the *novice* was wounded.

    a. experienced worker

    b. leader

    c. apprentice

    d. convicted criminal

8. The carabinieri, or state police, had *elite* and dedicated officers.

    a. common

    b. top-quality

    c. tough

    d. newly trained

9. In *retaliation* for the jailings, numerous high-ranking officials were murdered.

    a. willing acceptance

    b. the escape

    c. taking control

    d. revenge

10. The Camorra competed with the Mafia for *supremacy* in America.

    a. acceptance

    b. benefits

    c. control

    d. support

Organize

conduct/manage/run/supervise

The verbs above all mean to organize. They differ as follows:

conduct = to direct others or to lead. The person who conducts does the work him/herself.

manage = to use one's organizational skills. To see that something runs smoothly and gets done.

run = means the same as manage but has the added meaning of doing the work oneself.

supervise = to make sure others are doing their work.

Put each of the words in the box below under the correct heading. You may place the same word(s) under more than one heading.

a store   a company   negotiations   a meeting   a hotel
theater   a family business a trial   an experiment   a country
an organization   a research program

conduct	manage	run	supervise

Guilty People

....

criminal/felon/convict/culprit/delinquent

The above words all mean guilty people. They differ as follows:

criminal = a person guilty of a serious crime punishable by imprisonment or death.

felon = the legal term for someone convicted of a crime punishable by a lengthy jail sentence or death.

convict = a criminal who is serving a prison sentence.

culprit = a person or thing that has done something wrong and is causing an undesirable situation.

delinquent = a young person who has committed a crime, usually for fun.

Use one of the words above to best complete the following sentences.

1. The three young _____ were charged today with painting graffiti on the school walls.

2. The highly dangerous _____ escaped from prison yesterday and there is a statewide search for him.

3. The telephone went out of order again and it turned out that a faulty line was the _____ .

4. According to the police, the _____ who committed the bank robbery was disguised as a computer repair person.

5. He is a hardened _____ and even a long prison sentence won't change him.

6. We caught the _____ who was stealing paper from the photocopying machine at the office.

A. Looking for the Main Ideas

Some of the following statements from Reading 1 are main ideas and some are supporting statements. Find the statements in the reading. Write M in the blank in front of each main idea. Write S in the blank in front of each supporting statement.

_____ 1. The society grew like mold on cheese, rapidly extending its power and its operations.

_____ 2. Statesmen, dignitaries, even members of the church were involved in the society's criminal activities.

_____ 3. In Naples, the capital of the Camorra, city officials, the police force, and business owners were held tightly under the society's ironfisted rule.

_____ 4. Officers were paid to ignore Camorra thugs who tore apart the shops of owners who refused to pay a weekly fee to the local Camorra chief.

_____ 5. Neopolitan politics was dominated by the society and with few exceptions all political candidates were Camorristas.

_____ 6. The Camorra was divided into classes.

_____ 7. Whatever their eventual ranks in Camorra society, all new recruits were required to serve a one-year apprenticeship to a Camorrista and after that time to give proof of courage and loyalty through the initiation ceremony.

_____ 8. In early times the initiation had been quite severe, but it later entailed a pretend duel in which only the arm of the novice was wounded.

_____ 9. After the initiation, there was a ceremony to receive the novice into society.

_____10. They arrested more than 3,000 top members and the society's leading assassins.

B. Skimming and Scanning for Details

Scan Reading 1 quickly to complete the following sentences.

1. The Camorra society started out in the _____ of Naples.

2. One of the secret methods of communication among Camorra gangsters was to _____ if a victim was with someone else.

3. The leaders of the Camorra society went from petty thievery and thuggery to _____ , _____ , and _____ .

4. Although members of the Camorra originally came from the criminal classes, the society eventually recruited members from the _____ families of Naples.

5. Political control of the provinces was in the hands of _____ made up of _____ .

6. A new recruit spent _____ years as a lowest-grade member.

7. The only organization that dared to confront the Camorra was the _____ .

8. In 1907, _____ went after the Camorra with government soldiers and eventually gained the upper hand after trying and convicting hundreds of _____ .

9. Camorra leaders who escaped to the U.S. set up operations in major cities like _____ , _____ , _____ , and _____ .

10. In the United States, the Camorra fought for power with the _____ .

C. Making Inferences and Drawing Conclusions

Some of the following statements are facts from the reading. Other statements can be inferred. Write F in the blank in front of each factual statement. Write I in the blank in front of each inference.

_____ 1. Were it not for the weakness and corruption of those in authority, the Camorra would never have had such power.

_____ 2. The society's power attracted young men from aristocratic families.

_____ 3. The Camorra rituals were barbaric in nature.

_____ 4. Common people were helpless to stop the power of the Camorra.

_____ 5. The Camorra had political control over the provinces.

_____ 6. Camorra members had different ranks and functions.

_____ 7. The state police were very courageous to try to fight the Camorra.

_____ 8. Challenging the Camorra was a dangerous undertaking.

_____ 9. The better-organized Mafia broke the power of the Camorra in the United States.

_____10. Although less powerful than they once were, the Camorra is still in existence today.

DISCUSSION

Discuss these questions with your classmates.

1. Many groups have their own rituals and ceremonies. Describe the ceremony of a group you belong to or have heard about.

2. Explain how groups like the Camorra became so powerful.

3. Why do people like to join clubs and organizations?

Reading 2: Stranglers in a Strange Land

The following article, *"Stranglers in a Strange Land"* by Janet Milhomme, appeared in *Escape Magazine,* in 1994.

Figure 1   17th/18th century Indian Thugs. The Manson family of their day in India, called "Thags" in Hindustani, which means "deceivers." They traveled in gangs of up to 900 with one leader who directed all the moves and preyed on innocent travelers.

In the annals[1] of travel, there has never been a road hazard like them. Thugs were their name. Strangulation their game.

The Thugs, or Thugees as they were called then by the British, turned travel in 17th- and 18th-century India into a state of emergency. They murdered as many as 40,000 people a year for decades while authorities looked the other way and counted the protection profits.

Almost without exception, the Thugs preyed on travelers making their way along dusty Indian roads. They would insinuate themselves into the confidence of the traveler until the opportunity arose to strangle, rob and bury them. Master con men, they were called Thags in Hindustani, meaning "deceivers."

They were the Manson[2] family of their day and no traveler was safe from their wiles. To carry out the supposed wishes of the goddess Kali, cult[3] members, who numbered in the tens of thousands, staged elaborate pro-

---

[1] annals = historical records.

[2] the Manson family = a group headed by Charles Manson who committed some shocking murders in the 1960s.

[3] cult = a group of people believing in a particular set of religious beliefs or principles.

ductions to ensnare unsuspecting travelers. Each gang (which might consist of as many as 900 men) had its leader who directed all the moves. Divided into separate parties of 10 to 20 persons, they either followed each other at a distance or, taking different routes, rendezvoused at appointed places, presumably by accident, and without appearing to know each other.

Thugs never acted without the strength of numbers or the element of surprise. Some of the gang were sent ahead to select a good killing site and dig graves while others brought up the rear to keep watch. If an advance party needed more assistance to kill their victims, they made certain marks on the roads, clues to the gang who followed that they were to hasten forward. So efficient was their system of communication that if travelers began to suspect one party, another group of Thugs would infiltrate. After getting rid of the first group, the second then strangled them. If travelers suspected or avoided both parties, two or more Thugs were ordered to keep them in sight, while signals were sent to other members in a production that might last a week or more before the victims were finally waylaid.[4]

Thugs traveled for days in the company of their prey, using every manner to gain their friendship and confidence, usually proposing that they travel together for safety reasons. The murders normally occurred when the party rested at an appropriate spot. The stranglers came up from behind with accomplices at their side. Two Thugs were considered indispensable and commonly three gave a hand.

Their weapon was a strip of twisted yellow or white silk knotted at one end with a silver coin consecrated to Kali. The Thug held the opposite end in his hand, and with a flick of the wrist, threw the weighted end around the victim's throat, and it was over in seconds. The bodies, dumped in shallow graves, were for Kali. Since Kali conveniently had no need for earthly treasures, the booty went to the Thugs.

Despite the mayhem,[5] there was no outcry from the authorities. Rajahs and Indian chiefs, corrupt police and petty local authorities offered protection for a price. It wasn't until Lord William Bentinck (British Governor-General of India, 1833–35) took steps to attack the system that the Thugees were seriously pursued. His chief agent was Captain William Sleeman, a young Bengal Army officer who led a 12-year campaign that finally broke up the Thugs through mass arrests and execution.

From 1831 to 1837, 3,266 Thugs were captured, of whom 412 were hanged, 483 turned state's evidence, and the rest were transported or imprisoned for life. Ironically, many of the arrests were achieved by exploit-

---

[4] waylaid = stopped from wherever they were going.

[5] mayhem = chaos.

ing the criminals' passionate devotion to family. Thugs turned themselves in after family members were captured and imprisoned, and to Sleeman's astonishment, they were not the brutes he had envisioned but in many cases were otherwise upstanding citizens and family men.

Their confessions, however, were stupefying—many Thugs proudly admitting to an unthinkable number of murders. Their diaries, mostly lacking in detail, were monotonous lists of their morbid deeds.

"Left Poona and on arrival at Sarora murdered a traveler."

"On nearly reaching Bhopal, met 3 Brahmins and murdered them."

One Thug claimed to have strangled 431 persons during 40 years of Thugee. He said there were many more, but he was so intent on luring them to destruction that he lost count.

For all those who thought the world was getting less safe, the Thugs provide a little perspective.

VOCABULARY

Select the letter of the answer that is closest in meaning to the italicized word or phrase.

1. The Thugs *preyed on* travelers making their way along dusty Indian roads.

   a. hunted

   b. traced

   c. challenged

   d. discovered

2. The Thugs *insinuated* themselves into the confidence of a traveler.

   a. gradually suggested

   b. completely concealed

   c. highly advised

   d. slowly introduced

3. The Thugs were master *con men* who were called Thags meaning "deceivers."

   a. learners

   b. tricksters

   c. thieves

   d. instructors

4. No traveler was safe from their *wiles*.

    a. jokes

    b. stories

    c. tricks

    d. humor

5. Thugs staged elaborate productions to *ensnare* unsuspecting travelers.

    a. trap

    b. fight

    c. blame

    d. ruin

6. The Thug parties would give clues to the gang who followed that they were to *hasten* forward.

    a. approach

    b. volunteer

    c. shoot

    d. hurry

7. Their system of communication was so efficient that if travelers began to suspect one party, another group of Thugs would *infiltrate*.

    a. run through

    b. go through

    c. join up

    d. spread out

8. Their weapon had a silver coin attached to it *consecrated to* the goddess Kali.

    a. prepared for

    b. dedicated to

    c. chosen for

    d. equipped for

9. Since the goddess Kali conveniently had no need for earthly treasures, the *booty* went to the Thugs.

    a. gains

    b. medal

    c. award

    d. payment

10. To Sleeman's astonishment, the Thugs were not the *brutes* he had envisioned.

    a. strong characters

    b. unstable characters

    c. degraded characters

    d. weak characters

Themes

Dangerous

....

risky/hazardous/dangerous

Risky, *hazardous*, and *dangerous* all have similar meanings. They differ as follows:

risky = dangerous, used to describe actions.

hazardous = dangerous, but involves chance.

dangerous = unsafe, full of risk.

Write dangerous, hazardous, or risky in the blanks below. More than one of these words may fit some sentences.

1. *The virus is* _____ .

2. *Hang gliding can sometimes be* _____ .

3. *The rattlesnake is* _____ .

4. *The criminal is* _____ .

5. *The journey through the jungle was* _____ .

6. *The route was* _____ *because of landslides.*

7. *The organization is* _____ .

8. *The robbery in broad daylight was* _____ .

Suggest

....

insinuate/imply/hint

Insinuate, imply and *hint* all mean to suggest in some way. Their usage differs as follows:

insinuate = to indicate something bad without saying it openly.

imply = to suggest without saying it in words.

hint = to intentionally suggest something.

Choose the correct word in the following sentences.

1. Her behavior (implied/insinuated) that she wanted to go home early.

2. Are you (insinuating/hinting) he was the murderer?

3. The manager (hinted/insinuated) at the possibility of a bonus if the work was completed on schedule.

4. He (implied/insinuated) that I had gotten the position by corrupt means.

5. She (hinted/implied) I would get the promotion.

6. The letter (implies/insinuates) that you will get the insurance money.

COMPREHENSION

A. Looking for the Main Ideas

Look at Reading 2 to find the answers to the following questions.

1. That is the main idea of paragraph 5?

2. Which line states the main idea in paragraph 6?

3. Which sentence contains the main idea in paragraph 8?

B. Skimming and Scanning for Details

Scan the article quickly to find the answers to the following questions. Write complete answers.

1. Who did the Thugs murder?

2. Why did the Thugs murder people?

3. How many Thugs were there in India?

4. What did the Indian authorities do about the Thugs?

5. According to the article, what would be done if travelers suspected a group of Thugs?

6. According to the article, why would a Thug travel with his victim?

7. When did they murder a party of victims?

8. What did they use to strangle their victims?

9. What does the word *system* in paragraph 8 refer to?

10. According to the article, why were their confessions stupefying?

C. Making Inferences and Drawing Conclusions

The answers to these questions are not directly stated in the passage. Circle the letter of the answer that best completes the sentence.

1. It can be inferred from the passage that Kali represented _____ .

   a. wealth

   b. travel

   c. destruction

   d. power

2. From the passage, it can be inferred that the Thugs _____ .

     a. were good actors

     b. worked alone

     c. did not care about money

     d. were outcasts of society

3. From the passage, it can be concluded that the Thugs _____ .

     a. were a government organization

     b. were a widespread and powerful organization

     c. could be recognized easily

     d. were bothered by their conscience

DISCUSSION

Discuss these questions with your classmates.

1. What are the pros and cons of belonging to an organized group?

2. Many people believe that crime today is worse than it was in the past. Argue for or against this statement.

3. If you belonged to a secret organization, could you keep its secrets all your life? If not, what do you think would happen?

WRITING

Writing a Summary

Write a one-paragraph summary of Reading 1. Compare your summary to the summary checklist on page 265.

How To | Write

HOW TO SUMMARIZE
PAGE 263

Paraphrasing

Paraphrase paragraph 5 in Reading 2.
Begin with either:
According to Milhomme, . . .
or
Based on Milhomme's article, . . .

How To | Write

HOW TO PARAPHRASE
PAGE 257

Research

You may use your research later to write your descriptive essay.

HOW TO DO LIBRARY RESEARCH
PAGE 248

How To Write

Choose a particular group of people and find two or three dominant characteristics particular to them. Consult appropriate sources in the library, and/or use your own experience or that of your friends to gather information.

The following are suggested topics:

The Amish	The Mormons	The Boy/Girl Scouts
The Shakers	The Masons	The Red Cross
Greenpeace	The Salvation Army	The Quakers

Read the following essay written by a student.

Rastafarians

It was when I visited Jamaica some years ago that I first learned about Rastafarians. Since then I have learned more about them through friends and my own research. Rastafarians are members of a Jamaican religious movement that started in the 1930s. According to their belief, the only true God is the late Ethiopian emperor Haile Selassie who was originally known as Ras Tafari. Rastafarians also believe that white Christian preachers and missionaries have distorted the Bible to hide the fact that Adam and Jesus were black. The Rastafarians can be described as a religious group popularly characterized by their special hairstyle, music, and ganja.

Rastafarians have a special way of wearing their hair in the form of dreadlocks. According to Rastafarian belief no comb or razor must touch their hair or beards. Following this rule, Rastafarians let their hair grow long and only wash it, leaving it to dry naturally. This results in a mass of long, knotted hair that looks like a lion's mane. These dreadlocks are protected by wearing a handknitted hat with the Rastafarian colors of red, green, and gold. The red color represents the blood lost in the fight for black freedom; the green stands for life and ganja, the holy herb; and yellow stands for the wisdom of their God, Jah.

Rastafarians have become known in the western world not because of their religion but because of their reggae music. Reggae is a style of Jamaican music similar to American soul music but with a special rhythm. Reggae songs express one or two ideas of Rastafarianism which are repeated over and over again. A reggae concert is like a religious ceremony where the musicians are like priests repeating the message of their God, Jah, in the reggae rhythm. Bob Marley and his group popularized reggae music internationally. Bob Marley died in 1982, but his music still keeps the spirit of Rastafarians alive.

Rastafarians are characterized by the smoking of the holy herb, ganja. Rastafarians get together and smoke puffs of the herb, ganja, which is rolled into a large cigar. This herb originally came from India, and means marijuana in Indian. According to Rastafarians ganja is a holy herb whose use was authorized in the Bible. For Rastafarians smoking ganja is the way to understand themselves and God.

In conclusion, Rastafarians are commonly characterized in terms of the way they wear their hair, reggae music, and the smoking of ganja. However, this does not mean to say that this religious and political movement does not have any other characteristics or rules and regulations. Rastafarianism is a whole way of life.

Tasos
Cyprus

STUDENT ESSAY FOLLOW-UP

Read about the dominant impression on the next page before answering the following questions.

1. Underline the thesis statement.

2. What three characteristics of Rastafarians does the writer focus on?

3. Are each of these characteristics then developed in the body paragraphs?

4. Examine paragraph 2. Do all the ideas support the main idea? Are descriptive words used to strengthen the dominant aspect?

5. Underline the dominant aspects or impressions in the three body paragraphs.

Description

Description is often used to make a narration or exposition more lively and interesting. Exposition may rely on some narration and description. Also, a narration may include exposition and description. A descriptive essay, therefore, does not have to be purely descriptive but can use narration and exposition as well.

▶ The Dominant Impression

A good description has two strong elements: a dominant impression and appropriate supporting details. The dominant impression is the main effect a place, an object, a person, or a group of people has on our feelings or senses. We create the dominant impression by selecting the most important characteristic or feature of the person or group of people or place and emphasizing that feature. We can then develop the dominant impression by providing details that support it.

In the student essay about Rastafarians the three elements of the dominant impression are clearly stated in the thesis and developed in the body paragraphs. The reading on the Camorra focuses on the society's power and crimes. The end of the first paragraph states, "The strength and prestige of the Camorra escalated through the years, and by the turn of the twentieth century, the insidious society had almost all of southern Italy under its control."

Examine paragraph 5. How does it describe their power? Paragraph 3 talks about the crimes of the Camorra. What kinds of crimes did they carry out?

When reading about the Thugs in Reading 2, the dominant impression of their deceptiveness and their cold-bloodedness comes to mind. Which paragraph clearly describes their cold-bloodedness?

▶ Figures of Speech

Figures of speech are often used by writers to make their descriptions more vivid. Figures of speech are colorful words and expressions that make some kind of comparison. We will look at two figures of speech: the simile and the metaphor.

Simile

Of the many types of figures of speech, the most direct comparison is made with the use of the simile. In a simile one thing is compared with another to show a similarity, usually using the word *like* or *as*.

Examples:

The society grew *like mold on cheese.*
They were sly *as foxes* and deadly *as poisonous snakes.*
The Thugs were as efficient and well organized *as an army of ants.*

Find the similes in paragraph 2 and 3 of the student essay.

When writing similes, avoid the very obvious and overused ones such as "easy as pie," "busy as a bee," and "he eats like a pig." Try and create your own fresh and interesting similes.

Exercise 1

Complete the similes in the following sentences.

1. *The Thugs were as cold-blooded as* _____

   _____.

2. *The Thugs preyed on their victims like* _____

   _____.

3. *The Thugs were as cunning as* _____

   _____.

4. *Captain William Sleeman was as courageous as* _____

   _____.

5. *The goddess Kali was as evil as* _____

   _____.

6. *The Camorra was as powerful as* _____

   _____.

7. *Some members of the Camorra were as influential as* _____

   _____.

8. The Camorra was as dangerous as _____

_____.

9. People were as afraid of the Camorra as _____

_____.

10. The Camorra was as difficult to control as_____

_____.

▶ **Metaphor**

A metaphor expresses a comparison more indirectly without using "like" or "as." A word or phrase is used in the comparison suggesting the strong likeness between them.

Examples:

The confrontation between the government and the Camorra had nearly reached the level of a civil war. (The confrontation is compared to a civil war.)

They were the Manson family of their day. (The murderous activity of the Thugs is being compared to the horrible murders committed by the Manson family in our times.)

Exercise 2

Work with a partner or a group. Explain the comparisons being made in the following metaphors.

1. The Thugs were wolves in sheep's clothing.
2. They communicated with each other with the efficiency of radar signals.
3. The tentacles of the Camorra reached into every aspect of Italian society.
4. The Thugs were tigers in the grass ready to pounce on unsuspecting victims.
5. The steps of the Camorra pyramid led to the top man in Naples.
6. The *carabinieri* finally succeeded in rescuing Italy from the jaws of the Camorra.

Choose one of the following topics.

1 Write a descriptive essay using three dominant aspects of the group you researched earlier in this chapter.

2 Write a descriptive essay on an organization, a society, or a club that you are familiar with or would like to research. Use two or three adjectives to give the dominant impression.

3 Write a descriptive essay on a tribe or group of people that you are familiar with or would like to research. Use two or three adjectives to give the dominant impression.

4 Write a descriptive essay on a person you know using two or three adjectives to give the dominant impression.

1. Pre-writing.

Work alone, with a partner, or in a group.

1 Brainstorm the topic. Choose a pre-writing technique you prefer.

2 Brainstorm for descriptive adjectives and supporting details.

3 Work on a thesis statement.

How To **Write**

HOW TO BRAINSTORM
PAGE 242

2. Outlining.

A. Organize your ideas.

Step 1: Write your thesis statement.

Step 2: Select two or three of the best descriptive adjectives from your brainstorming activity.

Step 3: Find relevant descriptive details to support your dominant impression.

B. Make a more detailed outline. The essay outline on page 22 will help you.

3. Write a Rough Draft.

DRAFTING
PAGE 245

4. Revise Your Rough Draft.
   Use the revision check-
   list on page 246.

5. Edit Your Essay.
   Use the editing symbols
   on pages 247—248.

How To Write

EDITING
PAGE 247

6. Write Your Final Copy.

Chapter 5: Psychology

PRE-READING QUESTIONS

Discuss these questions with your classmates.

1 Look at the picture of the muscular man above. What do you think he is like? Place a check mark next to the characteristics you think this man has.

____ shy	____ sensitive	____ athletic
____ outgoing	____ studious	____ quiet
____ reserved	____ bold	____ tough-minded
	____ imaginative	

Now look at the thin man. Place a check mark next to the characteristics you think he has.

____ passive	____ anxious	____ outgoing
____ intellectual	____ talkative	____ aggressive
____ easygoing	____ thoughtful	____ active
	____ calm	

2 On what basis did you characterize these people?

3 Is it possible for the thin man to be outgoing and athletic or for the athletic man to be shy? Describe an incident in which you have been wrong about how you have judged a person by their physical appearance.

4 Do we expect our leaders to look a certain way?

Reading 1: Body Language

"Let me have men about me that are fat," says Julius Caesar to Marcus Antonius in Shakespeare's play *Julius Caesar*. In his opinion, fat people were more trustworthy than thin ones, that is, those with a "lean and hungry look," who "are dangerous."

Shakespeare wasn't the first person to categorize personality according to body type. And if you've ever reacted to people based on the way they look, you know he wasn't the last. The relationship between physical characteristics and personality has been explored for thousands of years, and used to predict and explain the actions of others. Although prehistoric man probably had his own ideas about the skinny guy in the cave next door, the ancient Greeks historically have been responsible for Western theories about body and character.

The Greeks believed the body was composed of four humors, or fluids: blood, black bile, yellow bile, and phlegm. Whichever someone had the most of led to a certain temperament or personality type—sanguine (hopeful), melancholic (sad), choleric (hot-tempered), or phlegmatic (lazy or slow).

Although this ancient theory eventually lost its popularity, it was replaced over the next few thousand years by all kinds of other ways to identify and catalog people by type. One of the most popular modern theories was proposed by William Sheldon in the late 1940s and early 1950s. He suggested a relationship between body shape and temperament (see chart). According to Sheldon's system, the endomorph, with an oval-shaped body and large, heavy stomach, is slow, sociable, emotional, forgiving, and relaxed. The mesomorph, with a triangular shape and a muscular, firm, upright body, is confident, energetic, dominant, enterprising, and at times hot-tempered. The ectomorph, with a thin, fragile body, is tense, awkward, and meticulous.

A number of researchers since Sheldon have contributed their own ideas to the basic theory that body shape and personality are somehow connected. Going one step beyond basic shape is the idea of "body splits." This theory looks at the body in sections— top to bottom, front to back, torso and limbs—with the idea

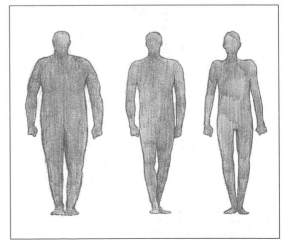

that each part of the body tells its own story. For example, the upper half of the body, consisting of our chest, head, and arms, is expressive and relates our feelings to others through gestures and facial movements. The lower body, on the other hand, is associated with more deeply felt emotions, particularly about family, children, and self-image.

According to this theory, someone with a well-developed upper body will be active and outwardly confident. However, if this same person has noticeably thinner legs and narrow hips, he or she might have trouble expressing themselves to others, lack self-confidence, and find it difficult to think about their deepest emotions. A person with a small chest but large hips will have opposite traits, such as being shy in public but emotional and loving toward friends and family. Look for the many clues to personality: weight distribution (heaviness and thinness in different parts of the body), muscular development, grace and coordination, and general health. For example, does one half of the body seem healthier, or more tense, or more relaxed than another? Look for tense shoulders or stiff legs and hips.

Backs and fronts are different, too. The front of the body is associated with our conscious self, the one we think about and show to others. The back, which is hidden from us most of the time, is associated with our unconscious self; that is, the feelings we hide from both ourselves and others. Many times we don't want to think about or show emotions such as anger and fear, and we tend to store these feelings in our back. If you're feeling stressful, your back is likely to be tense. People who find it hard to deal with problems without losing their temper are likely to have some kind of back trouble. Look around you at the stories backs tell. A stooped back is weighed down by burdens or troubles. A stiff and rigid back is hiding anger or stress. A straight and graceful spine is strong and flexible. Do you know what kind of back you have?

Finally, there is the split between torso, or body, and the limbs, or arms and legs. You express yourself with your arms and hands, and even your legs in the way you move about. People who are outgoing often use their hands and arms to gesture when they talk. They also walk with long, confident strides. Shy people hold their hands and arms quietly close to them and walk with small steps. Energetic people often tap their feet and move around a lot because it's hard for them to sit still. They can sometimes be impatient and are not the best listeners.

There is no end to theories about body shape and personality, and there is no doubt that certain people with certain bodies often have very predictable characters. However, there are some researchers who believe that the many instances in which body and personality go together are due to stereotyping; that is, we expect a certain type of person to have certain traits, so we see those traits whether they are there or not. For example, muscular people are believed to be dominant and forceful, so we treat them as leaders. But sometimes they are actually shy and timid. Fat people are supposed to be happy and warmhearted, but in reality they can just as easily be depressed or mean. Sometimes people will even act the way they think others expect them to act. By doing that, people fill the role in which we picture them.

No matter how you look at it, bodies and personalities are related, whether by chance or by choice. However, there are always exceptions to the rule and whenever that happens, there goes the theory. After all, we're only human, and hopefully that means we have a mind of our own—whether we're fat, skinny, or something in between.

VOCABULARY

Select the letter of the answer that is closest in meaning to the italicized word or phrase.

1. According to Shakespeare, people with a "*lean* and hungry look," were dangerous.

    a. wild

    b. thin

    c. weak

    d. angry

2. The Greeks believed a choleric was *hot-tempered*.

    a. lively

    b. romantic

    c. easily angered

    d. enthusiastic

3. The person with a triangular shape is confident, dominant, and *enterprising*.

    a. has courage to start new and difficult things

    b. is ready to attack at any time

    c. has special skills in business

    d. likes to be in control

4. The person with a thin, fragile body is tense and *awkward*.

    a. not friendly to people

    b. not very active or worried

    c. lacks skill in moving his/her body

    d. lacks ability to make decisions

5. The thin, fragile ectomorph is also *meticulous*.

    a. concerned about spending money

    b. concerned about details

    c. unable to decide

    d. unable to relax

6. Each section of the body—top to bottom, front to back, *torso* and limbs—tells its own story.

    a. the head and shoulders

    b. the front of the head and body

    c. the body without the head, legs, and arms

    d. the body with head, but without the legs and arms

7. Look at clues to personality such as weight distribution, muscular development, *grace* and coordination, and general health.

    a. beauty and harmony in movement

    b. beauty of physical features

    c. healthy color of physical features

    d. straight and flexible body

8. A *stooped* back is weighed down by troubles.

    a. hardened

    b. painful

    c. tense

    d. bent

9. People who are outgoing walk with long confident *strides*.

    a. movements

    b. steps

    c. gestures

    d. manners

10. Fat people can just as easily be depressed or *mean*.

    a. unkind

    b. moody

    c. anxious

    d. gloomy

Themes

Having Little Fat

Look up the words for having little fat *given below. Put each under the* **headings below. You may use a word more than once.**

lean	skinny	slim	slender
thin	scrawny	lanky	underweight

slice of bread	steak	favorable	not favorable

Having Much Fat

Look up the words for having much fat *given below. Then answer the questions that follow.*

obese	chubby	plump	flabby
stocky	dumpy	thickset	stout

1. Which of these words can describe cheeks?
2. Which of these words means very fat?
3. Which of these words mean short and broad?
4. Which of these words cannot be used to describe a man?
5. Which of these words are favorable?

Temper

Temper means your frame of mind or how you are feeling, and it is usually associated with anger.

1. According to the passage, what does *temperament* mean?
2. Which words in the passage mean to get angry?
3. What do you think the word *temperamental* means?
4. What kind of temper do you have?

COMPREHENSION

A. Looking for the Main Ideas

Circle the letter of the best answer.

1. The main idea of paragraph 4 is
   a. the Greek theory of personality lost its popularity over the years.
   b. many personality theories had been developed by the forties and fifties.
   c. William Sheldon's theory relates body shape to personality.
   d. large, heavy people are usually sociable and emotional.

2. Paragraph 7 is mostly about

    a. the difference between a person's front and back.

    b. how stress and anger can cause back problems.

    c. how we hide our feelings from ourselves and others.

    d. what a person's back can reveal about him or her.

3. Paragraph 9 is mainly concerned with

    a. the many theories about body shape and personality.

    b. how stereotyping affects the way we see ourselves and others.

    c. how muscular people tend to be leaders.

    d. how some people have very predictable characters.

B. Skimming and Scanning for Details

Scan the passage quickly to find the answers to these questions. Write complete answers.

1. According to the passage, how has the relationship between physical characteristics and personality been used?

2. What are the four fluids and their related personality types as they are found in the Greek theory?

3. What are the three shapes into which William Sheldon divided people?

4. In paragraph 5, sentence 1, to what does the word "their" refer?

5. In the theory of "body splits," what is the significance of the upper body?

6. To what do the words "this theory" refer in paragraph 6, line 1?

7. What are four clues to personality that you should look for, according to the theory of "body splits"?

8. With which part of the personality is the front of the body associated?

9. According to the passage, what type of person may not be a good listener? Why?

10. What is the stereotype of fat people?

C. Making Inferences and Drawing Conclusions

The answers to these questions are not directly stated in the passage. Circle the letter of the best answer.

1. The passage implies that
    a. ancient people didn't know enough to understand personality theories.
    b. very few theories that categorize people by their appearance have been popular.
    c. it's natural for people to look for relationships between physical characteristics and personality.
    d. it takes a scientific mind to identify and categorize people according to body type.

2. From the passage, it can be concluded that
    a. our emotions and attitudes can affect our health and appearance.
    b. a person with a pleasant personality is most likely to be pear-shaped.
    c. the shape of the body as a whole tells the most about personality.
    d. it's easy to hide our emotions from others.

3. It can be inferred from the passage that
    a. people have lost interest in theories linking personality to looks.
    b. when we expect people to behave in a certain way, we're often disappointed.
    c. there is nothing to support theories about body shape and personality.
    d. stereotyping can make it difficult for us to see others as they really are.

4. The author's attitude toward theories that categorize people according to body type is

      a. disbelieving.

      b. interested.

      c. shocked.

      d. disappointed.

DISCUSSION

Discuss these questions with your classmates.

1. Which physical characteristics do you use to categorize people?

2. What do you think of Sheldon's theory of relating body type with personality?

3. How can gestures and body movement be used to classify people?

4. Give some examples of how people are stereotyped.

Reading 2: Extraversion and Introversion

The following passage is taken from a college psychology text called *Personality* by Jerry Burger. In Chapter 9, The Biological Approach, Hans Eysenck's theory of personality is described. Eysenck claims that differences in personality are based on biological differences.

Figure 1 *Traits Associated with Eysenck's Two Major Personality Dimensions* Adapted from Eysenck and Eysenck (1968); reprinted by permission of Educational and Industrial Testing Service.

Eysenck's research strategy begins by dividing the elements of personality into various units that can be arranged hierarchically. The basic structure in this scheme is the *specific response* level, which consists of specific behaviors. For example, if we watch a man spend the afternoon talking and laughing with friends, we would be observing a specific response. If this man spends many afternoons each week having a good time with friends, we have evidence for the second level in Eysenck's model, a *habitual response*. But it is likely that this man doesn't limit himself to socializing just in the afternoon and just with these friends. Suppose this man also devotes a large part of his weekends and quite a few evenings to his social life. If you watch long enough, you might find that he lives for social gatherings, discussion groups, parties, and so on. You might conclude, in Eysenck's terms, that this person exhibits the *trait*[1] of sociability. Finally,

---

[1] trait = characteristic.

Eysenck argues that traits such as sociability are part of a still larger dimension of personality. That is, people who are sociable also tend to be impulsive, active, lively, and excitable. All these traits combine to form the *supertrait* Eysenck calls **extraversion.**

How many of these supertraits are there? Originally, Eysenck's factor analytic research yielded evidence for two basic dimensions that could sub-sume[2] all other traits: *extraversion-introversion* and *neuroticism.* Because the dimensions are independent of one another, people who score on the extraversion end of the first dimension can score either high or low on the second dimension. Further, as shown in Figure 1, someone who scores high on extraversion and low on neuroticism possesses different traits than does a person who scores high on both extraversion and neuroticism.

Where do you suppose you fall in this model? If you are the prototypic[3] extravert, then Eysenck describes you as "outgoing, impulsive and uninhibited, having many social contacts and frequently taking part in group activities. The typical extravert is sociable, likes parties, has many friends, needs to have people to talk to, and does not like reading or studying by himself." An introvert is "a quiet, retiring sort of person, introspective, fond of books rather than people; he is reserved and distant except to intimate friends." Of course, most people fall somewhere between these two extremes, but each of us is perhaps a little more of one than the other.

Eysenck argues that extraverts and introverts differ not only in terms of behavior but also in their *physiological*[4] makeup. Eysenck originally maintained that extraverts and introverts have different levels of *cerebral cortex arousal*[5] when in a nonstimulating, resting state. Although it may sound backward at first, he proposed that extraverts generally have a *lower* level of cortical arousal than do introverts. Extraverts seek out highly arousing social behavior *because* their cortical arousal is well below their desired level when doing nothing. In a sense, highly extraverted people are simply trying to avoid unpleasant boredom. Their problem is feeding their need for stimulation. Introverts have the opposite problem. They typically operate at an above-optimal cortical arousal[6] level. These people select solitude and nonstimulating environments in an effort to keep their already-high arousal level from becoming too aversive. For these reasons, extraverts enjoy a noisy party that introverts can't wait to leave.

---

[2] subsume = classify within a larger category.

[3] prototypic = an original after which something is modeled.

[4] physiological = biological (concerned with how the body works).

[5] cerebral cortical arousal = part of the brain that is activated by the nervous system.

[6] above-optimal cortical arousal = more than desirable activation of the brain.

Unfortunately, a great deal of research has failed to uncover the different level of base-rate cortical arousal[7] proposed by Eysenck. For example, introverts and extraverts show no differences in brain-wave activity when at rest or when asleep (Stelmack, 1990). But this does not mean that Eysenck's original theorizing was entirely off base. Rather, there is ample evidence that introverts are more sensitive to stimulation than extraverts are (Stelmack, 1990). That is, introverts are more quickly and strongly aroused when exposed to loud music or the stimulation found in an active social encounter. Introverts are even more responsive than extraverts when exposed to chemical stimulants, such as caffeine or nicotine.

Consequently, many researchers now describe extraverts and introverts in terms of their different sensitivity to stimulation, rather than the different base rate of cortical activity Eysenck proposed. However, the effect is essentially the same. Because of physiological differences, introverts are more quickly overwhelmed by the stimulation of a crowded social gathering, whereas extraverts are likely to find the same gathering rather pleasant. Extraverts are quickly bored by slow-moving movie plots and soft music because they are less likely to become aroused by these subtle sources of stimulation than introverts are.

---

[7] base-rate cortical arousal = low degree activation of the brain.

VOCABULARY

Select the letter of the answer that is closest in meaning to the italicized word or phrase.

1. Eysenck divided the elements of personality into units that can be arranged *hierarchically.*

   a. evenly spaced

   b. randomly organized

   c. ranked higher to lower

   d. combined in groups

2. Traits are part of a larger *dimension* of personality.

   a. subject

   b. part

   c. division

   d. range

3. People who are sociable also tend to be *impulsive.*
   a. kind
   b. arrogant
   c. hasty
   d. cautious

4. Eysenck describes extraverts as "outgoing, impulsive and *uninhibited.*"
   a. generous with money
   b. free and open
   c. unimaginative
   d. undependable

5. An introvert is "a quiet, *retiring* sort of person."
   a. possessing an excellent memory
   b. attending to duties willingly
   c. not fond of work
   d. avoiding the company of others

6. Eysenck thinks introverts are *introspective* and fond of books.
   a. thoughtful
   b. tolerant
   c. patient
   d. easygoing

7. Highly extraverted people try to feed their need for *stimulation.*
   a. excitement
   b. relaxation
   c. knowledge
   d. success

8. Introverts select nonstimulating environments in an effort to keep their already high arousal level from becoming too *aversive.*
   a. unimportant
   b. unpleasant
   c. unnecessary
   d. unsafe

9. There is *ample* evidence that introverts are more sensitive to stimulation than extraverts are.

    a. less than might be expected

    b. only a part of

    c. more than enough

    d. exactly what is needed

10. Extraverts are less likely to become aroused by *subtle* sources of stimulation than introverts are.

    a. hardly noticeable

    b. very unusual

    c. extremely displeasing

    d. constant

Themes

Show

show/exhibit/display/expose

The verbs *show*, *exhibit*, *display*, and *expose* are all similar in meaning. They differ slightly in meaning as follows:

show = to let something or someone be seen.

expose = to make visible by uncovering so as to leave without protection.

exhibit = to show in public, usually to attract attention as for a sale or a competition, or to show evidence of a quality.

display = to spread objects out so that they can be easily seen by the public.

Put each of the words in the box below under the correct headings.
You may use the words more than once.

skin to the sun	paintings	new cars for sale
fruit in a store	books to a friend	danger in the wild
a flag in a window	a large knowledge of vocabulary	
the foundation of an old building		a quality of endurance

show	expose	exhibit	display

Prefixes

The adjectives used in the phrases below can all be used to describe people. Make them negative by filling in each blank with an appropriate prefix from the box.

ir	im	in	un

1. an ___offensive person

2. an ___sincere woman

3. an ___flexible boss

4. an ___consistent behavior

5. an ___practical way

6. an ___corruptible officer

7. an ___discreet manner

8. an ___decisive child

9. an ___fallible judge of character

10. an ___elegant posture

11. an ___efficient worker

12. an ___judicious judgment

13. an ___reproachable character

14. an ___responsible person

15. an ___rational thinker

16. an ___personal judge

17. an ___patient onlooker

18. an ___bending father

19. an ___enlightened colleague

20. an ___pretentious millionaire

A. Looking for the Main Ideas

Write complete answers to the following questions about Reading 2.

1. What is the main idea of paragraph 1?

2. Which lines state the main idea of paragraph 2?

3. What is paragraph 3 mostly about?

4. Which sentence contains the main idea in paragraph 4?

B. Skimming and Scanning for Details

Scan the reading quickly to complete the following sentences.
Circle the letter of the best answer.

1. According to the passage, the basic structure of Eysenck's scheme for determining someone's personality type is _____ .
    a. habitual response
    b. supertraits
    c. specific response
    d. extraversion

2. If a person often does the same activity, then that behavior is considered _____ .
    a. not unusual
    b. a trait
    c. a habitual response
    d. model behavior

3. According to the passage, if a man enjoys parties, gatherings, and discussion groups, he is exhibiting the trait of _____ .
    a. sociability
    b. leadership
    c. optimism
    d. neuroticism

4. _____ is *not* an element of the supertrait "extraversion."
    a. Impulsiveness
    b. Activeness
    c. Liveliness
    d. Restlessness

5. Eysenck's original theory divided personality into _____ .

    a. three basic dimensions

    b. several supertraits

    c. impulsive and outgoing behavior

    d. extraversion-introversion and neuroticism

6. According to Eysenck's theory, an introvert _____ .

    a. has many friends

    b. likes books more than people

    c. goes to parties several times a week

    d. is impulsive

7. According to Eysenck, extraverts and introverts differ _____ .

    a. only in their behavior

    b. both behaviorally and physiologically

    c. only in their physiological makeup

    d. mostly in the way they think

8. Eysenck was interested in comparing levels of cerebral cortex arousal in extraverts and introverts when _____ .

    a. they were resting

    b. they were meeting other people

    c. they were feeding their need for stimulation

    d. they were alone

9. Eysenck thought that, compared to introverts, extraverts had _____ .

    a. a higher level of cortical arousal

    b. nearly the same level of cortical arousal

    c. a lower level of cortical arousal

    d. a different kind of cortical arousal

10. According to Eysenck, extraverted people like busy, noisy places because _____ .

    a. they're lonely without other people

    b. they're not very emotional

    c. they're shy

    d. they need the stimulation

C. Making Inferences and Drawing Conclusions

Some of the following statements can be inferred from the passage and others cannot. Circle the number of each statement that can be inferred.

1. Eysenck didn't spend enough time studying people to come up with a good personality theory.

2. People who don't have many friends are unhappy.

3. You can't categorize a person according to his or her behavior in a single situation.

4. An extravert isn't easily embarrassed.

5. Introverts are more intelligent than extraverts.

6. An introvert would like a museum better than a crowded movie theater.

7. An extravert likes people more than he needs them.

8. An introvert's discomfort might be mistaken for unfriendliness.

9. It's difficult to categorize people because our personalities are too complex to fit into defined categories.

10. You would most likely find more extraverts than introverts at a packed, high-energy nightclub.

DISCUSSION

Discuss these questions with your classmates.

1. Do you see yourself as an extravert or an introvert? Why?

2. Do you think Eysenck's theory makes sense? Why?

3. To what extent is personality hereditary? What other factors do you think affect the development of someone's personality?

4. Do you think people look for a partner who is a personality type like themselves? Do relationships with opposites work well?

Writing a Summary

Write a one-paragraph summary of Reading 1. Compare your summary to the summary checklist on page 265.

How To Write

HOW TO SUMMARIZE
PAGE 263

Paraphrasing

Paraphrase paragraph 4 in Reading 2.
Begin with either:
According to Burger, . . .
or
Based on Burger's article, . . .

How To Write

HOW TO PARAPHRASE
PAGE 257

Research

You may use your research later to write your classification essay.

How To Write

HOW TO DO LIBRARY RESEARCH
PAGE 248

Choose a particular subject that can be classified into three to five groups. Consult appropriate sources in the library, and/or use your own experience or that of your friends to gather information.

The following are suggested topics:

Socioeconomic groups	Blood groups	Personality types
Political groups	People's Looks	Types of pollution
Types of TV shows	Types of wars	Types of emotions

Read the following essay written by a student.

Classifying Personalities by Way of Astrology

The ancient Greek scientists observed the dazzling stars in the sky and created basic astronomy. They named each constellation after the characteristics of Greek gods. They used the twelve signs that appear in different periods in a year cycle to represent twelve human personalities. The twelve signs are: Aries, Taurus, Gemini, Cancer, Leo, Virgo, Libra, Scorpio, Sagittarius, Capricorn, Aquarius, and Pisces. Each sign projects the character and personality of one specific Greek god. The person born under a certain sign has a personality related to the characteristics of that Greek god. These twelve astrological signs can be classified into the four elements in this world which are: wind, earth, fire, and water.

The three signs in the first category are Gemini, Libra, and Aquarius. The characteristics of this element are just like the name of the element, wind. The people in this category are natural-born debaters. Their skills allow them to have more advantages than others in their careers and enable them to overcome difficulties easily. A lot of people in this element are often important people in big companies. They are remarkable people compared to other groups. People in this category do not like steady jobs; they like work with challenges and prefer exciting jobs. Nobody knows what is going on inside their heads just as you cannot catch the wind.

The second element, earth, includes the signs of Taurus, Virgo, and Capricorn. People born in this element have a rooted mind. They do not change their minds after making decisions. Their personality can be described as solid or immovable. Earth people usually exhibit a lot of patience. They can keep doing the same thing for years and often manage their lives into routines. Since they prefer doing stable tasks, they can often be found working for the government. These people are obstinate as stones but show higher loyalty to what they are doing than other groups. Earth people are often reliable partners in life.

Fire, the third element, includes the astrological signs of Aries, Leo, and Sagittarius. People born under this element tend to hurry, and do not have a lot of patience. In the battle of their lives, they like to charge ahead and take their enemy's position. They also have a strong desire for success. Because of their personalities, they become leaders of groups. Also, since they are not afraid of taking risks they often become pioneers in new fields such as explorers and inventors. Fire people are fighter types.

The last in the four elements is water, which includes the signs of Cancer, Scorpio and Pisces. People in these three astrological signs have sensitive feelings in the areas of emotions and love. They are born with talent in the field of art. Many artists, poets, sculptors, and musicians belong to one of these three signs. They use their natural-born skills to create many delicate articles of brilliance unequaled by their contemporaries. The way they express themselves is as soft and tender as water. Water people may be the closest friends or relatives in one's life. They are often perfect lovers, and there are many romantic stories about water people.

Classifying personality by using the four elements is not a foolproof method and there are many exceptions. A person with the element water may have an impatient personality as in the element fire; a fire person may be interested in the field of art or music; a person in the element of wind may enjoy working in a steady job; and an earth person may have multiple lifestyles. Psychiatrists use many techniques to classify human personality. Although using astrological signs and the elements is a way of classifying human personality, there is not much evidence to support it since we have multiple personalities in general—but it is a fun way of classifying personality.

Hsing Chueh
Taiwan

STUDENT ESSAY FOLLOW-UP

1. Underline the thesis statement.

2. How does the writer classify astrological signs?

3. What signs are in the first category? What are the characteristics of the first category? What signs are in the second category? What are the characteristics of the second category? What signs are in the third group? What are the characteristics of the third group? What signs are in the fourth group? What are the characteristics of the fourth group?

4. Does the writer use supporting examples for each element?

5. Can all the members of your class fall into one of the elements?

ORGANIZING

Classification

Classification means dividing people, objects, places, or ideas into various groups that share similar characteristics. With this method we put the many things in this world into order. Sociologists classify people into different classes; biologists classify plants or animals into species; and psychologists classify people's personalities into various types.

▶ The Principle of Classification

In order to be clear a classification should be made according to a single principle. This means that you choose one criterion to make your classification. For example, in Reading 1, "Body Language," Sheldon classifies people into three types—the endomorph, the mesomorph, and the ectomorph—on the principle of people's body type. In Reading 2, Eysenck classifies people into extraverts and introverts on the principle of personality. In your classroom, you can classify the students according to their ethnicity: Hispanic, Asian, European. You can also classify the same students according to their age: under 20, between 20 to 25, over 25. Another classification of the same students could be according to their work in class: hard-working students, average students, lazy students. Yet another classification could be made according to where they sit in class: in the front rows, in the middle, in the back rows. As you can see there are many principles that can be used; however, you must choose *one* principle of classification in your essay.

Once you have chosen a principle of classification, make sure the classification includes all members of the group. For example, you have decided to classify the students in your class by race. All the students fit nicely into the categories of Asian, Hispanic, and European except for one who is Arabic and does not fit. You must, therefore, add another category so that this student will fit, or look for another principle of classification.

To avoid omitting members, it is usually a good idea to divide the group into more than two categories. Most classification essays have three or four categories.

Exercise 1

Choose the one category that does not belong for each of the following classification groups. Give your reason.

Example:

    Vehicles: car, truck, van, jeep, motorcycle.
    Motorcycle does not belong. All the others have four wheels.

1. Sports: football, baseball, tennis, volleyball, swimming.
2. Literature: poetry, newspaper article, short story, drama, novel.
3. Transportation: by land, by air, by sea, by bus.
4. Teachers: bachelor's degrees, master's degrees, Ph.Ds, brilliance.
5. Style of clothes: formal, semi-formal, casual, beachwear.
6. Sport: hiking, skiing, swimming, ice-skating, tennis.
7. Animals: tortoise, crocodile, snake, lizard, monkey.
8. Food: protein, carbohydrates, fats, minerals, sugar.
9. Drugs: stimulants, depressants, hallucinogens, sedatives.

Exercise 2

Look at the following subjects and categories. Identify the principle of classification being used.

Example:

> Students: intelligent, average, below average
> Principle of classification: level of intelligence

1. *Teachers: tough graders, fair graders, easy graders*

   Principle of classification: _____

2. *People: round faces, diamond faces, rectangular faces, square*

   faces, triangular faces

   Principle of classification: _____

3. *People: dark hair, blond hair, red hair*

   Principle of classification: _____

4. *Drivers: very careful, careful, careless, reckless*

   Principle of classification: _____

5. *Bats: plant-eaters, blood-eaters, fish-eaters*

   Principle of classification: _____

6. *Burns: first-degree, second-degree, third-degree*

   Principle of classification: _____

7. *People: U.S. citizens, permanent legal residents, illegal residents*

   Principle of classification: _____

Introduction in the Classification Essay

Introduce the categories of classification you will be using in your thesis statement.

Examples of Thesis Statements:

The students in my class can be classified according to their level of intelligence: those who are intelligent, those who are average, and those who are below average.

People can be classified according to the shape of chin they have: those who have a pointed chin, those who have a round chin, those who have a broad chin and those who have a small chin.

Wrinkles fall into two categories: horizontal and vertical.

Fish fall into three basic classes: jawless fish, bony fish and cartilaginous fish.

When stating your categories in the thesis, remember to use parallel structure, or words of the same grammatical form, in the series.

FAULTY PARALLEL CONSTRUCTION
PAGE 284

Example:

Teachers can be classified as *those who dress formally, those who dress semi-formally*, and *those who dress casually*. (clauses)

In terms of body language, people can be classified according to *movements, postures*, and *facial expression*. (nouns)

The Greeks categorized people as *melancholic, phlegmatic, sanguine*, and *choleric*. (adjectives)

Transitions in the Classification Essay

For your classification essay, you will need several types of transitions:

1. Transitions that introduce categories:

the first	first	in addition
the next	second	finally
the last	third	besides

Examples:

The first group consists of students who are intelligent.
The next category includes students who are average.

2. Transitions that show comparison and contrast:

unlike	in contrast to	while
whereas	different from	like

Examples:

Unlike the slow endomorph, the mesomorph is energetic.
The temperament of the sanguine type, *in contrast to* the melancholic type, is hopeful.

3. Transitions that show examples:

one example	a good example	typical

Examples:

A good example of an extravert is the director of our company.
Your tennis coach is a *typical* mesomorph.

Exercise 3

Fill in the blanks using the following transition words. Each word can be used only once.

next	third	a good example	last
typical of	besides	first	fourth
whereas	in addition to	on the other hand	

According to Dr. Li Tao in his book *How to Read Faces*, people can be divided into two broad categories: those who are mentally inclined and those who are firmly practical people. The faces of mind-oriented people have balanced faces that can be divided into three roughly equal sections. _____ , physical types tend to have larger jaws and shorter faces. _____ these two broad categories, Dr. Tao divides faces into five basic shapes. The _____ is the round face with strong bone structure. It is _____ a mentally active person with self-confidence, resistance to illness, and potentially long life. _____ is the diamond-shaped face, which indicates a generally warm, strong-willed, and lucky person. _____ is the rectangular face and _____ is the square face. _____ the rectangular face indicates creativity, intelligence, and self-control, the square face belongs to an honest, well-balanced a person with leadership qualities. _____ is the triangular face, with its wide forehead, prominent cheekbones and pointed chin. _____ having a brilliant and sensual temperament, the triangular-faced person is intelligent and ambitious. _____ of such a person is the famous Elizabeth of Austria.

▶ WRITING PRACTICE

Choose one of the following topics.

1 Use one of the topics researched in this chapter to write a classification essay using three to five categories of classification.

2 Write an essay about major types of food using a principle of classification.

3 Write an essay classifying people by the way they dress. Establish your principle of classification and give examples of each group.

4 Write an essay classifying your friends into three or four major categories.

1. Pre-writing

Work alone, with a partner, or in a group.

How To Write

BRAINSTORMING
PAGE 242

1 Brainstorm the topic. Choose a prewriting technique you prefer.

2 Brainstorm for a principle of classification that includes all the members of the group. Do not have more than five categories since you need to write a paragraph on each.

3 Work on a thesis statement.

2. Outlining

A. Organize your ideas

Step 1: Write your thesis statement using parallel structure.

Step 2: Identify each category, defining or describing it.

Step 3: Give examples and specific details for each category.

B. Make a more detailed outline. The essay outline on page 22 will help you.

3. Write a Rough Draft.

How To	Write

Drafting
Page 245

4. Revise Your Draft. Use the revision checklist on page 246.

5. Edit Your Essay. Use the editing symbols on pages 247—248.

How To	Write

Editing
Page 247

6 Write Your Final Copy.

Chapter 6: Fashion in History

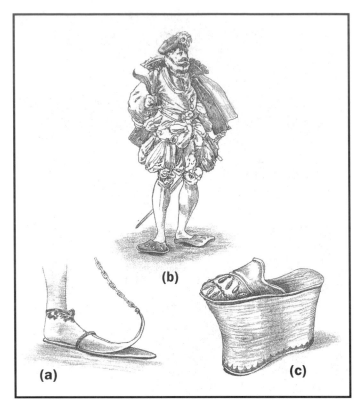

Figure 1 Drawings of different kinds of shoes: (a) very long toes (held up by fine chains to the knees); (b) wide toe (10 inches wide); and (c) platform shoes of the past.

PRE-READING QUESTIONS

Discuss these questions with your classmates or teacher.

1 Describe this season's shoe fashions.

2 Why do fashions come and go?

3 Do you dress according to the latest fashions? Why or why not?

The clothing and artifacts we wear send messages to others which may be intentional or unintentional. Look at the six people in the photos below. Judging from their clothes and artifacts, what can you say about their:

   a. economic status

   b. occupation

   c. nationality

   d. identification with a specific group

   e. likeability

   f. age.

Reading 1: The Toe of the Shoe

There are no creatures on earth less practical than humans, and nothing shows our frivolity better than fashion. From women's hoop skirts[1] to men's high hats, fashion victims through the ages have endured the ridiculous, the uncomfortable, and the absolutely dangerous in an effort to be fashionable. Even our feet, which are normally planted firmly on the ground, have suffered the pains of keeping up with the latest craze.

Since shoes are meant to protect the feet, it's hard to believe that some styles have made walking nearly impossible. In ancient China, it was the custom to bind the feet of upper-class girls so that when they became women they could squeeze their stunted feet into silk shoes only four inches long. The binding process involved bending the toes under the feet, which were bound with tight wrappings worn day and night until the feet stopped growing. The girl's deformed "lily feet" left her capable only of being admired. In other words, she had to be waited on hand and foot.[2] In spite of the painful process, the girl considered the binding a great honor, as girls with "large" feet were often ridiculed.

According to legend, the practice started when a royal princess was born with very small, deformed feet. To save her from embarrassment in later years, it was decided that no lady of the court would be considered truly noble unless she had feet as tiny as the princess. However the trend got started, Chinese poets helped it along by writing poems about the beauty of feet that were like "little golden lilies." A lady's tiny shoes and unsteady walk, if she could walk at all, were the pride of her wealthy husband who saw that she was carried about and waited upon in the style to which she was accustomed. When a man chose a wife with "lily feet," he sometimes took a second wife to act as her servant.

In the 1800s, the ruling Manchus passed a law forbidding the foot-binding practice, but many families ignored the command and continued the ancient tradition. It wasn't until China became a republic in 1912 that the binding of a girl's feet was finally considered a criminal offense.

In contrast to the Chinese, in other parts of the ancient world men were usually the ones undergoing discomfort, as well as incredible inconvenience, because of their shoes. And in this case the problem was not too

---

[1] hoop skirt = a skirt made to stand out from the body with a circle of flexible material to stiffen it.

[2] waited on hand and foot = constantly served or attended.

small, but rather oversized shoes, or at least shoe toes. Shoes with long, pointed toes were in fashion nearly 5,000 years ago in the Orient. The trend then spread to Asia Minor[3] where the toe underwent one slight change to an upturned look. Eventually the fashion "turned up" in Egypt, Greece, and surrounding countries.

Some Egyptian rulers preferred their five-inch shoe tips stuffed and formed in the shape of an uplifted elephant's trunk. Other Egyptian slippers spared no cloth with their eight-inch curled-up points. Although not quite as long, Greek and Roman magistrates[4] also wore shoes with turned-up toes as a symbol of their office when court was in session.

For more than 400 years, long-toed shoes went in and out of fashion, in a manner similar to the way hemlines[5] today fall below the calf[6] one year, and touch the thigh the next. Long-toed shoes got a second chance in Europe when the Crusaders[7] brought back samples of the style from Syria. By the thirteenth century, shoe tips were stretching out across Europe in all kinds of extravagant designs. Long-toed shoes characterized the man who didn't have to perform any physical labor, so the longer the toe, the wealthier the man. Imagine trying to work in a field while wearing shoes with foot-long toes!

Like a well-watered weed, long-toed shoes continued to grow until the fourteenth century when some measured thirty inches from heel to toe. Toes alone extended up to a full foot beyond the human foot inside the shoe. Some toes turned out; some arched up and down like a miniature roller coaster;[8] others simply went outward and upward. Toes defied gravity by being stuffed with moss,[9] hay, or wool, and were often stiffened with whalebone.

---

[3] Asia Minor = Turkey.

[4] magistrates = officials who judge cases in the lowest law courts.

[5] hemlines = the length of skirts or dresses.

[6] calf = fleshy back part of the leg between the knee and the ankle.

[7] the Crusaders = men who went on military expeditions undertaken by Christian powers in the eleventh, twelfth, and thirteenth centuries to win the Holy Land from the Muslims.

[8] roller coaster = a kind of small railroad with sharp slopes and curves, popular in amusement parks.

[9] moss = a small flat flowerless plant that grows like fur on wet soil or a wet surface.

Long-toed shoes got so ridiculous that in the 1300s, Pope Urban V and France's King Charles V condemned them as "an exaggeration against good manners" and "a worldly vanity." But these protests fell on deaf ears, or toes in this case, because the wearing of long-toed, flip-flopping shoes only increased. In England, the toes were sometimes adorned with tiny silver bells, called "folly bells." Some shoes became so absurdly long that to keep from tripping over them, the wearers held up the toes with fine chains attached to garters at their knees. So popular were long-toed shoes that the fashion continued through most of the fifteenth century and spread from nobles and wealthy people to other citizens, although many wore shoes with round and pointed toes of a more practical length.

Finally, long-toed shoes became such a nuisance that King Edward IV of England had laws enacted in 1463 to limit their length. But the laws didn't apply to everyone. In contrast to the privileged class, commoners were forbidden to wear shoes with toes more than two inches long. Any shoemaker who made shoes or boots that exceeded that limit was subject to a heavy fine. By 1470, French shoemakers were also forbidden to make shoes with long toes.

The fashion for long-toed shoes finally died out, but people couldn't seem to control their obsession with toes. In the early 1500s, in contrast to the previous century, toes went wide instead of long. The toes of some shoes were shaped in the form of a spread-open fan ten inches wide! Various styles had names like duck's bill, bear's paw, and cow's mouth. The silly-looking shoes invited mischief and it's said that a favorite practical joke in both England and France was to come upon a gentleman unobserved and nail the broad toes of his shoe to the floor. Once again, like the long toe, the wide-toe style became so foolish and troublesome that a law was passed to limit toe width to six inches.

In comparison to the extreme fashion of men's shoes, women wore only mildly wide shoes. Their shoe fronts were frequently stuffed with hay or cloth and shaped into a series of giant toes. Sometimes they had grooves with linings of contrasting colors.

In seventeenth-century France, unlike previous eras, it was women who became the foot fashion leaders. They started a trend that has influenced ladies' footwear ever since. Small, tight-toed shoes were the French ladies' preference. They were so small in fact that some women, like the girls in ancient China, bound their feet with waxed linen tape so they could squeeze into the dainty shoes. So painful was this process that it was not uncommon for several of the queen's ladies to faint during court ceremonies because of the bindings.

A century later, American women still followed French fashion with tight, high-buttoned shoes with long, pointed toes. Although relief was at hand in the form of open-toed shoes in the 1930s, it wasn't long before ladies again were hobbling along in high-heeled pointy-toed shoes that continue to reappear every few seasons to torment women anew.

Why, one might ask, have men and women subjected their feet to silly, clumsy, cumbersome, painful, even dangerous footwear over the years? The answer, of course, is vanity. In spite of the fact that the first shoes were no doubt designed for protection, they eventually served as symbols of religion, wealth, rank, and social position. More than anything else, however, they have given their wearers a means of satisfying the human desire for adornment. Once the foot was enhanced with a bit of fur or a leather strap, appearance became more important than usefulness. Vanity went straight to man's feet and we've been victims ever since.

VOCABULARY

Select the letter of the answer that is closest in meaning to the italicized word or phrase.

1. Nothing shows our *frivolity* better than fashion.

    a. habits

    b. pride

    c. intelligence

    d. foolishness

2. Chinese women who had their feet bound as girls could squeeze their *stunted* feet into silk shoes only four inches long.

    a. undersized

    b. narrow

    c. fragile

    d. injured

3. Toes *defied* gravity by being stuffed with moss, hay, or wool.

    a. condemned

    b. delayed

    c. controlled

    d. opposed

4. King Charles V condemned long-toed shoes as "a worldly *vanity*."

    a. pretence

    b. disgrace

    c. pride

    d. imitation

5. Long-toed shoes became such a *nuisance* that King Edward IV had laws enacted to limit their length.

    a. amusement

    b. popular item

    c. inconvenience

    d. risk

6. In the seventeenth-century France, unlike previous *eras*, it was women who became foot fashion leaders.

    a. time periods

    b. places

    c. special events

    d. groups of people

7. Some French women bound their feet with waxed linen tape so they could squeeze them into their *dainty* shoes.

    a. highly decorative

    b. small and delicate

    c. embroidered

    d. sharp-pointed

8. High-heeled, pointy-toed shoes still reappear every few seasons to *torment* women anew.

    a. make proud

    b. cause to suffer pain

    c. prevent from having

    d. improve the looks of

9. Why have men and women subjected their feet to *cumbersome* and even dangerous footwear over the years?

    a. useless

    b. foolish

    c. fashionable

    d. awkward

10. Shoes have given people a means of satisfying the human desire for *adornment.*

    a. approval

    b. decoration

    c. honor

    d. youthfulness

Themes

Time Periods

period	spell	term	span	epoch	age	era

period = a general word for an extent of time of any length or for whatever purpose.

Example:

The Civil War was the climax of a very important period in the growth of the United States of America.

spell = an unbroken period of time that is not usually very long.

Example:

The southern part of the country has been experiencing a very hot spell for the last three weeks.

term = a limited period of time.

Example:

The president of the United States can only serve two terms of four years.

span = a length of time stretching from one point to another.

Example:
He built his empire in a span of eight years.

epoch = a period of time in history marked by remarkable changes or events.

Example:
Picasso started a new epoch in painting.

age = a particular period in history, sometimes centuries long, usually marked by a common feature.

Example:
In the Stone Age people wore animal skins.

era = a period of time of a few years or decades that is characterized by something new.

Example:
The era of space exploration started in the 1960s.

Choose the correct answer to complete the following sentences.

1. The computer _____ has improved world communications.

   a. age   b. era   c. term

2. On my way back from Tokyo I will stop in on my friends in Hawaii for _____ .

   a. a term   b. an epoch   c. a spell

3. Our bank manager was a waiter for a short _____ .

   a. era   b. age   c. period

4. The governor was elected for a third _____ .

   a. epoch   b. term   c. age

5. The Pony Express lasted for a _____ of eighteen months.

   a. span   b. term   c. spell

6. The discovery of gold began _____ of great development in California.

   a. a spell   b. an era   c. an epoch

Make sentences of your own using each of the time period words.

Compound Adjectives

A compound adjective is often made by joining a past participle, or adjective ending in *ed*, to another word with a hyphen:

> a well-watered weed (a weed that has a good supply of water)
> high-buttoned shoes (shoes that are buttoned to the top)
> high-heeled shoes (shoes that have high heels)

Adjectives with an *ed* ending can be made using words for parts of the body or parts of clothes.

> eye: blue-eyed, dark-eyed
> toe: long-toed, tight-toed
> hair: long-haired, short-haired
> heel: low-heeled, high-heeled

Change each italicized phrase into a compound adjective.

Example:

> A man *who has gray hair.*
> A gray-haired man.

1. Shoes *that have rubber soles.*

2. Shoes *that have open toes.*

3. A shirt *that has long sleeves.*

4. A shoe *that has leather straps.*

5. A shirt *that has an open neck.*

6. A man *who has wide shoulders.*

7. A girl *who has rosy cheeks.*

8. A pair of glasses *that has metal frames.*

Describe a person using as many compound adjectives as you can.

A. Looking for the Main Ideas

Write complete answers to the following questions.

1. What is the main idea of paragraph 2?

2. Which line states the main idea of paragraph 7?

3. Which sentences contain the main idea in paragraph 13?

4. What is paragraph 15 mostly about?

B. Skimming and Scanning for Details

Scan Reading 1 quickly to complete the following sentences. Circle the letter of the best answer.

1. According to the passage, the Chinese practice of binding a girl's feet began because _____ .

    a. the poets encouraged it

    b. it made a girl more beautiful

    c. a royal princess was born with deformed feet

    d. it gave men an opportunity to take a second wife

2. In the Orient five thousand years ago, the shoe fashion was _____ .

    a. long, pointed toes

    b. upturned toes

    c. flat, wide toes

    d. toes with silver bells

3. Long-toed shoes were brought to Europe by _____ .

    a. oriental traders

    b. the Crusaders

    c. the Egyptian rulers

    d. French aristocrats

4. In Europe, a long-toed shoe was a sign of _____ .

    a. royalty

    b. poverty

    c. wealth

    d. vanity

5. _____ was *not* used to stuff long toes.

    a. Moss

    b. Newspaper

    c. Hay

    d. Wool

6. The laws enacted by Edward IV of England limiting the length of long-toed shoes applied mostly to _____ .

    a. women

    b. the privileged classes

    c. shoemakers

    d. commoners

7. Shoes in the 1500s were very _____ .

    a. practical

    b. silly-looking

    c. long

    d. heavy

8. In seventeenth-century France, ladies' shoes were _____ .

    a. small, with very narrow toes

    b. very wide, with shoe fronts shaped into big toes

    c. open-toed and sandal-like

    d. high-buttoned

9. In the eighteenth century, American women _____ .

    a. developed their own comfortable shoe style

    b. went back to the Greek style

    c. were influenced by French fashion

    d. began to bind their feet

10. The first shoes ever made were most likely designed for _____ .

    a. adornment

    b. religious reasons

    c. attracting the opposite sex

    d. protection

C. Making Inferences and Drawing Conclusions

Some of the following statements can be inferred from the passage and others cannot. Circle the number of each statement that can be inferred.

1. Fashion may not only be impractical but harmful as well.

2. Girls of ancient China either suffered the humiliation of having large feet or suffered the pain of bound feet.

3. Some Chinese girls died because of the foot-binding practice.

4. For some people, fashion is more important than comfort.

5. The Egyptian rulers didn't like the styles of the Orient.

6. What is silly or ugly in one era can be high fashion in another.

7. Thirteenth-century Europeans weren't open to new styles.

8. Throughout the ages, it has been women who have set the fashion trends.

9. It has always been easier for the wealthy to be fashionable than the common people.

10. Styles really haven't changed much over the years.

DISCUSSION

Discuss these questions with your classmates.

1. What kinds of fashions have been or are physically harmful?

2. How do today's fashions show social or class distinctions?

3. What can you tell about a person from the clothing he or she wears?

Reading 2: Trousers and Skirts

The following reading is reprinted from *Men and Women: Dressing the Part* **(Washington, D.C.: Smithsonian Institution Press), pages 13-15, by permission of the publisher. Copyright 1989. It compares and contrasts the wearing of trousers and skirts.**

How did modern Western men come to wear trousers and women skirts? As the history of dress evolved, two basic types of clothing developed. In warm countries, where weaving was invented more than 10,000 years ago, a draped or wrapped-and-tied style predominated (like the Roman toga, the Indonesian sarong, and the Indian sari). In cold countries, by contrast, nomadic people favored clothing made of animal skins cut and sewn together to follow the lines of the body (like the trousers and jackets of central Asian and northern European people). An intermediate type of clothing was the binary[1] style, made of pieces of fabric sewn together and loosely following the lines of the body (like the Japanese kimono and the North African caftan). Binary clothes and wrapped garments could be folded flat, unlike the tailored clothes of the north, which fitted together with darts[2] and were three-dimensional. All three types entered the European tradition as a result of cultural contact, population movement, and invasion. The same thing happened in China.

---

[1] binary = consisting of two things or parts.

[2] darts = folds sewn into a garment to make it fit better.

But whereas in Europe, over the centuries, flowing robes became associated with femininity and tailored trousers with masculinity, this was not the case in China, where robes and trousers indicated not different gender, but different social status.

Trousers seem to have been invented in Persia in the later prehistoric period. They were then adopted by many northern European and central Asian "barbarians" (as they were referred to by "civilized" members of the Roman and Chinese empires), such as the Saxons. In many cases, barbarian women also wore trousers, especially when horseback riding was part of the nomadic way of life. In the cities of the two empires, however, both men and women of the elite wore long flowing robes (whether draped or binary). Even after the Roman Empire collapsed into a fragmented feudal Europe, noble men and women continued to wear long, quasi[3]-Roman robes. Peasants[4] wore short robes, and occasionally male peasants wore loose "barbarian" trousers.

Thus, the indigenous trouser tradition essentially died out in Europe—except in the clothing of soldiers. An aristocrat might wear a long robe at court, but he wore hose-like[5] trousers on the field of battle, often under his armor.[6] European men did not admire trousers, per se, but they did admire soldiers: the raison d'être[7] of the ruling aristocracy was its status as a warrior caste.[8] Women in Europe did not wear trousers because the garment had acquired such strong masculine connotations: what could be more masculine than a soldier?

In China, also, soldiers wore trousers (sometimes incorporated into suits of armor), but Chinese soldiers had no such exalted status, since the Chinese masculine ideal was the scholar-bureaucrat,[9] who wore a robe. In China, peasants of both sexes wore trousers, so there was a basic division between rulers in robes, on the one hand, and peasants and soldiers in trousers on the other. Women could and did wear trousers. Even upper-class Chinese ladies (and gentlemen) wore trousers for horseback riding or on less formal occasions.

---

[3] quasi = in some sense or degree.

[4] Peasants = in former times, people who worked on the land.

[5] hose-like = like stockings.

[6] armor = strong protective metal covering worn in battle by fighting men.

[7] raison d'être = reason or justification for existence.

[8] warrior caste = class of soldiers.

[9] bureaucrat = a person working for the government.

Back in medieval Europe, aristocratic men gradually developed a new, high-fashion type of trousers. First, however, they shortened their robes. Not that they adopted the coarse short robes of peasants, rather they developed elaborate and very short robes worn over tight stockings. Eventually, this new robe turned into a doublet,[10] and the top of the stockings into short, puffy bloomers[11] which turned into knee breeches. At the end of the eighteenth century, knee breeches[12] merged with plebian[13] long trousers to become modern men's pants. Women continued to wear long skirts—very long skirts for high-born women and their middle-class followers, and shorter skirts for peasants and working-class women.

The Victorians opposed female trousers and short skirts, not so much because they were prudish about female legs, but because they vehemently rejected clothing with mixed gender and class messages. Women could wear bifurcated[14] garments only under special conditions: at fancy dress parties (Turkish trousers were popular), sometimes for hunting, as part of bathing dress, and eventually as underpants. A few peasant and pioneer women wore trousers, as did some women who worked in mines.

Trousers [for women] were only very gradually accepted after World War I. But in the 1920s, "Conspicuous Outrage"[15] began to become as much a part of fashion as "Conspicuous Consumption." Even so, we forget how restricted most trouser-wearing really was during the Jazz Age.[16] Trousers were acceptable in the form of beach pajamas, lounge wear, riding jodhpurs,[17] and eventually blue jeans. But it was only in the 1940s and 1950s that casual trouser-wearing became common among teenagers, college coeds, and suburban housewives ("a little blue denim number for Eve to garden in . . ."). Trousers were still unacceptable as urban street wear or for work. As late as 1960, *Harper's Bazaar* ran an advertisement showing a woman, first in a black shirtwaist dress and again in a white (bifurcated) jumpsuit,[18] with the caption. "First we stole his shirt . . . now we steal his overall" indicating that both the button-down shirt and trousers were still regarded as masculine articles of clothing, no matter how long women had worn them.

---

[10] doublet = a man's close-fitting jacket worn in Europe in earlier times.

[11] bloomers = loose trousers gathered at the knee.

[12] knee breeches = short trousers fastened at the knee.

[13] plebian = of the common people.

[14] bifurcated = split in two.

[15] outrage = offense.

[16] Jazz Age = period between World War I and 1929.

[17] riding jodhpurs = riding pants.

[18] jumpsuit = a one-piece garment consisting of a blouse attached to trousers or shorts.

Look at the reading to answer the following questions.

1. What does the word *elite* in paragraph 3 mean?

    a. upper class

    b. scholars

    c. people who travel

    d. political candidates

2. Which word in paragraph 4 means *native*?

3. What is another way of saying *per se*?

    a. in order

    b. all things considered

    c. as such

4. Which of the following could substitute for *connotations* in paragraph 4?

    a. differences

    b. associations

    c. complications

    d. similarities

5. Which of these statements is true?

    a. An *exalted* status is a lower level.

    b. *Exaggerated* means the same as *exalted*.

    c. Something *exalted* is honored.

6. Which word is closest in meaning to *coarse* in paragraph 6?

    a. poor quality

    b. superior kind

    c. highly decorated

    d. square in shape

7. Which word in paragraph 7 means *shy and proper*?

8. What is another word for *vehemently*?

    a. quietly

    b. politely

    c. humorously

    d. strongly

9. Which word in paragraph 8 is similar in meaning to *noticeable*?

10. What does *coeds* in paragraph 8 mean?

    a. fashionable women

    b. female students

Rough and Not Rough

· ·

Some of the words in the box below mean *rough* and some mean *not rough*.

coarse	harsh	crude	rugged
even	smooth	sleek	dainty
glossy	fragile	refined	

They differ in meaning as follows:

    coarse = rough, not fine.

Example:

    Linen is a coarse fabric compared to silk.

    harsh = giving an unpleasant sensation when touched with the hand, or giving an unpleasant feeling to a sensitive person.

Example:

    The climate of Siberia is harsh.

    crude = something crude is still in its natural state. It is the opposite of highly developed or civilized.

Example:

    Crude oil is taken from the ground and then refined.

    rugged = something or someone so strong that it can survive almost anything, often used in nature to mean rough or untouched.

Example:

    The rugged coastline looked beautiful.

    even = regular, equal, the same level across the surface.

Example:

    The surface of the desk was not even because one of its legs was broken.

smooth = of a very even surface, polished.

Example:

The surface of the table was polished and smooth.

sleek = smooth and shiny, indicating an excellent physical condition.

Example:

It was a healthy dog with bright eyes and a sleek coat.

dainty = delicate and small.

Example:

The little ballet dancer gave a dainty bow.

glossy = extra smooth and shiny either by nature or art.

Example:

A book with a glossy cover looks more appealing.

fragile = delicate, easily broken.

Example:

Don't use that antique glass dish because it is very fragile.

refined = without impurities. When used of people, it means educated or well-mannered.

Example:

Crude oil must be refined before it can be used in automobiles.

*For each of the following sentences, circle T if the sentence is TRUE,
and, F if the sentence is FALSE.*

1. Something fragile can easily be broken.   T   F

2. A natural, undeveloped thing is in a crude state.   T   F

3. A harsh voice is unpleasant to listen to.   T   F

4. Sleek means shiny and in the best of health.   T   F

5. Something refined has been made pure.   T   F

6. Coarse means easily broken.   T   F

7. Something rugged is delicate and light-weight.   T   F

8. A dainty vase is small and delicate.   T   F

9. A smooth surface is very even and looks shiny.   T   F

10. A glossy finish is dark and dirty.   T   F

11. Even means equal in shape and measurement.   T   F

Choose the answer that best completes each of the following sentences.

1. Sheep's wool is _____ compared to fox fur.
   a. dainty   b. sleek   c. coarse

2. He survived _____ conditions alone in the mountains.
   a. rugged   b. fragile   c. crude

3. Long, dark hair looks _____ when wet.
   a. dainty   b. glossy   c. refined

4. Diplomats normally behave in a _____ manner.
   a. smooth   b. crude   c. refined

5. Life in prison is a _____ punishment for taking a peach.
   a. crude   b. harsh   c. even

6. The waters of the lake looked _____ in the sunset.
   a. even   b. smooth   c. fragile

7. A stone ax is a _____ thing to cut down trees with.
   a. refined   b. rugged   c. crude

8. Small and light in weight, she was too _____ to play ball.
   a. dainty   b. refined   c. sleek

9. Old people's bones are often very _____ .
   a. rugged   b. dainty   c. fragile

10. The cat looked _____ because it was so well fed.
    a. sleek   b. glossy   c. smooth

11. The roof fell in because the walls were not _____ .
    a. rugged   b. refined   c. even

Foreign Words and Phrases

Many expressions from other languages have been absorbed into English so that we no longer consider them as foreign. However, some words and phrases such as *per se* (Latin) and *raison d'être* (French) have retained their original spelling and pronunciation.

Use a dictionary to look up the following French and Latin words or expressions. Then choose the appropriate one to complete the sentences.

cul-de-sac	carte blanche	chic	gourmet
coup	debut	avant-garde	vice versa
per capita	curriculum vitae		

1. The application form for the position should be accompanied by a detailed _____ .

2. He likes fine food and wine, so we had better take him to a _____ restaurant.

3. She's a very _____ artist. I really do not follow what she is trying to say, and even some of the art critics are confused.

4. When one of them sleeps, the other works and _____ .

5. It would be better for you to buy the house in the _____ because there won't be any through-traffic noise to bother you.

6. Even though she is in her seventies, she always wears the most elegant clothes and looks very _____ .

7. He didn't know how he wanted his house decorated, so he just gave me _____ to do whatever I liked.

8. The _____ income in the United States in 1987 was about $22,000.

9. She made her _____ as a dancer in a movie when she was twelve.

10. In last week's _____ , the president was arrested and the military took over.

COMPREHENSION

A. Looking for the Main Ideas

Some of the following statements from Reading 2 are main ideas and some are supporting statements. Find the statements in the reading. Write M in the blank in front of each main idea. Write S in the blank in front of each supporting statement.

____ 1. As the history of dress evolved, two basic types of clothing developed.

____ 2. In cold countries, by contrast, nomadic people favored clothing made of animal skins cut and sewn together to follow the lines of the body (like the trousers and jackets of central Asian and northern European people).

____ 3. Binary clothes and wrapped garments could be folded flat, unlike the tailored clothes of the north, which fitted together with darts and were three-dimensional.

____ 4. Peasants wore short robes, and occasionally male peasants wore loose "barbarian" trousers.

____ 5. Thus, the indigenous trouser tradition essentially died out in Europe—except in the clothing of soldiers.

____ 6. Back in medieval Europe, aristocratic men gradually developed a new, high-fashion type of trousers.

____ 7. Eventually, this new robe turned into a doublet, and the top of the stockings turned into short, puffy bloomers, which turned into knee breeches.

____ 8. Trousers for women were only very gradually accepted after World War I.

____ 9. Trousers were acceptable in the form of beach pajamas, lounge wear, riding jodhpurs, and eventually blue jeans.

____ 10. Trousers were still unacceptable as urban street wear or for work.

B. Skimming and Scanning for Details

Scan the passage to complete the following sentences.

1. In warm countries, the early form of dress was a _____
    style, such as the Roman _____ , Indonesian _____ ,
    and the Indian _____ .

2. The _____ style is clothing made from pieces of fabric sewn
    together and loosely following the shape of the body.

3. The three early styles of dress from various parts of the world
    became incorporated into European tradition as a result of
    _____ , _____ , and _____ .

4. In China, robes and trousers indicated a difference not in gender
    but in _____ .

5. Trousers are believed to have been invented in _____ in the
    _____ time period.

6. Members of the Roman and Chinese empires considered them-
    selves civilized compared to the people of northern Europe whom
    they called _____ .

7. In medieval Europe, trousers were something the _____
    wore, and therefore became associated with _____ .

8. In medieval Europe, the peasants wore _____ robes while
    the nobility wore _____ robes.

9. The Victorians were opposed to having females wear both
    _____ and _____ because they preferred styles that
    gave a clear message regarding _____ and _____ .

10. In the 1940s and 1950s, trousers became popular clothing among
    _____ , _____ , and _____ .

C. Making Inferences and Drawing Conclusions

Some of the following statements are facts from the reading. Other statements can be inferred. Write F in the blank in front of each factual statement. Write I in the blank in front of each inference.

_____ 1. Climate and geography have influenced the evolution of clothing styles.

_____ 2. The Japanese and the North Africans had similar clothing styles.

_____ 3. Although flowing robes were worn by both male and female Europeans in early times, they eventually became associated with femininity.

_____ 4. In nomadic societies for whom horseback riding was a way of life, women often wore trousers.

_____ 5. It is most likely that the peasants' clothing was made more practical so it wouldn't interfere with their work, unlike the noblemen who didn't have to go out and build things and plow fields.

_____ 6. Unlike the Europeans, the Chinese valued intellect over brute force.

_____ 7. Aristocratic women of medieval Europe wore long skirts while the peasant women wore shorter skirts.

_____ 8. Victorian women were repressed by strict social codes.

_____ 9. Even in the 1950s, trousers were not acceptable attire for the working woman.

_____10. No matter how modernized society becomes, it is still difficult to break from traditional social ideas.

DISCUSSION

Discuss these questions with your classmates.

1. What do you consider to be a masculine look for men and a feminine look for women?

2. Do you think men and women should dress alike? Why or why not?

3. Fashionwise, which period would you like to have lived in? Why?

Writing a Summary

Write a one-paragraph summary of Reading 1.

Check your summary against the Summary Checklist on page 265.

How To Write

HOW TO SUMMARIZE
PAGE 263

Paraphrasing

Paraphrase paragraph 5 in Reading 2 with either:

According to Kidwell and Steele, . . .

or

Based on Kidwell and Steele's research . . .

How To Write

HOW TO PARAPHRASE
PAGE 257

Research

You may use your research later to write a compare and contrast essay.

How To Write

HOW TO DO LIBRARY RESEARCH
PAGE 248

Choose two styles and find three points of comparison and contrast between them. Consult appropriate sources in the library, and/or use your own experience or that of friends to gather information.

The following are suggested topics:

Two styles of architecture	Two styles of furniture
Two periods in fashion	Clothing styles in two different countries
Forms or styles of housing in two different countries	Two cars

Read the following essay written by a student.

Short Skirts of the Twenties and Sixties

Fashion always adjusts to periods and tells the truth about an age without benefit of hindsight. Many of the social changes of the twentieth century are reflected in the changes of fashion. The decades of the "Swinging Sixties" and the "Roaring Twenties," were the fun periods of the century, conveying the lighter side of life. They are also remembered as the decades of short skirts. In this essay, the rise and fall of short skirts and other features of fashion of the Twenties and Sixties will be compared and contrasted as relating to social changes and economical, political conditions.

Electro-technological advances after World War I like the refrigerator and vacuum cleaner, encouraged more women to work outside and a degree of female emancipation progressed. The new mass media such as movies, the radio, and records captured more audiences than ever and sped up the standardization of society. Such social development forced the style of women's clothes to become simpler and more practical so that women could lead active lives. Consequently, in the mid-1920s, the real revolution of short skirts began. In the Sixties, there was also a similar social development to that of the Twenties. The wave of female emancipation which affected women's clothes was irreversible. The new mass media, TV, was well installed in Europe and the United States, and music and dancing through TV influenced women's clothes. More advanced female emancipation and electro-technology in the Sixties made women's skirt lengths shorter than in the Twenties. Short skirts in the Twenties were just above the knee; on the other hand, the young women of the Sixties exposed the greater part of their thighs. Thus, short skirts came into fashion.

In both decades of the Twenties and Sixties, a new accepted type of beauty was the unisex type, that is, girls strove to look as much like boys as possible. French women, who had had the initiative of fashion for a long time, were too feminine and differed much from the unisex type. This time it was England and the United States who were the initiators of fashion rather than Paris. For the unisex look, short skirts went well with short hair. Women's hair in the Twenties was the shingle, that is, the top of the head was flat and the sides softer, straight or curly. The shingle became one of the most significant symbols of women's liberation in the Twenties. Compared with the hair fashion of the Twenties, the Sixties had a diversity of hair fashions. The most famous hair fashion was the Vidal Sassoon hair cut which was cleverly shaped by layering to an even overall length, and it was easy to manage and keep.

The fall of short skirts was influenced by economical and political conditions. Skirts suddenly became long again as the decade of the Twenties drew to its close. In the United States, the Wall Street Crash in October 1929 triggered off the slump and the Great Depression. Also, in Europe, the rise of Hitler began. The focus of interest on legs had lost its appeal so another one had to be found. With the fall of short skirts in the Twenties, the emphasis shifted from legs to the back. Backs were bared to the waist instead of bare legs. On the other hand, at the end of the Sixties, the fashion never shifted from its focus of attention. While young women exposed their legs, they began to expose their tops in see-through blouses. As the decade of the Seventies began the age of the mini-skirt ended, giving rise to the longer midi-skirt. This change in fashion was influenced by the oil crisis and distrust of politics like Watergate, and Vietnam in the Seventies.

It is said that fashion repeats itself every thirty or forty years. According to this theory, mini-skirts in the Sixties came into fashion almost forty years after the short skirts of the Twenties. Short skirts in both decades were accompanied by similar social changes, and the political and economical conditions in both decades affected their fall. Although these fun decades have gone into the past, they still sparkle in history. Fashion is always a mirror of the period.

Nubia
Peru

STUDENT ESSAY FOLLOW-UP

1. Underline the thesis statement.

2. From what point of view will the fashion of the Twenties and Sixties be compared and contrasted?

3. In paragraph 2, what conditions were similar for women in the Twenties and Sixties?

4. What is the similarity in paragraph 3?

5. What influenced the end of short skirts in the Twenties and Sixties?

6. Underline the topic sentences in paragraphs 3 and 4 that show comparison (similarity).

ORGANIZING

Comparison and Contrast

Comparison and contrast is a very useful and common method of essay organization. Many college essay topics require you to compare and contrast ideas, theories, facts, characters, principles, and so on. In your personal life, too, you find similarities and differences in a whole array of subjects from the products you buy to the friends you make and the jobs you get.

When you *compare* two items, you show how aspects of one item are similar to aspects of another. A comparison tells you what features are *similar.*

When you *contrast* two items, you show the differences between them. You point out the features that are not alike or are *different.*

▶ Finding Two Comparable Items

In order to make a comparison, you need to choose two items that share a similar feature or have the same function. In Reading 1, "Toe Fashion in Comparison," the toes of shoes were compared in different periods; in the student essay, short skirts of the Twenties were compared with short skirts of the Sixties. It would not be a good comparison if you compared the clothes of a rich woman with the uniform of a nurse. However, two kinds of uniforms can be compared and contrasted.

Exercise 1

Work with a partner. Write the names of two comparable examples for each group. Say why they can be compared.

1. fast food restaurants: _____ _____

2. amusement parks: _____ _____

3. computers: _____ _____

4. cars: _____ _____

▶ Basis of Comparison

The basis of comparison is an important aspect in the organization and development of your essay. When comparing two items, the same aspects of each must be compared. For example, when comparing two people, the basis of comparison could be appearance, behavior, or personality. Whatever bases of comparison you choose, you must use the same ones to discuss each person. You cannot compare the personality of one person to the appearance of the other.

The following is an example of some of the possible bases for comparing two universities:

	University A	University B
Bases of comparison:	size	size
	location	location
	reputation	reputation
	specialty	specialty

▶ Thesis Statement

In a comparison-and-contrast essay, you may want to compare and contrast two items to show that one is better than the other, or that the two are totally different, or that they have some similarities and some differences. Your purpose will vary.

The thesis statement for a comparison and contrast essay should include the names of the two items being compared and the dominant impression of the items.

Sample thesis statement:

University A is a better choice for me than University B because of its size, location, reputation, and specialty.

Task:

1. Write a thesis statement for an essay in which you compare two fast-food restaurants.

2. Write a thesis statement in which you compare two kinds of cars.

Organizing a Comparison and Contrast Essay

There are two basic ways to organize a comparison-and-contrast essay: (1) block organization and (2) point by point organization.

In block organization, one item such as University A is discussed in one block (one or more paragraphs) and University B is discussed in another block. In Reading 1, "Toe Fashion Comparison," small-sized feet were discussed in one block and then oversized shoes were discussed in another. In Reading 2 on trousers and skirts, the European association of flowing robes with femininity and trousers with masculinity was discussed in one block, and then in another block, what these garments were associated with in China.

Imagine you were going to write a comparison-and-contrast essay about the clothing styles in Los Angeles and New York City. The following outlines show how you might organize your essay using either the block or point-by-point approach.

▶ **Block Organization Outline**

Topic: A Comparison and Contrast of the Clothing Styles in Los Angeles and New York City.

Thesis Statement: The clothing style in Los Angeles is quite different from that of New York City in terms of fabrics, colors, and style.

   I. Los Angeles

       A. Fabrics (light, same for summer and winter)

       B. Colors (bright)

       C. Style (casual)

  II. New York City

       A. Fabrics (heavy, different for summer and winter)

       B. Colors (not bright)

       C. Style (formal)

Conclusion

Topic: A Comparison and Contrast of the Clothing Styles in Los Angeles and New York City.

Thesis Statement: The clothing style in Los Angeles is quite different from that of New York City from the point of view of fabrics, colors, and style.

    I. Fabrics

        A. Los Angeles (light, same for summer and winter)

        B. New York City (heavy, different for summer and winter)

    II. Colors

        A. Los Angeles (bright)

        B. New York City (not bright)

    III. Style

        A. Los Angeles (casual)

        B. New York (formal)

Conclusion

As can be seen, the block organization is simpler because fewer transitions are required, and one subject is discussed completely before going on to the other. The point-by-point organization in which similarities and differences of each point are discussed together requires the constant use of comparison-and-contrast indicators.

Comparison and Contrast Indicators

A good comparison-and-contrast essay should be sprinkled with comparison-and-contrast indicators, or structure words. The following is a list of some of these structure words.

Comparison Indicator Words

Sentence Connectors	Clause Connectors	Others
similarly	as	like (+ noun)
likewise	just as	similar to (+ noun)
also	and	just like (+ noun)
		(be) similar to
		(be) same as
		both . . . and
		not only . . . but also

Task:

Underline all the comparison structure words in Reading 1 and Reading 2.

Contrast Indicator Words

Sentence Connectors	Clause Connectors	Others
however	although	
nevertheless	even though	but
in contrast	while	yet
on the other hand	whereas	despite (+ noun)
on the contrary		in spite of (+ noun)

Task:

Underline all the contrast structure words in Reading 1 and Reading 2.

Join each of the following two sentences using the comparison or contrast structure words indicated. Make any necessary changes.

Example:

   although

In China foot-binding was a painful process for girls. Girls considered it a great honor.

Although foot-binding was a painful process for girls in China, they considered it a great honor.

1. *whereas*

In China women experienced inconvenience over shoes. In other parts of the world, men experienced inconvenience over shoes.

2. *likewise*

The long-toed shoe became foolish and ridiculous. The wide-toed shoe became foolish and ridiculous.

3. *just as*

A law was passed to limit shoe-toe length. A law was passed to limit shoe-toe width.

4. *however*

Women wore moderately wide shoes. Men went to extremes with the fashion.

5. *In contrast*

In Europe robes were associated with femininity. In China robes were associated with social status.

6. _whereas_

In China rulers wore robes. Peasants and soldiers wore trousers.

7. _while_

At the end of the eighteenth century, high-born and middle-class women wore long skirts. Peasant and working-class women wore shorter skirts.

8. _just like_

The fashion of short skirts ended in the 1920s because of troubled economical and political conditions. Short skirts went out of fashion in the 1970s because of troubled economical and political conditions.

WRITING PRACTICE

Choose one of the following topics.

1 Use one of the topics you researched in this chapter to write a comparison-and-contrast essay using three points of comparison and contrast.

2 Write a comparison-and-contrast essay about two people you know or know something about. Use three or four bases of comparison.

3 Write an essay about a place you know, comparing and contrasting the "way it was" to "the way it is" now.

4 Compare and contrast two groups of people in your native country. Compare their lifestyles, social status, and feelings toward each other.

1. Pre-writing

How To **Write**

BRAINSTORMING
PAGE 242

Work alone, with a partner, or in a group.

1 Brainstorm the topic. Choose the pre-writing technique you prefer.

2 Brainstorm for your bases of comparison and supporting ideas.

3 Work on a thesis statement.

2. Outlining

A. Organize your ideas

Step 1: *Write your thesis statement.*

Step 2: *Select three or four bases of comparison from your brain-storming activity.*

Step 3: *Find relevant supporting details for each point.*

B. Make a more detailed outline. Choose between the block and point-by-point organization outlines on page 22.

3. Write a Rough Draft.

How To	Write

DRAFTING
PAGE 245

4. Revise Your Draft. Use the Revision Checklist on page 246.

5. Edit Your Essay. Use the Editing Symbols on pages 247—248.

How To	Write

EDITING
PAGE 247

6. Write Your Final Copy.

Chapter 7: Nutrition

INGREDIENTS: **CRUST:** ENRICHED FLOUR (FLOUR, NIACIN, FERROUS SULFATE, THIAMINE MONONITRATE, RIBOFLAVIN), WATER, HYDRO-GENATED SOYBEAN OIL. CONTAINS LESS THAN 2% OF THE FOLLOW-ING: DRY YEAST, SOY FLOUR, SALT, BAKING POWDER (MONOCAL-CIUM PHOSPHATE, BAKING SODA), DEXTROSE, SORBITAN MONOSTEARATE. **TOPPINGS:** COOKED PORK SAUSAGE (PORK, SALT, SPICE, NATURAL FLAVOR), MOZZARELLA AND PASTEURIZED PRO-CESS AMERICAN CHEESE SUBSTITUTES (MADE FROM WATER, CASEIN, HYDROGENATED SOYBEAN OIL, MALTODEXTRIN. CONTAINS LESS THAN 2% OF THE FOLLOWING: SODIUM ALUMINUM PHOS-PHATE, SALT, LACTIC ACID, SODIUM CITRATE, SODIUM PHOSPHATE, ARTIFICIAL COLOR, SORBIC ACID [PRESERVATIVE], CITRIC ACID, ZINC OXIDE, FERRIC ORTHOPHOSPHATE, VITAMIN A PALMITATE, RIBOFLAVIN, FOLIC ACID, MAGNESIUM OXIDE, VITAMIN B6 HYDROCHLORIDE, NIACIN, THIAMINE MONONITRATE), PEPPERONI (PORK, MECHANICALLY SEPARATED PORK, BEEF, SALT, WATER, DEX-TROSE, SPICE AND COLORING, LACTIC ACID STARTER CULTURE, GARLIC POWDER, SODIUM NITRITE, BHA AND BHT AND CITRIC ACID ADDED TO PROTECT FLAVOR, SMOKE FLAVOR. MAY ALSO CONTAIN BEEF STOCK), GREEN PEPPERS, ONIONS, COOK CHEESE (SKIM MILK, CHEESE CULTURE, CALCIUM CHLORIDE, ENZYMES), TEXTURED VEG-ETABLE PROTEIN (SOY FLOUR, CARAMEL COLOR), HYDROGENATED SOYBEAN OIL. **SAUCE:** TOMATO PUREE (WATER, TOMATO PASTE), WATER, SUGAR, MODIFIED CORN STARCH, SALT, SPICE, HYDRO-GENATED SOYBEAN OIL, BEET POWDER, XANTHAN GUM, NATURAL FLAVOR, ARTIFICIAL COLOR.

PRE-READING QUESTIONS

Discuss these questions with your classmates or teacher.

1 Why do products have labels?

2 Do you know why it is important to read the labels on products?

3 Do people use additives in food in your country?

4 How long do you think additives have been used in food?

Match the labels to the products.

MADE WITH WATER, ENRICHED FLOUR (BARLEY MALT, NIACIN, IRON (FERROUS SULFATE), THIAMIN MONONITRATE, RIBOFLAVIN), HIGH FRUCTOSE CORN SYRUP, WHEAT GLUTEN, SOY FIBER, COTTONSEED FIBER, CONTAINS 2% OR LESS OF: YEAST, CALCIUM SULFATE, SALT, CORN BRAN, FLAVORS (NATURAL), SOY FLOUR, CORN GRITS, ETHOXYLATED MONO- AND DIGLYCERIDES, CELLULOSE GUM, MALTODEXTRIN, SODIUM STEAROYL LACTYLATE, MONO- AND DIGLYCERIDES, YEAST NUTRIENTS (AMMONIUM SULFATE), STARCH, VINEGAR, SOY PROTEIN, PRESERVATIVES (CALCIUM PROPIONATE).

Margarine

CURED WITH WATER, HONEY, POTASSIUM LACTATE, SALT, CARRAGEENAN, DEXTROSE, SODIUM PHOSPHATE, SODIUM ERYTHORBATE, SODIUM NITRATE.

Mayonnaise

INGREDIENTS: WATER, CANOLA OIL, PARTIALLY HYDROGENATED CORN OIL, MALTODEXTRIN, SALT, VEGETABLE MONOGLYCERIDES (EMULSIFIER), POTASSIUM SORBATE AND CALCIUM DISODIUM EDTA AND CITRIC ACID TO PRESERVE FRESHNESS, ARTIFICIAL FLAVOR, COLORED WITH BETA CAROTENE (SOURCE OF VITAMIN A), VITAMIN A PALMITATE AND VITAMIN D_3 ADDED.

Ham

INGREDIENTS: WATER, CORN SYRUP, LIQUID SOYBEAN OIL, MODIFIED FOOD STARCH, EGG WHITES, VINEGAR, MALTODEXTRIN, SALT, NATURAL FLAVORS, GUMS (CELLULOSE GEL AND GUM, XANTHAN), ARTIFICIAL COLORS, SODIUM BENZOATE AND CALCIUM DISODIUM EDTA USED TO PROTECT QUALITY.

Bread

Reading 1: The Story on Food Additives

What's that on your pizza? You can bet it's not just the extra cheese and onions you ordered. As a matter of fact, you can count on at least a dozen other "extras" that you never asked for, including dextrin, mono- and diglycerides, potassium bromate, sodium aluminum phosphate, sodium citrate, sodium metabisulfite and xanthan gum. These common food additives make your pizza, among other things, lighter, tastier, and generally more pleasing to the palate. Because we like our pepperoni[1] without mold, our crackers crispy, our peanut butter smooth, and our tomatoes red, chemicals are added to just about everything we eat. They make food more flavorful and easier to prepare; they make it last longer, look more appetizing, and feel better in our mouths (no lumps!).

Today's additives read like a chemistry book, so many people believe they're a modern invention. However, additives are nothing new, and neither is the controversy surrounding them. London in the eighteenth century could have been called the "adulterated[2] food capital of the world," though it's likely that other cities in other countries were just as guilty of the practice. One might think that food in the "old days" was pure and simple, but in many cases, what people paid for was not what they were getting. Pepper, for example, was adulterated with mustard husks,[3] pea flour, fruit berries, and sweepings from the storeroom floor. Tea, which was very expensive and brought all the way from China, was mixed with the dried leaves from ash trees.[4] China tea was green, and fake China tea was often made from dried thorn leaves[5] colored with a poisonous substance called verdigris. When black Indian tea became popular, it was common for manufacturers to buy up used tea leaves, which they stiffened with a gum solution and then tinted with lead, another dangerous substance. Even candy was contaminated with highly poisonous salts of copper and lead to give it color. These practices eventually came to the public's attention, and in 1860 the first British Food and Drug Act was passed. Despite the regulations on food purity that currently exist in almost every country, there are still problems. One of the most alarming cases occurred in 1969 when an Italian gentleman was charged for selling what was supposed to be grated parmesan[6] cheese that turned out to consist of grated umbrella handles!

---

[1] pepperoni = a very spicy pork or beef sausage often put on pizzas.

[2] adulterated = made impure or of poorer quality by adding substances of lower quality.

[3] mustard husks = the dry outer coverings of mustard seeds.

[4] ash trees = trees belonging to the olive family.

[5] thorn leaves = the dry, hard, pointed leaves from thorn bushes.

[6] parmesan = a hard, dry, strong-flavored cheese that is often sold grated.

Believe it or not, food adulteration is not all bad. Salt has been used as a preservative for thousands of years, and, thanks to some basic and other quite complicated substances, we have "fresh" vegetables in January, peanut butter that doesn't stick to the roof of the mouth, stackable potato chips, and meat that doesn't turn green on the way home from the grocery store. But as they say, there's a price to pay for everything.

In the case of vegetables and fruits, the price is taste. Bred[7] for looks and long hauls[8] we have plump, red tomatoes with fine body and perfect skin but very little for our taste buds[9] to smile about. The reason is that the tomatoes are picked green and then "gassed" along the way; that is, they're treated with ethylene gas, the same gas tomatoes give off internally if allowed to ripen on the vine.[10] The artificial gassing tricks the tomatoes into turning red. They don't really ripen; they just turn a ripe color. The price we pay for packaged foods that are ready in an "instant," however, is sometimes more than lack of stimulation for our mouths.

The federal government recognizes about thirty-five different categories of additives, which are used for various purposes. Antioxidants are added to oil-containing foods to prevent the oil from spoiling. Chelating agents stop food from discoloring. Emulsifiers keep oil and water mixed together. Flavor enhancers improve the natural flavor of food. Thickening agents absorb some of the water present in food and make food thicker. They also keep oils, water, and solids well mixed. About 800 million pounds of additives are added to our food every year.

What happens when we consume this conglomeration of chemicals? The average American ingests about five pounds of food additives per year. The good news is that the majority of the hundreds of chemicals that are added to food are safe. In some cases, they're even good for us, such as when vitamins are added. The bad news is that some of them are not safe, and these are the ones with which we need to concern ourselves.

The first of the "unsafe" additives is artificial sweeteners. The sugar substitute aspartame is sold commercially as Equal or NutraSweet and is used in many diet beverages.[11] However, studies have shown that about one out of 20,000 babies cannot metabolize one of the two substances that aspartame is made from and that toxic levels of that substance, called phenylala-

---

[7] bred = produced.

[8] hauls = distances of transportation.

[9] taste buds = small groups of receptor cells on the tongue that distinguish different tastes.

[10] the vine = the climbing plant.

[11] beverages = drinks other than water, alcohol, or medicine. Coffee and tea are hot beverages.

nine, can result in mental retardation.[12] Some scientists also believe that aspartame can cause problems with brain function and behavior changes in people who consume it. Some people who have consumed aspartame have reported dizziness, headaches, and even seizures.[13] Another controversy over aspartame involves its possible link to an increased risk of brain tumors. Aspartame is still widely added although many lawsuits have been filed to block its use. Another sugar substitute called saccharin has also been linked to cancer in laboratory animals.

The additives sodium nitrite and sodium nitrate are two closely related chemicals that have been used for centuries to preserve meat. These additives keep meat's red color, enhance its flavor, and stop the growth of dangerous bacteria. Nitrate by itself is harmless but it is quickly changed into nitrite by a chemical reaction that occurs at high temperatures and may also occur to some degree in the stomach. During this chemical reaction, nitrite combines with other chemicals to form some very powerful cancer-causing agents. Bacon is a special problem because it is thinly sliced and fried at a high temperature. Other processed meats, such as hot dogs, ham, and bologna are less of a risk. Nitrite has been considered an important cause of stomach cancer in the United States, Japan, and other countries. In the United States, in fact, the rate of stomach cancer has been declining for a number of years due to reduced use of nitrite and nitrate preservatives.

Artificial colorings, often used in combination with artificial flavorings, replace natural ingredients that are more costly to produce. Lemon-flavored "lemonade" is much cheaper to make than a real lemon product. Artificial colorings are synthetic dyes such as Blue No. 1, Blue No. 2, Citrus Red No. 2, Green No. 3, Red No. 3, Red No. 40, Yellow No. 5, and Yellow No. 6. They are widely used in foods to make them look more natural and more attractive. All those colored breakfast cereals for kids are loaded with food dyes, as are ice cream, cakes, and other tasty treats. For decades, questions about the safety of synthetic food dyes have been asked and many dyes have been banned for being toxic or cancer-causing. There are still questions of safety about the dyes that are currently in use. Yellow No. 5, for example, causes allergic reactions in some people. Red No. 3 has been banned for some uses because it caused tumors in rats. Other dyes are under investigation, but all are in wide use.

It's good to know that no single food additive poses a severe danger to the entire population. But several additives, such as those we have mentioned, do pose some risks to the general public and should be avoided as

---

[12] mental retardation = underdeveloped mental ability.
[13] seizures = sudden or violent attacks as of epilepsy.

much as possible. Fortunately, people are more aware than ever of the dangers of pesticide residues on fruits and vegetables, and of additives in our processed foods. There is intense pressure on the federal government to ban unsafe substances. But it is also our responsibility as consumers to read labels and be aware of what we're putting into our bodies, and to learn how to eat safe and healthy food for long and healthy lives.

VOCABULARY

Select the letter of the answer that is closest in meaning to the italicized word or phrase.

1. We like to have pepperoni without *mold*.
    a. yellow fat
    b. strange spices
    c. greenish growth
    d. reddish color

2. The *controversy* surrounding additives is nothing new.
    a. purpose
    b. debate
    c. idea
    d. judgment

3. *Fake* China tea was often made with dried thorn leaves and colored with a poisonous substance.
    a. Imitation
    b. Cheap
    c. Ordinary
    d. Light

4. Even candy was *contaminated* with highly poisonous salts.
    a. injured
    b. destroyed
    c. diseased
    d. made impure

5. What happens when we consume this *conglomeration* of chemicals?
    a. arrangement
    b. collection
    c. discovery
    d. preference

6. The average American *ingests* about five pounds of additives per year.
    a. cleans in the body
    b. changes to liquid
    c. takes in as food
    d. discharges from the body

7. Studies have shown that some babies cannot *metabolize* a substance that aspartame is made from.
    a. change into food
    b. grow with
    c. sleep with
    d. live on

8. All the colored breakfast cereals for kids are *loaded with* food dyes.
    a. pleasing with
    b. destroyed by
    c. improved with
    d. packed with

9. No single additive *poses* a grave danger to the entire population.
    a. transmits
    b. maintains
    c. presents
    d. donates

10. People are aware of the dangers of pesticide *residues* on fruits and vegetables.
    a. remainders
    b. samples
    c. trash
    d. portions

ingest/digest/consume
imbibe/assimilate

ingest = to take in as food into the body.

Example:

It is dangerous to ingest food before surgery.

digest = to be changed into a form that the body can use.

Example:

Vegetables are easier to digest than meat.

consume = to eat or drink.

Example:

Americans consume more meat per year than any other country.

imbibe = (formal) to drink or take in.

Example:

Americans imbibe millions of sodas every day.

assimilate = to absorb food into the body system.

Example:

It takes several hours for food to be assimilated by the body.

Place one of the verbs above in the blanks below. Use the correct tense of the verb.

1. *It is dangerous to _____ food before swimming.*

2. *Food is _____ in the stomach.*

3. *Babies can only _____ milk.*

4. *If you _____ too much alcohol your liver will have problems.*

5. *Americans _____ more food than any other nation.*

To Make Impure

contaminate/pollute

Both *contaminate* and *pollute* mean to make impure. However, the two words differ as follows:

> **contaminate** = to make impure by adding poisonous matter especially harmful bacteria, poison, and radioactivity.

> **pollute** = to make impure or dirty by harmful waste products.

Fill in each of the blanks with either contaminate or pollute. In some cases both can be used. Use the correct form of the verb.

1. Industrial waste has _____ the lake.

2. Air in big cities is _____ by carbon monoxide.

3. The water in the village was _____ by dead rats.

4. The wound was _____ by harmful bacteria.

5. All the ice cream made in the production plant was called back because some of the milk was _____ .

6. The meat from the cows in the area was _____ by high levels of radioactivity.

COMPREHENSION

A. Looking for the Main Ideas

Circle the letter of the answer that best completes the sentence.

1. The main idea of paragraph 2 is that
   - a. food additives are chemical substances.
   - b. some suppliers adulterate food to save money.
   - c. food adulteration has a long and sometimes dangerous history.
   - d. even something as innocent-looking as candy can be dangerous if it has additives.

2. Paragraph 7 is mostly about

      a. how phenylalanine can cause brain problems and behavior changes.

      b. the fact that lawsuits have failed to block the use of aspartame.

      c. the uses of the sugar substitute aspartame.

      d. the dangers posed by the substances in some artificial sweeteners.

3. Paragraph 9 is mainly concerned with

      a. the questionable safety of food dyes.

      b. the money-saving value of artificial flavorings and colorings.

      c. the banning of toxic and cancer-causing food dyes.

      d. the most popular foods in which food dyes are used.

B. Skimming and Scanning for Details

Scan Reading 1 to find the answers to these questions. Write complete answers.

1. What are five reasons why additives are put into food?

2. According to the passage, why was tea adulterated in eighteenth-century London?

3. What negative effect does *gassing* have on tomatoes?

4. What are five categories of food additives and their uses?

5. In the last sentence of paragraph 6, what does the word *these* refer to?

6. What is a common use of NutraSweet?

7. To what does the word *its* in paragraph 8, sentence 2, refer?

8. Why does bacon pose a special problem concerning the use of nitrite?

9. Give two reasons why dyes are widely used in foods.

10. Why has Red No. 3 been banned for some uses?

C. Making Inferences and Drawing Conclusions

The answers to these questions are not directly stated in the passage. Circle the letter of the best answer.

1. The passage implies that
    a. today's food additives are more dangerous than those used in the past.
    b. economics has always played a role in the use of food additives.
    c. food additives have more to do with making food look good than anything else.
    d. regulations on food purity have eliminated most problems with food adulteration.

2. From the passage, it can be concluded that
    a. the health risk posed by some additives must be weighed against their positive value, such as food preservation.
    b. Americans gain weight as a result of the large amount of food additives they consume.
    c. the majority of food additives are bad for us and should be banned.
    d. there is no evidence to prove that banning certain additives reduces the risk of cancer.

3. It can be inferred from the passage that
    a. when questions of safety are involved, getting a substance banned is a quick and easy process.
    b. there is no reason to be concerned about the safety of food additives because the government is doing all it can to protect consumers against unsafe substances.
    c. the goal of some consumer groups is to pressure the government to ban all forms of food adulteration.
    d. in spite of the government's role involving food additives, our health and safety also depend upon our own education and awareness.

4. The author's purpose is to

    a. entertain.

    b. inform.

    c. persuade.

    d. argue.

DISCUSSION

Discuss these questions with your classmates.

1. Are there some foods that you think are safer than others?

2. What are some of your favorite foods? Say why you like them.

3. Have you ever been sick as a result of eating or drinking a particular type of food? Describe what it did to you and the possible causes.

4. If you had a choice between healthy food that didn't look very appetizing and was more expensive and food that looked good and appetizing but was chemically treated, which would you choose and why?

Reading 2: BGH: The Debate Goes On

The following article is from *Harper's Magazine* (October 1994). It examines the debate over BGH, a growth hormone given to cows. Cows given BGH produce more milk but require more antibiotics. The debate is whether or not the milk from the cows given the growth hormone is safe to drink.

A quart of milk purchased in the United States today originates in a milk supply divided between two streams: one treated with synthetic bovine growth hormone (BGH) and another that is BGH-free. A bill currently before Congress would require labels on all milk, butter, cheese, yogurt, and ice cream sold in the country. But until it, or something like it, becomes law, most people won't know what they're eating or drinking. Right now, nearly all of the milk bottled in Vermont and Wisconsin is likely to be BGH-free or close to it. Dairy farmers in California, Texas, and Florida have generally been more enthusiastic about BGH.

Some of the potential dangers to cows treated with BGH were brought to light through the efforts of Dr. Marla Lyng, a Chilean-born veterinarian at the University of Vermont. Lyng observed several dozen Holstein cows that had undergone BGH testing in a clinical trial sponsored by Monsanto, the manufacturer of Posilac, a synthetic growth hormone. (The Monsanto study used a form of BGH that differs somewhat from Posilac.) In a meeting with representatives from Rural Vermont, a family-farm advocacy group, Lyng said that many of the cows she looked at had open wounds around their hocks (the hock, or heel, is located about halfway up the hind leg[1]). Many cows also had mastitis, an udder infection[2] that produces great quantities of pus,[3] which can get into the milk.

Rural Vermont prepared a report, based on Lyng's data and on computerized health records of cows in the university herd, that stated: "While definitive conclusions cannot be drawn to prove that BGH is a definite health hazard for dairy animals, there seem to be many reasons for concern." The data showed that Holsteins injected with BGH were twice as likely to suffer from hoof rot[4] and foot and leg injuries as non-BGH cows. The BGH cows also experienced more than twice the rate of uterine infections, and three or four times the rate of ketosis and retained placentas. Cows with ketosis go off-feed, milk production falls, and their milk gives off an odd, acidy-sweet smell. Retained placentas, or after-births, frequently get infected and, like uterine infections, are routinely treated with antibiotics, which can be passed on to humans. Hoof rot is also commonly treated with antibiotics, as are some foot and leg injuries.

"Given the increased use of antibiotics," the Rural Vermont report concludes, the BGH test "raises questions not only of animal safety but of human health as well." Although all milk sold in the United States is tested for antibiotic residues, routine testing looks for the presence of only four drugs, all of them from the penicillin family. A 1989 *Wall Street Journal* survey found antibiotic residues in nineteen of fifty milk samples that testers bought in ten cities. Unnecessary doses of antibiotics in humans can bring on allergic reactions or increase resistance, making the drugs less effective. The Centers for Disease Control call antibiotic resistance "a major public health crisis."

Monsanto vigorously disputes the validity of the Rural Vermont report. Company dairy research director Bob Collier argues that the herd in the University of Vermont trial was too small to justify the broad conclusions contained in the report. Collier also says that any higher incidence of infections in test cows is "related to the increase in milk yield, not to [BGH] use."

The Rural Vermont report was front-page news throughout Vermont, although it failed to get picked up by most of the national press. But Dr. David S. Kronfeld, a BGH expert and professor of veterinary medicine at

---

[1] hind leg = back leg.

[2] udder infection = an infection of the bag-like organ of a cow, which produces milk.

[3] pus = thick liquid from an infected wound.

[4] hoof rot = a disease of the hard foot of the cow.

Virginia Polytechnic Institute, believes Monsanto unwittingly[5] vindicated the Rural Vermont findings this year when it printed an insert that is distributed in Posilac packages. The insert details eighteen potential side effects on cow health that have been associated with the drug. Six of these were revealed to the public in the Rural Vermont study.

After the report appeared, the FDA sent a letter discussing the Monsanto trials to Representative Bernie Sanders of Vermont. According to the letter, Posilac had been administered to a herd of Jerseys[6] a year before the Holstein trials began. The study found that 43 percent of the Jerseys contracted mastitis[7] that required treatment, four times the rate of treatment among control cows.[8] And when BGH cows got sick, they stayed sick far longer—8.9 days on average, whereas control cows with mastitis were sick for only a day and a half. (Monsanto maintains that the herd suffered an abnormally high incidence of mastitis *before* the trial began.)

BGH doesn't cause mastitis directly, but it brings on conditions that may cause the condition. The drug acts on a cow by turning back her hormonal clock to the first months of a milk cycle. At that stage, cows just can't eat enough food; they're under such hormonal pressure to make milk that they have to draw on their own body tissues. Prolonging this stressed state makes them far more vulnerable to infections. "We now know that overall clinical mastitis, which requires antibiotic treatment, is up by almost 80 percent in BST [BGH] cows," Kronfeld said.

The Clinton Administration has shown little enthusiasm for regulating BGH or examining its safety record. A federal study[9] released in January argued that American leadership in biotechnology "would be enhanced by proceeding with (BGH), and would be impeded if there were new Government obstacles to such bio-tech products."

---

[5] unwittingly = not knowingly.

[6] Jerseys = a breed of cattle noted for their rich milk.

[7] mastitis = an inflammation of the breast of the cow caused by infection.

[8] control cows = cows in the scientific experiment.

[9] a federal study = an investigation by the central government.

Look at the reading to answer the following questions.

1. Which word is closest in meaning to *potential* in paragraph 2?

   a. related

   b. possible

   c. certain

   d. obvious

2. In paragraph 2, what does *sponsored by* mean?

   a. paid for by

   b. advertised by

3. What does *a family farm advocacy group* (paragraph 2) do?

   a. defend family farms

   b. reject family farms

4. Which word in paragraph 3 means a group of cows?

5. Which word is similar in meaning to *validity* as used in paragraph 3?

   a. cruelty

   b. reliability

   c. originality

   d. complexity

6. What does the word *incidence* in paragraph 6 mean?

   a. rate of happening

   b. speed

   c. relationship

   d. comparison

7. What word in paragraph 7 means *caught a disease*?

8. Which of these words is closest in meaning to *vulnerable* as used in paragraph 8?

   a. accustomed to

   b. guarded against

   c. exposed to

   d. dying of

9. Which of these words is closest in meaning to *enhanced* in the last paragraph?

    a. more weakened

    b. more powerful

    c. less opinionated

    d. less criticized

10. Which word is closest in meaning to *impeded* in the last paragraph?

    a. obstructed

    b. lost

    c. helped

    d. embarrassed

Themes

To Get in the Way

impede/obstruct/block/hinder

The verbs *impede*, *obstruct*, *block* and *hinder* all mean to get in the way of. They differ as follows:

impede = to get in the way of by making something difficult to do and slowing down its progress.

obstruct = to get in the way of by slowing down its progress and by putting obstacles or barriers in its way.

block = to make passage impossible by the use of obstacles.

hinder = to stop someone from doing something or prevent an activity from being done by slowing down its progress.

Choose the correct verb in the following sentences.

1. My colleague (hindered/blocked) me from doing my work this morning because she wanted to talk about her problems.

2. The road was (impeded/blocked) by a fallen tree.

3. The foreign student's problem with English spelling (impeded/obstructed) him from quick progress in class.

4. The putting into effect of the government's new policy on immigration was (hindered/obstructed) by protests and rallies.

5. The breakdown of his car (impeded/blocked) his movements this week.

COMPREHENSION

A. Looking for the Main Ideas

Write complete answers to the following questions.

1. What is the main idea of paragraph 2?

2. What is paragraph 4 mostly about?

3. Which line states the main idea of paragraph 6?

4. Which sentence contains the main idea in paragraph 8?

B. Skimming and Scanning for Details

Scan Reading 2 quickly to find the answers to these questions. Circle the letter of the best answer.

1. According to the passage, nearly all the milk bottled in Vermont and Wisconsin is likely to
    a. be contaminated with antibiotics.
    b. have an odd, acidy-sweet smell.
    c. be free of BGH.
    d. be tested for residue.

2. Which of the following would *not* require a label identifying the use of BGH?
    a. meat
    b. yogurt
    c. butter
    d. cheese

3. Dr. Marla Lyng observed that many cows treated with BGH had
    a. gained weight.
    b. been producing more milk than usual.
    c. lost their appetites.
    d. been afflicted with udder infection.

4. According to the Rural Vermont report, the Holsteins in their study were more likely to have foot and leg injuries if they were
   a. milked too often.
   b. treated with BGH.
   c. free of growth hormones.
   d. given antibiotics.

5. According to the passage, if a cow is given antibiotics,
   a. they can be passed on to humans.
   b. the cow will get more infections.
   c. the cow's milk production will increase.
   d. they can turn back the cow's hormonal clock.

6. Unnecessary doses of antibiotics in humans can cause
   a. fatal illness.
   b. allergic reactions.
   c. changes in hormonal levels.
   d. loss of appetite.

7. Monsanto disagreed with the Rural Vermont report, saying their conclusions weren't justified because the test herd was
   a. not all Holsteins.
   b. overstressed.
   c. too small.
   d. not given antibiotics.

8. A study found that when cows treated with BGH got sick, they
   a. stayed sick for only a day and a half.
   b. stopped eating.
   c. took longer to recover.
   d. often died.

9. BGH
   a. directly causes mastitis in cows.
   b. makes humans ill.
   c. has been banned.
   d. can make cows more vulnerable to disease.

10. The government is expected to

    a. examine the safety of BGH.

    b. do very little regarding BGH.

    c. regulate the use of BGH.

    d. ban the use of BGH.

C. Making Inferences and Drawing Conclusions

Some of the following statements can be inferred from the passage and others cannot. Circle the number of each statement that can be inferred.

1. People don't have enough information about the use of BGH to be able to make a choice about buying BGH or non-BGH products.

2. California cheese is more likely to have BGH than Wisconsin cheese.

3. It is not in Monsanto's interest to have negative BGH studies revealed to the public.

4. Cows treated with BGH are more likely to have lung disease than those not treated with BGH.

5. BGH has been definitely proven to be a health hazard to both cows and humans.

6. From the Rural Vermont study, it can be concluded that non-BGH cows are likely to be healthier than BGH-treated cows.

7. The use of BGH can indirectly affect the health of humans.

8. The question of the safety of BGH has caused widespread panic.

9. By giving cows antibiotics, humans will be safer from disease.

10. The results of the Rural Vermont study regarding the side effects of BGH are most likely accurate.

DISCUSSION

Discuss these questions with your classmates.

1. Do you know any other animals that are harmed by methods used to make them more productive?

2. What do you think the government should do to control the safety of our food supply?

3. Why do you think that substances like BGH and pesticides are allowed to be used?

Summary

How To Write

HOW TO SUMMARIZE
PAGE 263

Write a one-paragraph summary of Reading 1.
Check your summary with the Summary Checklist on page 265.

Paraphrasing

How To Write

HOW TO PARAPHRASE
PAGE 257

Paraphrase paragraph I, in Reading 2.
Begin paraphrasing with either:
According to Harper's Magazine, . . .
or
Based on the article in Harper's Magazine, . . .

Research

How To Write

HOW TO DO LIBRARY RESEARCH
PAGE 248

You may use your research later to write a cause-and-effect essay.

Choose a particular additive or food or drink and find out three effects it has; or find a disease and find three things that cause it.

The following are some suggested topics:

Effects of lead poisoning	Effects of caffeine
Effects of vitamin supplements	Effects of DDT use
Causes of obesity	Causes of anorexia

Read the following essay written by a student.

The Negative Sides of Fast Food

With today's fast lifestyle, it is very hard to keep up with the traditional way of taking care of all human needs. Eating habits are no exception. According to an article in *Success* magazine (Nov. 1994), America today eats more fast food than ever before. Ninety-six out of every one hundred Americans eat fast food on some kind of regular basis. There are many side effects related to this popular eating habit, most of which are damaging to our health and personal care. Eating fast food regularly may cause our bodies to be deficient in the vitamins and minerals we need to maintain good health; also, eating fast food can be very addictive, and people accustomed to it rarely change their eating habits.

The food sold in most fast food restaurants may not be all that good for us. The majority of those restaurants are franchises, which means that everything has to look, taste, and smell the same way in all the restaurants of a particular franchise. A franchise controls this by having a main food distribution center, which implies that the food has to go through a long frozen storage period, then a transportation period before it gets to the consumer. In order for the food to still taste fresh after all this time, a lot of artificial preservatives have to be added. As if that were not enough, the main element that the fast food market competes for is not good food or fresh ingredients, but they advertise and compete for the lowest prices, and we all know what that means.

People who have the habit of eating fast food rarely even try to change their diet. Instead, people tend to get more and more used to the convenience and taste of fast food. According to a survey in *Industrial and Labor Relations Review* magazine (Oct. 1992), out of every ten fast food eaters only four will eat the same amount or less, the other six will double their "loads" of fast food within four years; and out of every ten people that finally get to control their eating disorder, six will come back to eating fast food within six years. These alarming figures seem to be in contradiction with today's convenient ways of cooking at home. Easy to make dishes like those for microwaves, soups, etc. would appear to be the solution for the fast food problem, but obviously the real problem was not the trouble of cooking at home, but the addicting simplicity of the fast food market.

In conclusion, eating fast food is not only an unhealthy habit but it is also a corrupting one. Chances are most of us will have to eat some kind of fast food over a period in our lives, but this would not be a problem if we planned a diet that could be combined with fast food. Simple meals such as cereals, yogurts, and dishes for microwave ovens can make a big difference and are just as fast and affordable as food from any of the popular franchises. All it takes is a little conscience and responsibility.

Pedro
Dominican Republic

STUDENT ESSAY FOLLOW-UP

1. Underline the thesis statement.

2. What two effects of eating fast food is the writer considering?

3. What is the topic sentence of paragraph 2? Is it clearly supported?

4. What effect is the writer considering in paragraph 3? What evidence of the effect does he give?

5. In the conclusion, does the writer restate the thesis statement in other words?

ORGANIZING

Cause and Effect Essay

Another popular type of essay organization is the cause-and-effect essay. This form of writing is frequently used in academic writing. In college, your history teacher may ask you to write about the causes of the American Civil War; your health teacher may ask you to write on the three effects of a snake bite; your psychology teacher may ask you to explain the high rate of alcoholism among American Indians.

There are three types of cause-and-effect essays:

1. The Cause Analysis Essay (explains causes)

2. The Effect Analysis Essay (explains effects)

3. The Causal Chain Essay (explains causes that lead to effects in a chain.)

The Cause Analysis Essay

There are few situations that can be traced back to a single cause. There are usually several causes for something, or a combination of causes that lead to an effect.

For example, why do some children have a low IQ? For some it may be caused by early malnutrition which slows brain growth; for others it may be caused by exposure to toxins such as lead which damage the nervous system. It may be caused by the lack of a stimulating environment. It may also be caused by parents who do not encourage their children or spend time with them. If you examine the topic further you might find that family size may also be a cause.

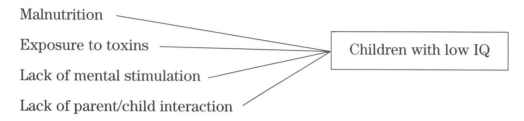

Malnutrition

Exposure to toxins

Lack of mental stimulation

Lack of parent/child interaction

Children with low IQ

Organizing the Cause Essay:

The Thesis Statement:

The thesis statement should state the causes to be discussed.

For example:

Low IQ in children is generally caused by the following factors: malnutrition in childhood, lack of a stimulating environment, and a lack of interaction with their parents.

The Body Paragraphs:

Although there are other causes for low IQ in children, these were picked out as the more important causes, and the ones that could be easily supported.

Each body paragraph will discuss one of the causes mentioned in the thesis statement.

The Conclusion:

The conclusion will restate the thesis and provide a general comment on the topic.

▶ The Effect Analysis Essay

Just as there can be many causes for something, a cause can have several effects. For example, many people consume caffeine in one form or another which has the effect of making them alert, but addiction to caffeine can have many negative effects such as restlessness, insomnia, heartbeat irregularities, and even high blood pressure which may lead to other serious problems.

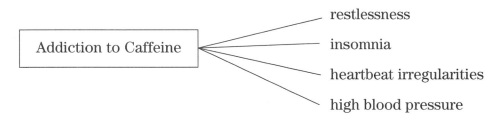

In the student essay on "The Side Effects of Fast Food," you can see the two negative effects of eating fast food regularly. Also, in Reading 1, "The Story of Food Additives," the effects of food additives are explained. Notice that reference is made to the cause before explaining the effect. It is important to understand which is the cause and which is the effect. Look at the following examples:

Cause: The additives sodium nitrite and sodium nitrate are two closely related chemicals that have been used for centuries to preserve meat.

Effect: Nitrite has been considered an important cause of stomach cancer in the United States, Japan, and other countries.

Cause: The sugar substitute aspartame is sold commercially as Equal or Nutrasweet and is used in many diet drinks as a substitute for sugar.

Effect: One out of 20,000 babies cannot metabolize one of the two substances that aspartame is made from and toxic levels of that substance can result in mental retardation.

Effect: Some people who have consumed aspartame have reported dizziness, headaches, and even seizures.

Effect: Its possible link to an increased risk of brain tumors.

Exercise 1

Identify which is the cause (C) and which is the effect (E).

1. ___ Accident death rates dropped by 30 percent.

   ___ A seat belt law was passed.

   ___ Motorists were required to wear seat belts.

2. ___ Carla burned 500 calories per week.

   ___ Carla's blood pressure was lower.

   ___ Carla exercised 45 minutes each day.

3. ___ Social and work-related pressures have increased in modern times.

   ___ People are more at risk for stress-related illnesses, such as heart attacks.

4. ___ The sun's ultraviolet rays penetrate the deeper layer of the skin.

   ___ Skin cancer is one of the most common forms of cancer in the United States.

   ___ The protective ozone layer in the atmosphere is decreased by pollutants.

5. ___ Most American women over the age of fifty consume half of their daily calcium requirements.

   ___ Calcium in bones gradually becomes depleted, leaving them weak and brittle, a condition called osteoporosis.

   ___ In this country, older women suffer approximately five million fractures each year.

6. ___ People who walk daily have healthier cardiovascular systems.

   ___ Aerobic exercises allow the heart and lungs to utilize oxygen more efficiently.

7. ___ Flu viruses are highly contagious and are spread through close contact with infected persons.

   ___ Flu epidemics spread rapidly through the workplace.

8. ___ Antibiotics have been over-prescribed by doctors for decades.

   ___ Over a period of time, bacteria can become resistant to antibiotics when repeatedly exposed to them.

   ___ A medical crisis exists because many antibiotics are no longer useful for combating diseases.

In each sentence of the paragraph, underline the cause once and the effect twice.

1. Ear pain occurs when there is a buildup of fluid and pressure in the middle ear. Often during a cold or allergy, particularly in small children, the ear tube becomes swollen shut, preventing the normal flow of fluid from the middle ear. Fluid begins to accumulate, causing stuffiness and decreased hearing. Sometimes a bacterial infection starts in the fluid, which results in pain and fever. Ear pain and ear stuffiness can also result from high altitudes, such as when descending in an airplane or driving in the mountains. Swallowing will frequently relieve the pressure in the ear tube.

2. Eating candy can produce acids in the body. Consuming carbohydrates can even produce an alcoholic condition in your body. One of our great orators, William Jennings Bryan, gave speeches nationwide about the bad effects of drinking alcohol, causing more than one person to change his drinking habits. Ironically, Bryan himself died of an alcoholic stomach as a result of eating thirteen pancakes with syrup for breakfast. Eating the pancakes, which are full of carbohydrates, and the sugary syrup, created a kind of alcoholic brew in his stomach. This innocently consumed brew produced alcoholic poisoning, which in turn led to his death.

3. Exercise is the central ingredient for good health because it tones the muscles, strengthens the bones, makes the heart and lungs work better, and prevents disease. It increases energy and vitality and gives you a good feeling about yourself. This sense of well-being helps you deal better with stress, eases depression, and aids sleep. There are three kinds of exercises, of which *strengthening* is the least important because it builds more bulky muscles, although it is important for increasing general strength. *Stretching* exercises keep the muscles loose and are a bit more important than weight-lifting. Stretching before doing other kinds of exercises warms up the muscles, and makes them looser and less susceptible to injury. *Aerobic* exercises are the key to fitness because they improve your heart and lungs. Your heart speeds up to pump larger amounts of blood. You breathe more frequently and more deeply to increase the oxygen transfer from the lungs to the blood. As a result of these efforts, the heart becomes larger and stronger and your lungs healthier.

Organizing the Effect Analysis Essay

The Thesis Statement:

The thesis statement, as in the causal analysis essay, should state the effects to be discussed.

Example:

Eating fast food regularly may cause our bodies to be deficient in vitamins and minerals we need to maintain good health and also it can be very addictive.

The Body Paragraphs:

Like the causal analysis select two or three major effects. In the thesis statement above two effects have been selected. Therefore, the first body paragraph will explain the effects on health of eating fast food and the second body paragraph will explain the addictive effect of eating fast food regularly. Support each effect with relevant examples and/or facts.

The Conclusion:

The conclusion will restate the thesis and provide a general comment on the topic.

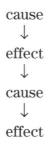 **The Causal Chain**

In this type of cause-and-effect essay, one cause will lead to an effect which will lead to another cause and so on, creating a chain of causes and effects.

cause
↓
effect
↓
cause
↓
effect

For example, bad weather conditions such as excessive rainfall may affect the farmers' vegetable crops causing the vegetable crops to die. This would make vegetables scarce, causing prices to rise in the supermarkets. This would result in people not buying vegetables very much because they are so expensive. Since people will be eating few vegetables, this will affect their health.

excessive rainfall
↓
damage to vegetable crops
↓
vegetable prices go up
↓
people eat less vegetables
↓
people are not as healthy

In Reading 2, "BGH: The Debate Goes On," a causal chain may be implied: cows are given BGH to increase their production of milk; the BGH causes the cows to get infections so the cows are given antibiotics. The antibiotics in turn get into our milk supply, creating cause for alarm.

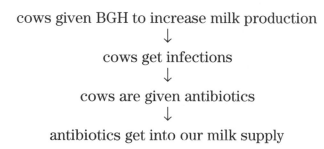

cows given BGH to increase milk production
↓
cows get infections
↓
cows are given antibiotics
↓
antibiotics get into our milk supply

The most frequent use of this type of essay is in the sciences where there are biological or weather cycles.

Practice:

Plan the causal chain for one of the topics below or choose a chain from geography or biology.

1. The cutting of forests in the Amazon.

2. The killing of elephants for ivory.

Organization of a Causal Chain

The Thesis Statement:

The thesis statement should state the three or four steps in the chain:

For example:
> The use of BGH to increase milk production indirectly affects human health since the cows that are given BGH get infections, and are treated with antibiotics, which then get into our milk supply.

The Body Paragraphs:

It is important to break the chain into three or four major steps. Each body paragraph will describe one step in the chain stated in the thesis statement. Each step should be supported with details.

The Conclusion:

The conclusion will restate the main points in the chain and provide a comment on the topic.

 **WRITING PRACTICE**

Choose one of the following topics.

1 Use one of the topics you researched in this chapter to write a cause or effect essay.

2 Write an effect analysis of eating junk food regularly focusing on three effects.

3 Write an essay on either the causes or the effects of pollution.

4 Write an essay on the causes or effects of the use of pesticides.

1. Pre-writing

Work alone, with a partner, or in a group.

1 Brainstorm the topic. Choose the pre-writing technique you prefer.

2 Brainstorm for three causes or three effects.

3 Work on a thesis statement.

2. Outlining

A. Organize your ideas.

Step 1: Write your thesis statement. Include the three causes or effects.

Step 2: Order the causes or effects.

Step 3: Provide supporting ideas and details for each cause or effect.

B. Make a more detailed outline. The essay outline on page 22 will help you.

3. **Write a Rough Draft.**

How To **Write**

DRAFTING
PAGE 245

4. **Revise Your Rough Draft. Use the checklist on page 246.**

5. **Edit Your Essay. Use editing symbols on pages 247—248.**

How To **Write**

EDITING
PAGE 247

6. **Write Your Final Copy.**

Chapter 8: Technology

PRE-READING QUESTIONS

Discuss these questions with your classmates or teacher.

1. What piece of technology have you used most recently?

2. What technological invention have you enjoyed the most?

3. What future technology do you look forward to using? Why?

A Hundred Years of Technology

Match the letter under each decade with the technological invention below.

1900s A	1910s B	1920s C	1930s D	1940s E
1950s F	1960s G	1970s H	1980s I	1990s J

A Dutch company called Philips, and the Japanese firm Sony, introduce the first compact disc.

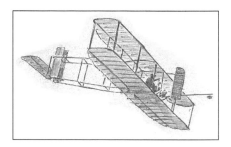

The first practical plane is flown by the Wright brothers.

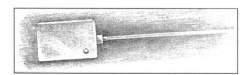

The first laser is built by Theodore Maiman, an American

The B.B.C. begins operating a black-and-white-television service from London. Within 3 years television sets are in 20,000 homes.

The U.S. launches Telstar, the first satellite to relay live television shows as well as telephone calls.

A U.S. company called IBM produces the first word processor.

The first personal computer is developed by Intel Corporation of California.

The first mass-produced car, the Ford Model T, appears on the market.

An American inventor named Chester Carlson invents the photocopier.

The American Rand Corporation and IBM discover robotics.

Plastic tape for the tape recorder was introduced by a German company, AEG.

Reading 1: The World of Virtual Reality

Imagine walking on the surface of Mars. You follow the channels where water is believed to have once flowed; hike across the flat plains covered with rocks of all sizes; and jump the basin called Hellas, measuring more than 930 miles across. After you explore the polar caps, you climb the huge volcano Olympus Mons, which is twice as high as Earth's highest peak. Seem impossible? It may be in the real world, but not in virtual reality.

Virtual reality (VR) is a new technology that allows you to look at, listen to, and move around a computer world every bit as fantastic as your wildest imaginings. Unlike a video game or computer art, virtual reality eliminates the computer screen and lets you "step into" a three-dimensional artificial world. All you have to do is put on the special video goggles and a wired glove, and the impossible becomes probable—you can climb mountains or fly above them, explore other planets or play with molecules, paint in three dimensions or design a house as you walk through it.

The Mars program described above was created from satellite pictures and information sent back by a Viking spacecraft stationed on the planet. It is just one example of the kinds of environments, or realities, that can be created by today's VR systems. At the heart of these systems are programs that continuously provide the sensory information, like the red dust and gray rocks you see on the Martian landscape and the rocket engines you hear as you land, that makes you feel like you're really there.

A different program might take you under the sea, where you're surrounded by colorful fish. An octopus appears and you chase it back into its cave. You can hear the distant sounds of whales and the rush of water in your ears. A starfish catches your eye and you pick it up and examine it before placing it carefully on the sea floor, next to a colorful shell.

You get the feeling that you are actually swimming in this incredible, undersea world because inside your headgear, called a head-mounted display (HMD), are special goggles with two miniature screens inside and headphones for sound. When you turn your head in the direction of the octopus, signals are processed by the computer to create another set of sights and sounds. Moving your hand inside the wired glove also sends signals to the computer and allows you to pick up the starfish and move it anywhere you want. Virtual reality is created because the user and computer work together. The computer creates an environment that responds to and is controlled by the user.

In one way, you can say that virtual reality makes dreams come true because you, the user, become immersed in an imaginary world that you can see, hear, and to some extent feel. Sensory immersion could someday become so deep that all of our senses would be stimulated by the computer to convince the mind that it's really in another world. In the future, total sensory immersion could include temperature, bodily movement, and the feel and even the smell of things.

Think of being in a movie. You know you're sitting in a theater surrounded by other people and that the people on the screen are actors. Nevertheless you do what is called "suspending disbelief," and for a while, what you are seeing and hearing becomes real enough to affect you. You might feel excited, scared, angry, or happy while you are watching. Virtual reality is better than a movie, however, because there are no distractions and the sense of being totally immersed in a virtual, three-dimensional world is much greater. The user has a real feeling of "being there," in another reality, experiencing some event that doesn't physically exist in the real world. Consider how you feel when you come out of a good movie or are in the middle of a good novel, and you'll understand how virtual reality has so much potential to teach and inspire.

Virtual reality's power of immersion is of great value because of its ability to focus the user's attention on a specific problem or experience. Distractions are blocked out, which allows participants to focus on just the information they want to work with. How many times have you been told to "pay attention" if you really want to learn something or get the most out of something? Everyone knows that concentration without distractions is the key to better learning and top performance. Scientists have solved complex problems by placing all their information in a virtual setting and then working with it.

Immersion is only half of the merit of virtual reality. The other important value is interaction. Without it, we're just observers, and little problem-solving or creative thinking can occur. If you're a landscape designer, for example, it is the ability to interact with the virtual world that allows you to design the landscape. You would enter a three-dimensional world of grass, trees, and flowers. You could pick the varieties you want and place them where you want, putting grass here and flower beds there; then walk around to the back of the house, perhaps creating a stone pathway as you go along. All this involves two unique aspects of interactivity in a virtual world: navigation within the world and the dynamics of the environment.

Navigation is simply a user's ability to move around independently as if inside the environment. You can fly, move through walls, walk around, or swim. It means moving your point of view through three-dimensional space.

Dynamics involves picking a particular element in the virtual world with the intent of performing an action with it, such as moving a tree from one spot to another, or changing the colors of the flowers or adding a fence. For a scientist, it might mean moving molecules around to create a new substance. For an architect, it might mean changing the placement of supports and coming up with a stronger building design.

Astronomers have used the tools of virtual reality to assemble complex, three-dimensional star fields of the galaxy and to fly around in the data to understand how the universe is structured. As a result of their studies, the astronomers have seen things in the data they couldn't experience before. They are coming up with many surprises, such as the way vast numbers of galaxies are clumped together in threads, ribbons, and clusters, leaving tremendous empty areas between them.

With the assistance of various computer tools, we can now enter and interact with new and interesting worlds. Because virtual reality gives us details and information in the most natural way possible through vision, sound, and sensations, we can look at problems in a different way, using all our human senses to find answers. The uses of VR are endless—in design and engineering, entertainment, education, business, medicine, and even sports. Through virtual reality we are truly entering a brave, new world.

VOCABULARY

Select the letter of the answer that is closest in meaning to the italicized word or phrase.

1. All you have to do is put on the special video *goggles* and a wired glove.
    a. wide glasses that fit tightly against the face
    b. a type of hat with wires inside
    c. an instrument attached to the chest
    d. a metal, wired arm extension

2. At the heart of VR systems are programs that provide *sensory* information.
    a. related to the thought processes
    b. associated with the internal organs of the body
    c. having to do with sight, hearing, etc.
    d. connected with sleep and dreams

3. The user becomes *immersed in* an imaginary world.
    a. connected to
    b. side by side with
    c. completely surrounded by
    d. in close contact with

4. VR is better than any movie because there are no *distractions*.
    a. noises that cause distress
    b. things that draw one's attention away
    c. commercials or advertisements
    d. concerns about how interesting the story is

5. Virtual reality has great potential to *inspire*.

    a. produce better quality products

    b. encourage people to do something good

    c. assist in problem solving

    d. give immediate results

6. Immersion is only half of the *merit* of virtual reality.

    a. form

    b. approach

    c. technique

    d. advantage

7. One aspect of interactivity in a virtual world is *dynamics*.

    a. feelings

    b. thoughts

    c. imagery

    d. actions

8. Dynamics involves picking an element in the virtual world with the *intent* of performing an action with it.

    a. purpose

    b. expectation

    c. interest

    d. method

9. Vast numbers of galaxies are *clumped together*.

    a. loosely organized

    b. spaced evenly apart

    c. set very closely in masses

    d. revolving around each other

10. Vast numbers of galaxies are clumped together in threads, ribbons, and *clusters*.

    a. lines

    b. groups

    c. pairs

    d. individuals

Helpful

· ·

advantageous/beneficial

The adjectives *advantageous* and *beneficial* both mean having a helpful or good effect. They differ as follows:

beneficial = helpful, useful, having a good effect.

advantageous = helpful, useful in reaching a particular goal.

Choose the correct word to complete the sentence.

1. A relaxing vacation that you needed for a long time would be _____ .

    a) beneficial   b) advantageous

2. Taking a course of treatment for a stomach problem is _____ .

    a) advantagcous   b) beneficial

3. Going to the right college has been _____ .

    a) beneficial   b) advantageous

4. When you want to sell your house it is _____ to put it on the market when the demand for houses goes up.

    a) advantageous   b) beneficial

5. The meeting with John was _____ for me because he gave a good offer on the product I was trying to sell.

    a) beneficial   b) advantageous

Task:

What would be advantageous about VR?
How could VR be beneficial to someone?

Examine

....

Both *explore* and *investigate* mean to examine carefully. They differ as follows:

to investigate = to try and find out more information or to try to find the reasons for something.

to explore = to travel to little known or unknown places to find out more, or to find out more about explanations and ideas.

Put the words or phrases in the box below under the correct headings. You may use the words or phrases under both headings when necessary.

a crime	a person	outer space	the ocean floor
a subject	Central Africa	an idea	Antarctica
the possibilities	clues		

to investigate	to explore

Task:

What would you like to investigate using VR?
What would you like to explore using VR?

COMPREHENSION

A. Looking for the Main Idea

Circle the letter of the answer that best completes the sentence.

1. The main idea of paragraph 2 is that
   a. virtual reality is a new technology that eliminates the need for a computer screen.
   b. virtual reality is an artificial world into which a user can "enter" and interact.
   c. special equipment is necessary to enter the world of virtual reality.
   d. there are many ways in which virtual reality can be used.

2. Paragraph 5 is mostly about
   a. how signals from the head-mounted display are processed by the computer.
   b. how the wired glove is used to move objects in the virtual world.
   c. how you feel when you're immersed in a virtual world.
   d. how the computer and user work together in the virtual environment.

3. Paragraph 9 is mainly concerned with
   a. how to use virtual reality for designing landscapes.
   b. why observation isn't enough to solve problems.
   c. the two aspects of interactivity in the virtual world.
   d. the value of the interactive aspect of virtual reality.

B. Skimming and Scanning for Details

Scan Reading 1 quickly to find the answers to these questions. Write complete answers.

1. According to the passage, what was used to create the Mars virtual reality?

2. According to the passage, what kind of information makes you feel as if you're really in the virtual world?

3. What are the two instruments that make up the head-mounted display?

4. What could total sensory immersion involve in the future?

5. What makes the immersive experience of VR more powerful than that of a movie?

6. In paragraph 9, sentence 2, to what does the word "it" refer?

7. What is navigation within the virtual world?

8. What does dynamics involve?

9. How have astronomers used the tools of virtual reality?

10. What are five areas in which virtual reality can be useful?

C. Making Inferences and Drawing Conclusions

The answers to these questions are not directly stated in the passage. Circle the letter of the best answer.

1. The passage implies that
   a. the environments that can be created by virtual reality systems are limited.
   b. the least important aspect of virtual reality is its ability to convince the user of being in an imaginary environment.
   c. with virtual reality, the user has less control over the program than with current computer programs and video games.
   d. without sensory stimulation, the feeling of being immersed in the virtual world would be greatly diminished.

2. From the passage, it can be concluded that
   a. the suspension of disbelief is not necessary in the virtual world.
   b. the value of VR technology is primarily in its ability to entertain.
   c. VR technology could discourage people from being creative.
   d. virtual reality can be a powerful tool for learning.

3. It can be inferred from the passage that

    a. experiencing an event that exists in an artificial world is one way to solve real-life problems.

    b. the impact of virtual reality lies in its ability to focus our thoughts without the distraction of sensory stimulation.

    c. virtual reality is a controversial technology because it prevents people from thinking for themselves.

    d. the goal of VR technology is to create artificial worlds for people to live in.

4. The author's tone is

    a. sarcastic.

    b. enthusiastic.

    c. indifferent.

    d. doubtful.

DISCUSSION

Discuss these questions with your classmates.

1. Does VR limit creativity or encourage it?

2. In what ways can VR be used in the domain of education and sports?

3. In what ways can VR be harmful to society?

Reading 2: Crippled by Computers

The following article by Janice M. Horowitz appeared in *Time* Magazine in October 1992.

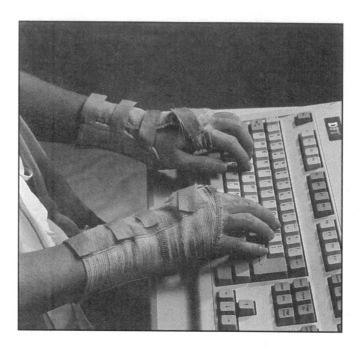

As more U. S. workers spend their days at keyboards, hand injuries and lawsuits are multiplying.

As jobs in journalism go, Grant McCool's was a plum[1] assignment. Based in Hong Kong for Reuters news service, McCool covered breaking news throughout east Asia, traveling to South Korea, China and Pakistan. But in 1989, after five hectic[2] years, the native of Scotland was ready for a change. That's when his bosses transferred him to New York City to be an editor.

That's also when the trouble started. After typing on his computer keyboard for hours a day over several months, McCool developed excruciating pain in his hands; some mornings he would wake with his arms throbbing and burning. "The doctor told me to stop typing immediately," recalls McCool, 32. He hasn't written or edited a story on deadline[3] since. Nor has he been able to clean house, carry heavy objects or play squash.[4] He cannot even drive a car; controlling the steering wheel with his injured hands is impossible.

---

[1] plum = very desirable.

[2] hectic = busy, full of excitement and hurried movement.

[3] deadline = a date or time before which something must be completed.

[4] squash = a game played in a walled court with rackets and a rubber ball.

McCool suffers from a severe case of cumulative trauma disorder, a syndrome that results from overusing the muscles and tendons of the fingers, hands, arms and shoulders. The condition brings pain, numbness, weakness and sometimes long-term disability. Such problems, more commonly known as repetitive stress injuries (RSI), now strike an estimated 185,000 U. S. office and factory workers a year. The cases account for more than half the country's occupational illnesses, compared with about 20 percent a decade ago.

A particularly fast-growing category of victims includes white-collar professional and clerical workers who spend their days pounding away at keyboards. An increasing number are responding in a white-collar way: with lawsuits. Hundreds of injured telephone reservationists, cashiers, word processors and journalists, McCool among them, are suing computer manufacturers, blaming the machines for their disabilities. IBM, Apple Computers, AT&T and Kodak's Atex-division, which produces a word-processing system designed for journalists, have all been named in the suits, which demand damages of up to a $1 million or more per victim.

Employers are quickly learning that they must face up to the problem. Already, RSI costs about $7 billion a year in lost productivity and medical costs. Moreover, under the provisions of the Americans with Disabilities Act, which went into effect this summer, employers are now required to accommodate "reasonably" workers with physical impairments. Companies may have to transfer employees with RSI to less stressful jobs or give them special help. Increasingly, union and other worker groups are demanding that companies provide better keyboards and office furniture and give employees more frequent breaks to reduce the risk of injury.

How ironic that computers, the very technology celebrated for making office work easier, would cause such harm. By now, nearly half the U. S. work force—some 45 million workers—use computers (though not all spend hour after hour punching keys). "We thought technology was going to help us, which it does. But we did not consider that we would also have to adjust the workplace at the same time," says Barbara Silverstein, research director of Washington State's department of labor and industries.

RSI involves not just one but an array of ailments resulting from tugging,[5] pounding and straining crucial tissues in the upper body. It usually begins innocuously.[6] "People think they've had a particularly hard day or that they're getting old," says Frank Fernandez, an Oakland, California, attorney who has filed suit against several computer manufacturers on behalf of RSI sufferers.

---

[5] tugging = pulling hard with a lot of effort.

[6] innocuously = harmlessly.

But as the hands continue to be overworked, symptoms worsen. Tendons,[7] which are like long pulleys[8] directing the movement of the fingers from many places in the hands and arms, can swell up, producing painful tendinitis. Soreness can also result from the inflammation of sheaths surrounding the tendons. Muscles in the forearm that control the movement of fingers may be irritated, a condition called myositis. As tissues become inflamed and swollen, they can press on nearby nerves, causing tingling and weakness in the fingers. Sometimes scar tissue develops in the area. All together these injuries, if not treated, can result in diminished coordination and strength: patients may literally lose their grip[9] and have trouble managing simple manual tasks.

Among the more extreme—and less common—cumulative traumas is carpal tunnel syndrome. It develops when tissues in the palmar side of the wrist swell, squeezing a vital nerve that runs through the area. Carpal tunnel syndrome can cause crippling pain for months or years, though surgery can sometime help.

It is hard to conceive how the gentle patter[10] of fingers over a computer keyboard could do such damage. People have, after all, been typing for decades, and computers would seem to be an improvement over clunky[11] typewriters. But word processors pose special problems. They allow workers to sit with their fingers flying across the keyboard at 240 strokes a minute for hours without a break. A typewriter, by contrast, forces workers to pause every so often to move the carriage or change the paper. The amount of time spent at the keyboard is critical: a study in Australia found that people who typed for more than five hours a day at a computer had 12 times as great a risk of developing RSI as those who spent less time.

The modern office has left many employees with little variation in their daily tasks. "Instead of running to the file cabinet to pull out information or going to the library, workers can do everything they need to by just sitting at the keyboard," says Silverstein. "They don't even have to get up to talk to each other. Now they have electronic messaging." Even today's phones with push buttons instead of dials strain the same tired tendons.

---

[7] tendons = thick, fibrous cords that connect muscles to bones.

[8] pulleys = apparatus used for lifting heavy things.

[9] grip = hold.

[10] patter = the sound of something hitting a hard surface lightly, quickly, and repeatedly.

[11] clunky = heavy and noisy.

Admittedly, personal traits and habits often influence who will develop RSI. A pioneer in treating the injuries, Dr. Emil Pascarelli, medical director of New York City's Miller Institute at St. Luke's–Roosevelt Hospital, points out how very heavy people can get into trouble. For their hands to reach the keyboard, they have to maneuver their arms around their own girth,[12] and wind up[13] contorting[14] their wrists inward. Double-jointedness can also be a risk factor. Smokers may have fewer injuries, thanks to their periodic breaks away from the terminal to satisfy nicotine cravings. And what goes on outside the office can be just as damaging as what happens in it. Observes Katy Keller, a physical therapist at the Miller Institute: "Injured people go home and talk on the telephone, stir the supper and carry the baby all at the same time. All this does is add to the physical stress of the workday."

New, more benign technology would help. In the U. S. and elsewhere designers are scrambling to create radically different keyboards that will be easier on the hands. But the ultimate goal is to do away with the keyboard. Reuters has given McCool a voice-activated computer that can type words and perform other functions in response to his verbal commands. Such machines are still slow and unreliable and can "understand" only a limited vocabulary, but the technology is improving rapidly. When voice-activated computers spread through the workplace, probably sometime early in the next century, the only occupational risk might be an occasional bout[15] of laryngitis.[16]

---

[12] girth = the thickness around something.

[13] wind up = end up.

[14] contorting = twisting in an unusual way.

[15] bout = bad attack.

[16] laryngitis = a painful condition of the larynx, where sounds are produced, making speech difficult.

Look at the reading on computers to answer the following questions.

1. Which word in paragraph 2 means "extremely painful"?

2. Which definition of "throbbing" as used in paragraph 2 is correct?

    a. a hard beating of the blood vessels

    b. an abnormal swelling of an area of the skin

3. Which of these answers describes a *cumulative* injury?

    a. happens all of a sudden

    b. occurs from time to time

    c. gets worse over time

    d. decreases in seriousness as time goes by

4. Which word means the same as *pounding*, as used in paragraph 4?

    a. practicing

    b. counting

    c. striking

5. What are *impairments*, as used in paragraph 5?

    a. injuries or weaknesses

    b. powers or qualities

6. Which is the best definition of *ironic*, as used in paragraph 6?

    a. in keeping with most people's ideas

    b. opposite to what might be expected

    c. unusual in form or meaning

    d. unbalanced or unequal

7. Which of these words could be substituted for *array* in paragraph 7?

    a. several similar

    b. commonly known

    c. directly opposite

    d. many different

8. What is another way of expressing *straining*, as used in the passage?

    a. damaging or weakening

    b. strengthening or making better

    c. twisting or turning

9. Which statement is correct?

     a. Diminished strength is a complete loss of strength.

     b. Diminished strength is a lessening or weakening of strength.

     c. Diminished strength is an increase in strength.

10. Which word or phrase is similar in meaning to *benign* as it is used in paragraph 13?

     a. easier to operate

     b. less noisy

     c. different

     d. not harmful

Themes

Damage

··

damage/harm/hurt/injure/impair

To damage, harm, hurt, injure and *impair* all have the same meaning but differ as follows:

damage – to harm but not completely destroy. It is used with objects (not people) or abstract nouns (health, beauty). When used with objects, a loss of value is implied.

Example:
The fire damaged the house.

harm = to have a bad effect on or cause an injury to.

Example:
Drinking too much can harm your liver.

hurt = to cause physical or mental pain.

Example:
She was hurt by what you said.

injure = to hurt a living thing by causing wounds, bruises, etc.

Example:
He injured his leg when he fell from his horse.

impair = to make weaker or worse.

Example:

Reading in the dark can impair your eyesight.

Put the words or phrases in the box below under the correct headings. You may put the word or phrase under more than one heading in some cases.

hearing	one's arm	a computer	a child
a camera	one's feelings	one's ability	crops
one's relationship	someone's pride	a building	one's finger

damage	harm	hurt	injure	impair

Legal Action

sue/take someone to court/bring a charge against/try

bring a charge against someone = when the authorities begin legal proceedings against someone for doing something wrong.

sue = to start legal proceedings against a person or company, usually in the hopes of being awarded damages (money).

take someone to court = same as sue but more informal.

try = when legal authorities begin proceedings against someone in a court of law.

Choose the correct word in the following sentences.

1. She is (suing/bringing a charge against) the computer company for $100,000 in damages.

2. He was (tried/taken to court) for murder and the case was well publicized.

3. The police officer (charged him/took him to court) for possessing an unlicensed gun.

4. She is (taking him to court/trying him) for not paying her for her work.

5. The woman cannot be (taken to court/tried) because she is mentally disturbed.

6. The officer (charged him/took him to court) for reckless driving.

Task:

Use each of the words for legal action in a sentence.

COMPREHENSION

A. Looking for the Main Ideas

Write complete answers to the following questions.

1. What is the main idea of paragraph 4?

2. Which line states the main idea of paragraph 5?

3. What is paragraph 8 mostly about?

4. Which sentence contains the main idea in paragraph 10?

B. Skimming and Scanning for Details

Scan Reading 2 quickly to complete the following sentences. Circle the letter of the best answer.

1. When Grant McCool developed a severe case of cumulative trauma disorder, his doctor told him to _____ .

   a. take some medication

   b. rest for a week

   c. stop typing right away

   d. exercise his hands

2. _____ is *not* a symptom of cumulative trauma disorder.

    a. pain

    b. fever

    c. weakness

    d. numbness

3. Union and worker groups are asking employers to _____ .

    a. stop buying computers

    b. provide better equipment

    c. raise employees' salaries

    d. give employees more vacation time

4. The condition called myositis occurs when _____ .

    a. muscles in the forearm become irritated

    b. tendons swell up and produce pain

    c. tissues in the wrist swell

    d. sheaths surrounding tendons get inflamed

5. When a nerve inside the wrist is squeezed because of swelling, it produces a condition known as _____ .

    a. tendinitis

    b. myositis

    c. carpal tunnel syndrome

    d. double jointedness

6. The reason why today's computer typists are more likely to suffer from RSI than typists in the past is because today's workers _____ .

    a. work longer hours

    b. are given more work to do

    c. have more complicated machinery

    d. take less breaks from the keyboard

7. Another contributing factor to RSI in the modern office is that _____ .

    a. work stations are too close together

    b. the lighting is not very good

    c. supervisors don't talk to their workers

    d. workers have little variety in the tasks they do

8. Workers who are overweight are more likely to get RSI because they _____ .

    a. must hold their wrists in an awkward position

    b. can't sit on small chairs at computer work stations

    c. can't reach their desks very easily

    d. don't place their feet on the floor correctly

9. People can make work-related injuries worse by _____ .

    a. refusing to talk about them with co-workers

    b. not consulting with a doctor when they get the injury

    c. aggravating them with bad habits outside the office

    d. blaming computer manufacturers for their pain and suffering

10. Perhaps the best solution to the problem of RSI is to design _____ .

    a. nicer office environments

    b. different keyboards

    c. more comfortable typing chairs

    d. voice-activated computers

C. Making Inferences and Drawing Conclusions

Some of the following statements can be inferred from the passage and others cannot. Circle the number of each statement that can be inferred.

1. Computers have solved all of the problems associated with office work.

2. Repetitive stress injuries are not serious conditions.

3. RSI is not a big problem for companies since they affect only a small portion of the work force.

4. As fast and convenient as computers are, they do have some drawbacks.

5. Companies would save money by taking steps to reduce the number of computer-related injuries like RSI.

6. Computer-related injuries can cause long-term disabilities.

7. It would be better if computer workers went back to using the old-style typewriters.

8. The computer age has made workers like their jobs less.

9. A physically fit and active office person is less likely to develop RSI than an overweight and passive worker.

10. Offices of the future will probably be designed differently than they are today.

DISCUSSION

Discuss these questions with your classmates.

1. What are the advantages or disadvantages of voice-activated computers?

2. Social interaction in the workplace is limited by the use of computers. Discuss.

3. Mental and physical health are negatively affected by the use of computers. Agree or disagree with the statement, giving reasons.

WRITING

Writing a Summary

Write a one-paragraph summary of Reading 1.
Check your summary with the Summary Checklist on page 265.

How To | Write

How to Summarize
Page 263

Paraphrasing

Paraphrase the last paragraph in Reading 2. Begin with either:
According to Horowitz, . . .
or
Based on Horowitz's article, . . .

How To | Write

How to Paraphrase
Page 257

Research

You may use your research later in the chapter to write your argument essay.

How To | Write

How to do Library Research
Page 248

Choose a particular technological invention and find three reasons for it or three reasons against it. Consult an encyclopedia as well as appropriate sources in the library, and/or use your own experience or that of your friends to gather information.

The following technological innovations are suggestions:

the laser	space stations	robotics
electric cars	video games	the personal computer

Read the following essay written by a student.

Traps of the Information Revolution

The explosion of computer technology is changing every aspect of our lives. Cyberspace, a recently coined term for the media space in which people interact with advanced computer technology, is causing an information revolution. Cyberspace includes the Internet, the world's biggest computer network, which began twenty years ago and is growing all the time. Now every computer company, nearly every publisher, most communications firms, banks, insurance companies and a lot of mail-order and retail firms use the Internet. In the near future, cyberspace including the Internet will overwhelm us. The progress of computer technology cannot be neglected any more, and we have to think about how the information revolution will influence our society and transform our lives. It is my belief that in the future, cyberspace may harm healthy human life, generate a number of new crimes, and widen the gap between the haves and the have-nots.

First, cyberspace will have the negative effect of making our lives less healthy. Our workplace will be redefined by cyberspace. More than three million employees in American companies are telecommuting and performing their work away from the office. These numbers are increasing every year. This means the employees' social lives which always revolved around their co-workers will change. Their creativity will be dampened because they won't be stimulated by co-workers, and they might not be able to divide their private lives from their social lives. Moreover, cyberspace makes us sit for long periods in front of the computer screen and we will gradually believe that a kind of actual space exists behind the screen. Our concept of reality will be shifted. Even if we don't visit Washington, we would be able to enjoy a virtual tour of the White House guided by the president. We would be able to see a battlefield in real time and soon we won't be able to distinguish between reality and virtual reality.

Secondly, advanced computer technology generates new crimes. E-mail, which is sent through the Internet, is more efficient than the mail. However, Internet hackers who are skilled programmers with mischievous bent can easily thieve the content of E-mail and may scatter viruses. Everyone can open a virtual dirty books store from a desktop, making it possible for children to see pornography on the screen. Commercial software, which is covered by the Copyright Act, as well as books, records, tapes, and films are easily copied over the Internet. At present neither the laws nor the enforcement structure are designed to deal with these new criminal activities effectively.

My opponents argue that cyberspace can create a real democracy. It is said that the idea of the information super-highway lessens the distance between the government and us because it puts politics on-line, creates virtual Washington, national referendums, making it possible for everyone to participate in debate and vote from home. Is this true? Indeed, cyberspace may be everywhere in America but it is only the privilege of the younger, more educated, and more affluent of the country's population. In future, cyberspace will widen the gap between rich and poor, educated and uneducated, blacks, whites and Hispanics. If the government depends on the idea of the information super-highway, it means to ignore the have-nots in our society. My opponents say that those who don't own computers can access a computer at public establishments such as libraries and schools. However, since computer technology is progressing at every moment, new computers soon become old and telecommunications companies tend to place the new information networks in more affluent communities. Even if all individuals could obtain a computer, they could not obtain equal services because the information network of rural areas and urban slums falls behind.

The computer has radically transformed everything since being invented about fifty years ago. Technology has an addictive power and the progress of computer technology is speeding up, creating with it its problems. Cyberspace, which is generated by computer technology, has some risk of harming healthy human life, generating new crimes, and widening the gap between the haves and the have-nots. It is time to consider where the information revolution and social transition are headed. We should think about the negative effects and reconsider where this transition will lead to.

Kiyoe
Japan

STUDENT ESSAY FOLLOW-UP

1. Underline the thesis statement.

2. Is the student's argument for or against cyberspace? State her three reasons.

3. Are each of the three reasons developed in the body paragraphs?

4. Examine paragraph 1. Do all the ideas support her opinion?

5. Are the main points restated in the thesis? Does the writer give a final comment on the topic?

ORGANIZING

Argument Essay

In an argument essay, just like in an oral argument, you must win the person over to your way of thinking. The difference between an oral argument and a written argument is that you must appeal to the other person's reason by being logical and by providing evidence.

First, assume that the reader does not agree with you. If the reader did agree then you would not have to write an argument. When arguing your point remember not to insult the reader in any way because he or she may have a different opinion than yours. Insulting your reader with a statement such as "People who believe that handguns should not be banned are all killers," will weaken your argument. Always be respectful and logical.

Just arguing your own reasons is not sufficient to convince the reader. In order to really convince the reader you must understand your opponents' position and the reasons they would give to support their opinion. It is therefore essential to know both sides of the argument in order to be convincing.

Look at both sides of the issue. Read each thesis statement, and then write two reasons that support it and two reasons against it. The first one is done for you.

1. Television is having a bad effect on society.

   For

   a. Society is visually informed about what is going on in the world.

   b. Television provides cheap, comfortable entertainment for masses of people.

   Against

   a. Families do not talk to each other any more.

   b. People are not interested in what is going on in their communities.

2. Radio talk shows, where people can phone in and express whatever opinion they have, should be censored.

   For

   a. _____
   _____

   b. _____
   _____

   Against

   a. _____
   _____

   b. _____
   _____

3. The government should keep records on everyone on computer files.

   For

   a. _____
   _____

   b. _____
   _____

   Against

   a. _____
   _____

   b. _____
   _____

4. Employees should work for the same employer all their lives.

   For

   a. _____
   _____

   b. _____
   _____

   Against

   a. _____
   _____

   b. _____
   _____

▶ Using Specific Evidence

Nothing will support your opinion better than pertinent facts and statistics. To find the evidence, go to the library where you will find facts, numbers, and data. These will give a definite view to your opinion that cannot be contested.

HOW TO DO LIBRARY RESEARCH
PAGE 248

Look at the following examples of strong and weak support:

Lack of support: Many American workers suffer from repetitive injuries annually.

Good support: According to a 1992 OSHA (Occupational Safety and Health Administration) report more than five million workers suffer from repetitive injuries annually.

Lack of support: Children spend more hours watching television than any other activity except sleeping.

Good support: According to A. C. Nielsen, in the average household, television-watching among children ages 2 to 12 occupies more of their time than any activity except sleeping—including hours spent attending school. Studies show the average child in that age bracket watched twenty-eight hours of television a week.

Use authority to support your argument. The authority you use must be recognized, reliable, and expert. In the above example, the authority for the injuries was OSHA, and the authority for television was A. C. Nielsen, a famous rating company. When using an authority, you should identify it by name, and enclose the exact words of the authority in quotation marks.

HOW TO QUOTE
PAGE 255

For example, in Reading 2, "Crippled by Computers," authorities are named to make a convincing argument:

"We thought technology was going to help us, which it does. But we did not consider that we would also have to adjust the workplace at the same time," says Barbara Silverstein, a research director of Washington state's department of labor and industries.

Avoid vague references to authorities using terms such as "authorities agree . . . ," "people say . . . ," "research says . . ." These are not acceptable in a logical argument.

Which of these sentences do not have a reliable authority?

1. Research indicates that most Americans spend their leisure time at home watching television, listening to music, and talking on the phone.

2. According to the United Media Enterprises *Report on Leisure in America*, eight out of ten of the most popular leisure activities were home-based, including watching television, reading the newspaper, listening to music, and talking on the phone.

3. Americans spend almost as much time listening to the radio as they do watching television according to a report.

4. Americans spend almost as much time listening to the radio as they do watching television, according to the Radio Advertiser's Bureau figures for 1985.

Organizing Your Argument

The Introduction

Introduce the topic by giving background information. It is important that the reader understand the issue to be argued. Define any terms that are unclear. If you were going to argue against virtual reality, you would first have to define virtual reality very clearly before taking your stand.

The Thesis Statement in an argument essay is different from those in other types of essays. In the argument essay thesis, you have to be persuasive and take a stand or choose a side on an issue. Look back at the thesis statement of the student essay.

Body Paragraphs

The body paragraphs give reasons for your opinion and support them with evidence or facts. Each body paragraph relates back to a point of the argument stated in your thesis. The body paragraphs should be ordered so that the strongest reason is the last.

A characteristic of the argument essay is that you must recognize the opposing view and prove it wrong, or **refute** it. This means that you start with one of your opponent's viewpoints and prove that it is wrong by your superior reasons. Generally, the refutation occurs in the last body paragraph. Look back at the student essay on "Traps of the Information Age" to see how the student refutes the opposing argument.

Read the following argument about spending on the space program, then read the sample refutation.

Argument

It's about time our government stopped wasteful spending on trips to outer space and started concentrating on our needs here on earth. While billions of dollars are being spent launching telescopes that don't work, space probes that don't reach their destinations, and manned flights that circle around the planet a few times, millions of people are dying from illness and starvation, are hopeless refugees living under horrible conditions in camps, or are innocent victims of ethnic slaughter and civil war. We need to spend money on education and medical research, on rebuilding and replenishing, and on finding a lasting solution to peace here on planet Earth.

Refutation

While it is true that the space program is costly, it is well worth the money spent. Yes, we have important needs here on Earth, but the space program also contributes to those needs. Satellites allow ships and planes to travel safely. Communication satellites bring information, and therefore education, to the farthest reaches of the planet. It's true that the Hubble telescope didn't perform up to design, but it has nevertheless provided scientists with invaluable information about our stars and planets. One space probe didn't reach its destination but others are on their way, performing gallantly as messengers from space. Furthermore, important medical and scientific experiments are performed on board manned flights. Finally, we cannot deny the human need for exploration that will one day see us populating Mars and other planets, and allow us to see life, and the need for peace, in a new perspective.

Read the following argument about the place of computers in educa-tion. Then write your own refutation.

It's time for computers to take over the classroom and introduce a new age in education. The classroom, the instructor, and the current formal system of education should be eliminated because computers have the ability to provide tailored, individual instruction. With com-puterized education, children could all learn at their own pace. Advancement to high school and college could be based solely on the achievement of certain levels of knowledge and skills based on com-petency tests, administered by computers of course. Smart ten-year-olds could work on advanced degrees while their less-gifted peers learn at their own pace. Multimedia programs would make learning fun and concepts easier to understand. No more lectures or over-crowded classrooms. The computer is the school of the future.

▶ The Conclusion

Summarize the main points of your argument or restate the thesis. End your conclusion with a stronger statement such as a demand for action or an alternative solution. In the conclusion, of Reading 2, "Crippled by Computers," the alternative offered is a voice-activated computer.

The following is a brief outline for an argument essay:

Introduction	Background information Thesis: Take a stand.
Paragraph 1	Argument that supports your opinion
Paragraph 2	Stronger argument that supports your opinion
Paragraph 3	Strongest argument that supports your opinion
Paragraph 4	Refutation
Conclusion	Restate thesis or summarize main points. End with an alternative or demand for action.

Choose one of the following topics.

1 Use one of the technologies you researched and write an argument for or against it. Use three reasons in your argument.

2 Write an argument for or against space exploration. Support your opinion with relevant facts.

3 Write an argument essay giving reasons for or against the use of cellular phones. Support your reasons with relevant facts.

4 Write an argument essay on either the pros or cons of electronic mail.

1. Pre-writing

Work alone, with a partner, or in a group.

1 Brainstorm the topic. Write three reasons for and three reasons against the topic.

2 Select the strongest points. Which side do you want to take a stand on?

3 Work on a thesis statement.

2. Outlining

A. Organize your ideas

Step 1: *Write your thesis statement including the three reasons for or against the topic.*

Step 2: *Order your reasons. Choose the opponent's argument that you can refute.*

Step 3: *Decide what kinds of support would be relevant. Go to the library to get relevant facts.*

B. Make a more detailed outline. The essay outline on page 22 will help you.

3. Write a Rough Draft.

4. Revise Your Rough Draft.
Use the essay checklist on page 246.

5. Edit Your Essay.
Use the editing symbols on pages 247–248.

6. Write Your Final Copy.

PART II

How to

Write

1. HOW TO GET IDEAS, DRAFT, REVISE, AND EDIT

A. Getting Ideas

Before starting to write on a specific topic, it is important to develop some ideas. In this section you will learn a number of strategies for generating ideas. These techniques are useful when you first start thinking about your topic or at any other time you find you have nothing to say about the topic.

▶ Brainstorming

To get ideas and stimulate your thoughts, you can use the strategy of **brainstorming.** You can brainstorm alone or with a group.

These are some guidelines to follow when brainstorming:

- Give yourself or the group a limited amount of time.

- Write down the word or phrase you need to get ideas about.

- Write down all the possible ideas that come to mind. Do not organize your points in any way.

- When time is up, look over the ideas to see if any can be grouped together.

The following is an example of a brainstorming session on the subject of video games for children.

VIDEO GAMES	
addictive	fun
time consuming	more exciting than T.V.
bad for eyes	too violent
expensive	takes time away from homework

Since there are more negative than positive points written down, the student might write about the negative sides of video games.

◆ Clustering

Clustering is another way of generating ideas. To cluster you make a visual plan of the connections among your ideas.

Use the following guidelines for clustering:

- Write your topic in the center of your paper and circle it.

- Draw a line from the circle and write an idea related to it. Circle the idea and from it draw lines and write ideas related to it. Keep making new circles and connecting them back to the ideas they came from.

- When you have no more ideas, look at your clusters and decide which ideas seem more important.

The following is an example of clustering on the subject of obesity. From this diagram, the writer can develop an essay on the causes or effects of obesity.

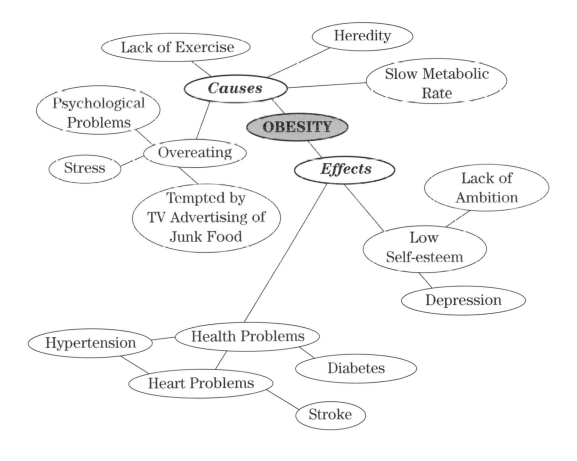

With the freewriting technique, you write freely on a topic without stopping. You don't stop the flow of your ideas by worrying about correct grammar or whether what you say is important enough to write down. After you freewrite, you can decide which of your ideas could be useful.

These are some guidelines to follow when freewriting:

- Give yourself a time limit.

- Write the topic at the top of your paper.

- Write as much as you can about the topic. Do not worry about grammar, spelling, organization, or relevance.

- Write until your time is up.

- Read your freewriting and underline the main idea(s).

- Repeat the process, this time using the main idea as your freewriting topic.

The following is an example of the freewriting technique applied to the subject of a vegetarian diet.

A Vegetarian Diet

I am not a vegetarian but two of my friends are. They always tell me how cruel it is to kill animals, and I tell them I need meat to get my protein. They tell me you can get protein from sources other than animal products. <u>Animal products contain fat which can be bad for health, whereas plants are high in fiber and good for health.</u> Even if it were good for me, I just think vegetarian food is boring. But they proved me wrong when I went out to eat with them. <u>The vegetarian dishes were very tasty and there were so many varieties.</u> There are so many cookbooks now for vegetarians I noticed.

The writer has underlined two ideas which could be explored further. These are "Animal products contain fat which can be bad for health, whereas plants are high in fiber and good for health," and "The vegetarian dishes were tasty and there were so many varieties." The writer can take one of these ideas and freewrite about it again.

B. Drafting

After you have developed some ideas for your essay, it is time to start drafting or actually writing your essay.

First, you should draft the thesis statement. The thesis statement will have to tell the reader the main idea you are discussing and your approach to the main idea. A thesis statement cannot simply state what you are going to do, for example, "In this essay I will describe my brother." It should present your approach to the main idea as in, "My brother is both an ambitious and sociable character." Here the words *ambitious* and *energetic* will be the focus of your description of your brother.

With the thesis statement written, your focus on the subject will be clear. You would write one paragraph on the "ambitious" aspect of your brother with supporting statements and details, and another paragraph on the "sociable" character of your brother with supporting statements and details.

The following are some questions to think about as you write your draft:

- What kind of supporting details do I need?

- How many supporting details do I have to give and how long do they have to be?

- How do I avoid overlapping supporting details?

As you are writing your first draft, remember these questions and check and change sentences that do not support the main idea clearly.

C. Revising

After the first draft, plan to revise your draft at least one time. Revising means changing the organization or content of the essay and also editing the sentences.

The questions on the checklist below will help you to see if your essay is focused and well developed. You may wish to ask another person (classmate) to revise your essay using the following checklist.

Revision Checklist

Thesis Statement	_____ Does the thesis statement state your main idea adequately?
	_____ Does the thesis statement show your approach or attitude to the main idea?
Unity	_____ Do the supporting ideas show the writer's attitude toward the main idea?
	_____ Do the supporting details and examples show the writer's attitude toward the main idea?
Development	_____ Are more supporting details needed?
	_____ Is enough evidence provided to support the main idea?
	_____ Is the evidence that is provided convincing?
Coherence	_____ Are all the paragraphs logically connected to each other?
	_____ Do the sentences flow logically one after the other?
	_____ Are transitions needed to make the sentences clearer?
Purpose	_____ Is the writer's purpose clear?
	_____ What did the writer want to convey to the reader? Was this achieved?

D. Editing

Editing means checking your essay to see if you have followed the rules for expressing your ideas clearly, and followed the rules of grammar, spelling, and punctuation.

When editing, go through one sentence at a time. Make sure your sentences are clear and grammatically correct. Mark them for fragments or run-ons. If you are unsure about a grammatical form, consult a grammar book. When you think you have misspelled a word, consult a dictionary.

The following is an editing checklist. The symbols on the left may be used by your instructor to indicate problem areas in your writing.

▶ Editing Symbols for Sentences and Paragraphs

Symbol	Meaning
frag	Is the sentence a fragment or an incomplete sentence? Check to see if it has a subject and a verb.
r/o	Is the sentence a run-on, or sentence which should really be two? [Check to see if each sentence is really only one.]
s-v agr	Does the subject agree with the verb in person and number?
//	Are two or more words in a series written in the same, or parallel, grammatical structure?
trans	Have you used transitions to connect your ideas clearly?
pro agr	Do the pronouns agree with the words they refer to in person and in number?
awk	Have you phrased your ideas in an awkward manner, perhaps by translating them from your native language?
choppy	Are your sentences short, unrelated, or choppy? Are ideas broken into paragraphs correctly? Are all your ideas related to the same topic in your paragraph?

Editing Symbols for Words and Punctuation

Symbol	Meaning
sp	Is the word spelled correctly? Check a dictionary.
om	Is there a word that has been omitted?
~	Check for incorrect word order.
wd form	Are the word forms correct? Check verb tenses and suffixes.
ww	Is the wrong word used? Check its meaning in a dictionary.
p	Are there any errors in punctuation? Check to see if commas, semicolons, and quotation marks are used correctly.
cap	Are words capitalized correctly? Check to see if proper nouns, names of places, religions, nationalities, names of books, and titles are capitalized correctly.

2. HOW TO DO LIBRARY RESEARCH

Libraries are information centers. They are your most valuable resource for the facts you need to write essays, term papers, reports, and theses. And now that they're catching up with the computer age, libraries have become more valuable than ever; they have become user-friendly ports of entry to the information superhighway.

Multimedia workstations for doing electronic research allow library users to retrieve information from government, business, and educational sources nationwide. Online hookups offer commercial and government databases and library files, delivering information as diverse as the latest White House press releases to analyses of the fishing industry in Canada.

Librarians have always provided information and assistance to library users. Today they are helping users conduct online research in computer centers, and teaching them how to use Internet hookups and electronic catalogs.

Not all libraries have the latest technological innovations, but regardless of their simplicity or sophistication, all libraries have in common reference librarians to help get you started and three basic places to begin looking for information—the catalog, reference books, and periodical indexes.

A. The Catalog

The heart of the library is its catalog. It contains an alphabetical listing of all the books in the library. Electronic (computer) catalogs often include the books held by all the participating libraries in a system and indicate at which library the book is located.

Every book has at least three listings in the catalog, under *author, title,* and one or more *subjects.*

▶ Finding the Listing

Card catalog: If you know the title of the book you need, look for its card in the title catalog. If you need a book on a particular subject, look in the subject catalog. If you know the author, look under the author's last name.

Electronic catalog: Instructions on the computer screen will tell you what commands to type to begin the catalog program and to search it for the book you need. For most electronic catalogs:

Type N for NAME search (author or subject)

W for WORD search (in title or subject fields)

SW for SUBJECT word search (subject headings)

B for BROWSE by subject, title, series, or call number

S to STOP or SWITCH to another database

Next to the electronic catalog computer there is usually an information sheet with searching hints and instructions on how to *display* or print the results of your search.

Every card or electronic display contains basic and helpful information about a book. Here is a sample author card from a card catalog:

① R
    813
    F263Gra

② **Gray, Richard J.**
③ The life of William Faulkner: a critical biography.
    Cambridge, Mass. Oxford Press, 1994.
④ xvi, 448p. [8] plates:illus.; 24 cm.
⑤ Bibliography: p.[422]-434.

⑥ 1. Faulkner, William, 1897-1962
    2. Novelists, American 20th century Biography

1. The call number of the book.

2. The name of the author.

3. The full title of the book, the place of publication, the name of the publisher, and the date of publication.

4. Number of pages in the book (xvi tells you there are sixteen introductory pages numbered in Roman numerals), the use of illustrations, and the size of the book (an inch is 2.54 centimeters).

5. The book contains a bibliography (brackets indicate the pages are not actually numbered but appear between numbered pages).

6. Tells you subject headings under which the book is listed.

Title and *subject* cards are simply copies of the author card, with the title or subject typed just above the author's name.

In the electronic catalog, you can conduct your search by author, subject or title, but the information appears the same way on the computer screen.

```
AUTHOR(S):      Gray, Richard J.
TITLE(S):       The life of William Faulkner:
                a critical biography
                Oxford Press, Cambridge, Mass.
                1994.
                xvi, 449p. [8] plates: illus.; 24 cm

                Includes bibliographical references
                (p.[422]-434) and index

SUBJECTS:       Faulkner, William, 1897-1962
                Novelists, American 20th century Biography

LOCATION:   ANGMSA REF        STATUS: In
CALL #:     813 F263Gra

LOCATION:   ANGMSA CIRC       STATUS: In
CALL #:     813 F263Gra
```

Notice that the computer provides the library location at which the book can be found (in the reference section and on the circulation book shelves at the Angeles Mesa [ANGMSA] Branch) and gives the status of the book (the book is available in both areas of the library).

▶ What to Look For

If you read the information carefully before looking for or requesting a book, you won't waste time retrieving books you may not need. You should scan the card or computer display for: 1) the date of publication; 2) the subjects under which the book is catalogued; 3) the total number of pages; 4) reference to a bibliography; 5) the letter R above the call number.

The *date of publication* will tell you whether the information the book contains is useful for your purposes. The *subjects* under which the book is catalogued will tell you whether they are relevant to your topic. The *length* of the book will give you an idea of how comprehensive it is and whether or not you'll have time to read it. The word or abbreviation for *bibliography* will tell you whether this book can quickly lead you to other sources. Finally, the letter R will tell you this is a reference book and can only be used in the library. If you have only ten minutes to spare at the library and were hoping to take out your books, you will have to leave this resource for another time.

If you think you have found the book you need, your next step is to write down the call number, the author's name, and the title of the book. In libraries that do not allow the public in the "stacks," or areas where the books are shelved, you will have to write this information on a call slip and give it to the proper person at the circulation desk.

If the stacks are open to the public, the call number will help you locate your book, since all books are shelved by their call numbers. Larger libraries often have information sheets that map the sequence of call numbers so you know which section or floor to go to find your book.

If the letter R is typed above the call number, it may either be found on the shelves with the rest of the books or it may be in a special reference section. Ask the librarian which system the library uses.

Task

Study the library card below and answer the questions that follow.

Colorado River

979.11
G75 LI

Lingenfelter, Richard E.
First through the Grand Canyon.
Los Angeles, Calif., Dawson Pub., 1958.
119 p. illus., facsims.; 19 cm.
Bibliography: p.[113] - 116.

1. White, James, 1837 -
2. Colorado River
3. Grand Canyon (Ariz.)
4. United States Exploring Expeditions

---

1. What type of card (subject, author, title) is it?

2. What is the call number of the book?

3. What is the name of the author?

4. What is the full title?

5. Where and when was it published?

6. Who published the book?

7. How many pages are there?

8. Are there any illustrations?

9. What size is the book?

10. Does the book contain a bibliography?

11. What are the other subjects under which the book is listed?

B. Reference Books

Reference books are very helpful when you are looking for concise information. They include encyclopedias, dictionaries, almanacs, indexes, directories, handbooks, yearbooks, atlases, and guides. In most libraries, reference books are located on open shelves in the reference area or behind the reference desk where they must be requested. You should browse through the reference section of your library to become familiar with the books available. If you cannot find the reference book you want, or if you don't know what reference book will help you most, consult the reference librarian.

▶ Going Online

In the computerized library, assistants will help you to research and retrieve information from online resources with access to hundreds of databases, from the Library of Congress to financial institutions to the local chamber of commerce. Moreover, dictionaries, encyclopedias, and other reference books can be consulted quickly and easily on a computer, making your search fast and efficient.

C. Periodical Indexes

A periodical is a publication that appears at regular intervals, such as magazines and academic journals. Periodical indexes are guides to the contents of periodicals published over a number of years. Indexes do not contain the actual articles but tell you where to find the articles you need on your subject of research.

Periodical indexes list articles in at least two places: under the *author's name* and under one or more *subjects*. Indexes use many abbreviations with which you should become familiar. Some of the most common are:

bibl.	bibliography
v.	volume
pp.	pages
ed.	edited, editor, edition
cond.	condensed
il.	illustrated

The names of periodicals are also abbreviated:

Sat R	Saturday Review
Am Hist	American History
Nat Geo	National Geographic
Sci Digest	Science Digest

There are many indexes in the library: *International Index to Periodicals, Bibliographic Index, Book Review Digest, New York Times Index, Ulrich's Periodical Directory*, and many others. The most widely known periodical index is the *Reader's Guide to Periodical Literature*.

Electronic indexes have all the information you need at your fingertips. Prompts on the computer screen guide you to select the index you need, and then to conduct your search in the index according to *topic* or *multiple keywords*, which include names, subject words, and phrases.

3. HOW TO QUOTE

In academic writing you are expected to support your ideas accurately to make them convincing to the reader. Writing about your own experience will not convince people all the time but reference to an authority in a newspaper or magazine article or book that agrees with you will make your ideas more valid.

The best way to use quoted material is to integrate it into your own writing. You should begin by saying something about the subject in your own words and then use the quotation to explain the significance of your statement.

Example:

> One aspect of the change in the nature of American society in the 1970s and the 1980s is the change in the pattern of immigration. In his book *The Unfinished Nation*, Brinkley reports, "The nation's immigration quotas expanded significantly in those years, allowing more newcomers to enter the United States legally than at any other point since the beginning of the twentieth century." (898)

The rules for quoting are as follows:

1. Put a comma after the reporting phrase, and put quotation marks before and after the words quoted. Capitalize the first word of the quotation.

Example:

He states, "In the 1970s, more than 4 million legal immigrants entered the United States."

2. If the quotation is broken, put quotation marks around both parts and separate with commas. Do not begin the second part with a capital letter unless it is a new sentence.

Example:

"In the 1970s," he states, "more than 4 million legal immigrants entered the United States."

A. Omitting Words and Adding Words

It is important to use the exact words of the author. However, if you have to omit part of a quotation to fit the context of your writing, use an ellipsis which is indicated by three spaced periods: (. . .).

Example:

> Brinkley states, ". . . the wave of immigration in the twenty years after 1970 was the largest of the twentieth century." (*The Unfinished Nation*, p. 898)

If you need to add words to the original in order to explain it or make it fit into the structure of your writing, put square brackets [ ] around the words you've added.

Example:

> "Many Asian immigrants [Koreans, Chinese, Japanese, Indian, Philippino, Vietnamese, Thai] were highly educated professionals seeking greater opportunity in the United States," Brinkley stated.

B. Reporting Words

When introducing a quotation, reporting phrases are used such as the ones below:

As Brinkley said, "_____ ."

As he stated, "_____ ."

As he reported, "_____ ."

As he wrote, "_____ ."

As he declared, "_____ ."

As he maintained, "_____ ."

As he insisted, "_____ ."

Other reporting phrases can be used without *as* with the present or past tense.

Mr. Brinkley said, "_____ ."

He believes, "_____ ."

He further stated, "_____ ."

He continued, "_____ ."

Examples:

> Mr. Brinkley further stated, "Already by the end of the 1980s, people of white European background constituted under 80 percent of the population (as opposed to 90 percent a half-century before)."

"It seemed likely that by the middle of the twenty-first century," he continued, "whites of European heritage would constitute less than 50 percent of the population."

Use the phrase "according to . . ." only when you are paraphrasing. Do not use "according to . . ." when citing with quotation marks.

Example:

According to the 1980 Census, 60 percent of Americans identified themselves as having English, German, or Irish ethnic origins.

or

Sixty percent of Americans identified themselves as having English, German, or Irish ethnic origins, according to the 1980 Census.

Remember *always* to document the source of your quotation even when it is not a direct quotation.

4. HOW TO PARAPHRASE

Paraphrasing and summarizing are useful alternatives to direct quotations when using material from books, magazines, and other sources.

When you paraphrase, you put the published information in different words, or in other words "rephrase" it, without changing the meaning of the original. When you paraphrase it is important to use your own words. A paraphrase is usually the same length as the original passage in order to include all the information.

Although you are using your own words when you paraphrase, you are expressing the author's ideas. Therefore, you must be sure to give the author credit for them or you will be plagiarizing. Begin your paraphrase with a reference to the author and/or title of the work, or the source of the article. Use phrases such as:

According to (author's name) . . .

Based on (author's name) article in (source) . . .

In his/her book (title), (author's name) indicates that . . .

The following are examples of paraphrases:

Example I:

Ancient Medicine

Original:

Medicinal practices in the ancient world *were as related to* religion and philosophy as they were to science. The Egyptians were *proficient* surgeons who *employed* an *array of medications* and surgical *practices.* Their *extensive expertise involving* the human anatomy was *derived mainly from* their *practice of embalming. The ideology behind this* was that the *deceased* person's spirit, or Ka, would *perish* if the body *decomposed. To furnish an eternal abode* for the spirit, the body was *meticulously preserved.* In *another part of the ancient world,* Chinese medicine *was also linked to ideology, in particular the belief* that people are *closely linked to* a universe *dominated* by two *opposing* types of forces known as *yin* and *yang,* the negative and the positive. Physicians *were part philosophers who believed* that the harmony of the universe and the health of people depended on keeping a balance between the two forces. (*Discovery,* Everett, Reid, and Fara)

Paraphrase:

In their book *Discovery,* Everett, Reid, and Fara indicate that the practice of healing in the ancient world had as much to do with religion and philosophy as it did with science. Extremely skillful surgeons, the Egyptians used a variety of drugs and surgical techniques. Their broad knowledge of the human anatomy was primarily due to their preservation of the dead. Their belief was that the dead person's spirit, or Ka, would die if the body rotted away. In order to provide a lasting home for the spirit, the body was mummified as carefully as possible. In the ancient Far East, Chinese medicine also involved philosophical beliefs, especially the idea that people are part of a universe controlled by two conflicting forces known as *yin* and *yang,* the negative and the positive. Physicians endorsed the philosophical belief that the harmony of the universe and the health of people depended on keeping a balance between the two forces.

These are the substitutions for the italicized words in the original:

Original	Paraphrase
Medicinal practices	the practice of healing
were as related to	had as much to do with
proficient	extremely skillful
employed	used
array of medications	variety of drugs
practices	techniques
extensive expertise involving	broad knowledge of
derived mainly from	was primarily due to
practice of embalming	preservation of the dead
The ideology behind this	Their belief was
deceased	dead
perish	die
decomposed	rotted away
to furnish an eternal abode	to provide a lasting home
meticulously preserved	mummified as carefully as possible
another part of the ancient world	ancient Far East
was also linked to ideology	also involved philosophical beliefs
in particular the belief	especially the idea
closely linked to	depended on
dominated	controlled
opposing	conflicting
were part philosophers who believed	endorsed the philosophical belief

Some words in the original text cannot be changed because there are no synonyms for them, such as the names of people, countries, religions, and scientific terms. In this passage, for example, there are no synonyms for *Egyptians*, *science*, *Ka*, *Chinese*, *yin*, and *yang*. Not every word has to be changed in a paraphrase and sometimes a few of the original words are kept to maintain the accuracy of a piece. In this passage, for example, important words like *ancient*, *religion*, *science*, *philosophy*, *anatomy*, *spirit*, *negative*, *positive*, *harmony*, and *universe* have not been changed.

Notice that the paraphrase is approximately the same length as the original passage and that all of the information is included.

Example II

> ### Personality Types
> ....
>
> **Original:**
>
> *What kind of people* are *likely candidates for* heart attacks and *what kind* are not? *Typical* Type A people are the most *susceptible to heart* problems *because* they are *strongly motivated* to *overcome obstacles* and are driven to *achieve and to meet* goals. They *are attracted to* competition, *enjoy* power and recognition, and *are easily aroused to anger and action. They dislike wasting time* and do things *in a vigorous and efficient manner.* On the other hand, Type B people are *relaxed* and unhurried. They may work hard *on occasion,* but *rarely* in the *driven,* compulsive *manner* of Type A people. *These people* are less likely than Type A's to *seek the stress of competition* or to be *aroused* to anger or action. *Naturally* not all people *classified* as Type A or Type B *fit* these profiles exactly, and *there are times when* Type A people *behave in a Type B manner* and vice versa. But, as with other traits, researchers can *identify the extent to which each of us behaves, on the average,* and *assign* us a personality type *on the basis of which some startling predictions can be made.* (*Personality,* Burger)
>
> **Paraphrase:**
>
> Which personalities are prone to heart attacks and which are not? According to Burger in his book *Personality,* classic Type A people are most at risk for coronary problems due to their intense desire to conquer barriers and their drive to realize their goals. They like competition, relish power and recognition, have quick tempers, and are readily provoked to action. Time is of the essence, so they do things energetically and efficiently. On the other hand, Type B people are calm and unhurried. Periodically, they may work hard, but hardly ever in the compelling, compulsive way of Type A people. Type B's are less likely than Type A's to be competitive or to be incited to anger or action. Of course, not all people identified as Type A or Type B conform to these profiles exactly. Occasionally, Type A people exhibit Type B characteristics and vice versa. But, as with other traits, researchers can determine the measure of our average behavior and attribute a personality type to us, which can tell some very surprising things about ourselves.

On the left are the words and phrases as they appear in the original. Find the rephrased expressions that correspond to the original and write them on the lines below.

Original	Paraphrase
1. What kind of people	_____
2. likely candidates for	_____
3. what kind	_____
4. Typical	_____
5. susceptible to heart	_____
6. because	_____
7. strongly motivated	_____
8. overcome obstacles	_____
9. achieve and to meet	_____
10. are attracted to	_____
11. enjoy	_____
12. are easily aroused to anger and action	_____
13. They dislike wasting time	_____
14. in a vigorous and efficient manner	_____
15. relaxed	_____
16. on occasion	_____
17. rarely	_____
18. driven	_____
19. manner	_____
20. These people	_____
21. seek the stress of competition	_____
22. aroused	_____
23. Naturally	_____
24. classified	_____
25. fit	_____

26. there are times when _____

27. behave in a Type B manner _____

28. identify the extent to

which each of us behaves,

on the average _____

29. assign _____

30. on the basis of which

some startling predictions

can be made _____

Steps for Paraphrasing

The following are useful steps to follow when paraphrasing:

1. Read the article over several times until you fully understand it.

2. Underline all the words you do not understand. Look them up in a dictionary or use a thesaurus to find a good synonym.

3. Begin your paraphrase with a reference to the author and/or title of the book.

4. Rewrite each sentence simplifying the structure and using synonyms. Rewrite each sentence one after the other.

5. Review your paraphrase. Make sure it sounds natural and like your own writing. Check to see if you have included all the information in the original and that the meaning has not been changed in any way.

With a partner or group or alone paraphrase the following selections. Use a dictionary or thesaurus to find synonyms. Follow the steps above.

1. Although many women throughout history have been involved in the development of science, their work has gained little recognition. For a number of reasons their achievements have been ignored and their names left out of books. (Reid and Fara, *Discovery*, p. 92)

2. Observe a group of listeners the next time a good storyteller tells an obscene joke. Skilled joke tellers elaborate on details. They allow the tension to build gradually as they set up the punch line. Listeners smile or blush slightly as the joke progresses. According to Freud, this long building creates greater tension and thus a louder and longer laugh when the punch line finally allows a tension release. (Burger, *Personality*, p. 99)

3. Three decades of research has demonstrated that people exposed to aggressive models sometimes imitate the aggressive behavior. This finding holds true for children as well as adults. But clearly, simple exposure to an aggressive model is not enough to turn us into violent people. Anyone who has watched television or attended a few movies recently undoubtedly has seen some murders, beatings, shootings, and the like. Yet rarely do we leave the theatre in search of victims. (Burger, *Personality*, p. 445)

5. HOW TO SUMMARIZE

A summary is very similar to a paraphrase, only shorter. When you summarize you put published information in your own words and include all the important information, without changing its meaning, just as you do when you paraphrase. However, when you summarize you reduce the amount of information. The length of a summary may vary. For example, the summary of a book may be several pages long while the summary of an article may be one paragraph.

In this exercise, you will summarize passages in the fewest possible sentences. This means you will only include the main points and supporting ideas, leaving out the details. As with the paraphrase, begin by referring to the author and/or title of the article. Include also the source (book, newspaper) of the article.

To clearly see the difference between a summary and a paraphrase, look at the following examples of paraphrases and summaries of the passages on ancient medicine and personality types.

Example I

Ancient Medicine

Original:

Medicinal practices in the ancient world were as related to religion and philosophy as they were to science. The Egyptians were proficient surgeons who employed an array of medications and surgical practices. Their extensive expertise involving the human anatomy was derived mainly from their practice of embalming. The ideology behind this was that the deceased person's spirit, or Ka, would perish if the body decomposed. To furnish an eternal abode for the spirit, the body was meticulously preserved. In another part of the ancient world, Chinese medicine was also linked to ideology, in particular the belief that people are closely linked to a universe dominated by two opposing types of forces known as *yin* and *yang*, the negative and the positive. Physicians were part philosophers who believed that the harmony of the universe and the health of people depended on keeping a balance between the two forces. (*Discovery*, Everett, Reid, and Fara)

Paraphrase:

In their book *Discovery*, Everett, Reid, and Fara indicate that the practice of healing in the ancient world had as much to do with religion and philosophy as it did with science. Extremely skillful surgeons, the Egyptians used a variety of drugs and surgical techniques. Their broad knowledge of the human anatomy was primarily due to their preservation of the dead. Their belief was that the dead person's spirit, or Ka, would die if the body rotted away. In order to provide a lasting home for the spirit, the body was mummified as carefully as possible. In the ancient Far East, Chinese medicine also involved philosophical beliefs, especially the idea that people are part of a universe controlled by two conflicting forces known as *yin* and *yang*, the negative and the positive. Physicians endorsed the philosophical belief that the harmony of the universe and the health of people depended on keeping a balance between the two forces.

Summary

In their book *Discovery*, Everett, Reid, and Fara indicate that in ancient times, medicine was part religion, part science. The expertise of Egyptian surgeons was derived from their religious practice of mummification to provide the spirit, or Ka, with eternal life. In ancient China, philosophy influenced medicine in the belief that health depended upon a balance between the negative and positive universal forces, or *yin* and *yang*.

Notice that only the main ideas and key points are stated and repetitions of the same idea are left out. Since you include only the main ideas in a summary, it is helpful to make a brief outline before you begin to summarize. Look at the paraphrase, outline, and summary for the passage on personality types.

Example II

Personality Types

Original:

What kind of people are likely candidates for heart attacks and what kind are not? Typical Type A people are the most susceptible to heart problems because they are strongly motivated to overcome obstacles and are driven to achieve and to meet goals. They are attracted to competition, enjoy power and recognition, and are easily aroused to anger and action. They dislike wasting time and do things in a vigorous and efficient manner. On the other hand, Type B people are relaxed and unhurried. They may work hard on occasion, but rarely in the driven, compulsive manner of Type A people. These people are less likely than Type A's to seek the stress of competition or to be aroused to anger or action. Naturally not all people classified as Type A or Type B fit these profiles exactly, and there are times when Type A people behave in a Type B manner and vice versa. But, as with other traits, researchers can identify the extent to which each of us behaves, on the average, and assign us a personality type on the basis of which some startling predictions can be made. (*Personality*, Burger)

Paraphrase:

Which personalities are prone to heart attacks and which are not? According to Burger in his book *Personality*, classic Type A people are most at risk for coronary problems due to their intense desire to conquer barriers and their drive to realize their goals. They like competition, relish power and recognition, have quick tempers, and are readily provoked to action. Time is of the essence, so they do things energetically and efficiently. On the other hand, Type B people are calm and unhurried. Periodically, they may work hard, but hardly ever in the compelling, compulsive way of Type A people. Type B's are less likely than Type A's to be competitive or to be incited to anger or action. Of course, not all people identified as Type A or Type B conform to these profiles exactly. Occasionally, Type A people exhibit Type B characteristics and vice versa. But, as with other traits, researchers can determine the measure of our average behavior and attribute a personality type to us, which can tell some very surprising things about ourselves.

Outline

A. Type A people

1. At risk for heart attacks

2. Are driven, competitive, quick-tempered, time-conscious, energetic, and efficient

B. Type B people

1. Calm and unhurried

2. Less competitive and slower to react

C. On the basis of average behavior, people can be categorized according to well-defined personality types.

You can see from the outline (item C) that the main idea is stated in the last sentence of the passage. In your summary, however, you will write the main idea first, then add one sentence for each of the two supporting ideas (items A and B).

Summary

According to Burger in his book *Personality*, people can be categorized into well-defined personality types on the basis of their average behavior. Type A people tend to be more at risk for heart attacks because they are driven, competitive, quick-tempered, time-conscious, energetic, and efficient. Type B people, on the other hand, are calm, unhurried, less competitive, and less reactive than their Type A counterparts.

Summary Checklist

1. Begin with a reference to the author and/or title of the article. Include the source of the article.

2. Identify and write the main ideas and key points.

3. Do not include details or repeat ideas.

Exercise 1

Summarize the following passages in a few sentences. Check your work against the summary checklist.

1. Music video is a relatively new entry into the world of television, having become common only in the 1980s. Music video is difficult to categorize and to illustrate with one example, because it includes so many different types of expression. The definitive characteristic is in its name: There is music and there is video imagery. Some music videos dramatize the words of a song or even create brief visual dramas that are only vaguely related to the music. Some offer a message or statement. Some are relatively straightforward recordings of the performers at work. Obviously, defining the art of music video is not an easy task. (*Living With Art*, Rita Gilbert)

2. Charles Darwin, an English naturalist and explorer, began a five-year expedition in December 1831 on a ship called the *Beagle*. The expedition reached Bahia in Brazil in the spring of 1832. Darwin was amazed by the number and dazzling colors of the flowers and birds he saw. The *Beagle* then sailed south along the coast of Patagonia where the crew discovered the fossil remains of several extinct animals. In September 1835 the expedition reached the

remote Galapagos Islands. There Darwin saw birds, animals and plants that are found nowhere else on earth because they had developed in isolation from their relatives in America. They were to play an important part in Darwin's theories on how animals and humans evolved. (*Discovery*, Everett, Reid, and Fara)

3. Beginning in the Middle East at least 10,000 years ago, some peoples began to purposely sow the seeds of their food plants. It was a practice that allowed them to produce adequate amounts of food in the areas near their settlements rather than pursuing game and living as nomads. At the same time, they gradually tamed and domesticated wild animals for their food, hides and labor. An agricultural lifestyle led to the first towns and cities, the development of tools, baskets and pots, which led to the development of commerce and new crafts and skills. Agriculture played a significant role in developing the control over our existence that distinguishes humans from other species. (*Biology!*, Postlethwait, Hopson, Veres)

6. HOW TO CONSTRUCT SENTENCES

A. Avoid Fragments

There are two kinds of clauses: dependent and independent. An independent clause has a subject and a verb, and it can stand alone. A dependent clause may or may not have a subject and a verb, but it cannot stand alone. When a dependent stands alone as if it were a sentence, it is called a **fragment**.

1. When a clause begins with one of the words below, it is dependent.

after	if, even if, whether	what, whatever
although, though	in order that, so that	when, whenever
as, as if	since	where, wherever
because	than	which, whichever
before	that	while
even though	unless	who, whom
how	until	whose

A clause may have a subject and a verb, but because it begins with one of the above words it is dependent.

Examples:

> After he wrote his essay
> Before he wrote his essay
> When he wrote his essay

The above clauses are not complete statements, but fragments. To correct a fragment, an independent clause must be added.

Examples:

> After he wrote his essay, he checked for errors.
> Before he wrote his essay, he researched the subject.
> He used a dictionary when he wrote his essay.

Note: When a sentence begins with a dependent clause, a comma is placed at the end of the dependent clause.

2. A group of words without a subject and a verb is also a fragment.

Examples:

> Gave no excuse to her instructor (no subject)
> Louise working on her assignment (no verb)
> Walking along the beach (no subject and no verb)

To make these fragments into sentences each must be given a subject and a verb.

> She gave no excuse to her instructor. (Added a subject)
> Louise was working on her assignment that day.
> (Made "working" into a verb.)
> Walking along the beach, she got an idea.
> (Added an independent clause.)

Exercise 1

Write an S for sentence or an F for fragment in each of the blanks below. Put a period after each sentence, and make each fragment into a complete sentence. Use correct punctuation for dependent clauses.

Example:

> **F** Although I didn't want to take any more courses, *I signed up for a painting class.*

___ 1. Since I've started taking art classes

___ 2. I'm learning to paint with watercolors for the first time

___ 3. Because I can find interesting subject matter in my own neighborhood

___ 4. After making a rough sketch

___ 5. The next step is to wet the paper and drop paint on the main areas, like the sky

___ 6. Which areas will be dark and which will have the lightest values

___ 7. Once the main colors are established, I can concentrate on the smaller details

___ 8. I've discovered that I prefer to use round brushes and seldom use flats

___ 9. Even though it's not necessary to finish a watercolor all at once

___10. Unless I paint outdoors, which I prefer

Exercise 2

Write S for sentence or an F for fragment in each of the blanks below. Put a period after each sentence, and make each fragment into a complete sentence. Use correct punctuation for dependent clauses.

___ 1. Looking for nonpolluting alternative sources of energy

___ 2. Sometimes a matter of going back to earlier times

___ 3. Wind power has been put to use since the seventh century

___ 4. A windmill uses sails to create power

___ 5. Works on the principle of the wheel and axle

___ 6. The modern wind turbine drives a generator rather than a grindstone

___ 7. Rotor blades up to 300 feet across to extract as much energy from the wind as possible

___ 8. Blades like aircraft wings operated by an efficient control system

___ 9. A computer ensures that the blades always face into the wind

___10. Areas like the windy California deserts

*The following short passages contain fragments. Correct the frag-
ments by adding them to an independent clause and crossing out the
period and capital letter. Use correct punctuation where necessary.*

Example:

> Although the common earthworm does not have an orga-
> nized breathing system. It does take in oxygen. The oxygen must
> dissolve. In the thin film of moisture on the skin before it can be
> absorbed. It is then carried in the blood.

> Although the common earthworm does not have an orga-
> nized breathing system, it does take in oxygen. The oxygen must
> dissolve in the thin film of moisture on the skin before it can be
> absorbed. It is then carried in the blood.

1. The Chinese always kept better records about earthquakes than
   any other country. So it only makes sense that they created the
   first seismograph. It was invented by an astronomer and geogra-
   pher named Chang Heng. In the second century A.D. It had eight
   carefully balanced bronze balls. Which were arranged in a circle
   around a compass. Whenever the instrument picked up movement from an earthquake. One of the balls would roll off.

2. An atlas can be used for many purposes. From planning a trip to
   finding locations in the news. To get the most out of an atlas. The
   user must be able to find places on the map. Measure distances
   and determine directions. Understanding map symbols is also
   important. Because in a sense the whole map is a symbol representing the world.

3. Because it is very expensive to put a criminal in prison.
   Electronic tagging has become a popular way to restrict a criminal's freedom while awaiting trial. A belt, fitted around the criminal's ankle. Carries an electronic device that sends out a coded
   radio signal to the criminal's home telephone. If the criminal tries
   to leave home. The signal is broken. And the telephone immediately contacts the police.

4. When pieces of matter fall to earth. They are called meteorites.
   They are very impressive in the night sky. Because a meteorite is
   visible as a bright fireball followed by a trail of gases and dust.
   About 500 meteorites fall every year. Although most go unno-
   ticed. Most of them fall into the sea.

The following passage contains fragments. Correct the fragments by adding them to an independent clause and crossing out the period and capital letter. Use correct punctuation where necessary.

Producing a film is a complicated process. Involving many people. During production of a film at a studio, there may be scenes that have to be shot away from the studio. This part of the film can be shot at the same time as the studio filming. By the Second Unit. The Second Unit is in itself a production company. Because it has a production manager, director, and assistants. Whenever scenes like car chases, stunt footage and outdoor backgrounds have to be shot. It is the Second Unit that does the job. The scenes are filmed. Then all the footage must be coordinated with the First Unit footage. So that all moves and directions will match the final film.

B. Avoid Run-on Sentences

A clause has a subject and a verb. It may be independent, that is, it can stand alone, or it my be dependent and cannot stand alone.

When two independent clauses are written together without any punctuation, or with just a comma, they are called a run-on sentence.

Examples:

I have worked hours on this essay it is beginning to read much better.
I have worked hours on this essay, it is beginning to read much better.
The program was interesting therefore I watched it with attention.
The program was interesting, therefore I watched it with attention.

These sentences can be corrected in one of three ways:

1. By making the independent clauses into two sentences.
   I have worked hours on this essay. It is beginning to read much better.
   The program was interesting. Therefore I watched it with attention.

2. By separating the two independent clauses with a semicolon.
   I have worked hours on this essay; it is beginning to read much better.
   The program was interesting; therefore I watched it with attention.

Words like *therefore, however, moreover, likewise, otherwise, furthermore, then, nevertheless, consequently,* and *thus* may come between independent clauses. They all require a semicolon in front of them.

3. By separating the two independent clauses with a comma and one of the following connectors: *and, but, yet, so, for, or, nor.*

> I have worked hours on this essay, and it is beginning to read much better.
>
> You must hurry, or you'll miss your plane.

Learn the three ways to avoid run-on sentences.

Exercise 1

In each independent clause, underline the subject once and the verb twice.

Example:

> Fossils are any remains of an animal or plant of past geological ages; they have been preserved in the earth's crust.

1. We studied fossils in science class last year, and since then I have been collecting fossils of plants and animals.

2. I search along river banks; then I dig in the rocks with a special hammer and chisel.

3. I clean the specimens, but my partner marks and sorts them.

4. Fossils are preserved in various ways; usually only a small part remains.

5. Complete animal fossils are very rare, but in some cases entire organisms have been found.

6. Frozen mammoths have been discovered in Siberia; their flesh and bones were still intact.

7. Some organic material is replaced by minerals; this is called petrifaction.

8. A petrified fossil has turned to stone, but a carbonized fossil has been pressed on rock, leaving a thin layer of carbon.

9. Sometimes the fossil dissolves away; a hollow mold of its shape is left.

10. Many fossils are lost by later earth movements and erosion; they are never seen.

Write C if the sentence is correct. Write R if the sentence is a run-on.

___ 1. I have always enjoyed water sports, so I've started taking sailing lessons.

___ 2. I thought I'd start sailing right away, but first I had to take some classroom instruction.

___ 3. In my first three classes, I studied all the parts of a sailboat, I also learned about the tides and weather.

___ 4. It's very important for sailors to have some knowledge of winds and clouds this helps them to identify approaching storms.

___ 5. Storms create dangerous conditions; not only is the wind strong, but waves also become very large.

___ 6. Fog is also dangerous to sail in, it can occur very quickly.

___ 7. At the onset of fog, you must establish your position as quickly as possible; knowing where you are is the key to safety.

___ 8. There are no roads on the water, yet there are definite rules of the road that all boaters must follow.

___ 9. The main purpose of the rules is to prevent boats from colliding, this risk exists when two boats are in sight of each other.

___ 10. I had my first sailing lesson yesterday it was fun to finally get out on the water.

Exercise 3

Correct the run-on sentences by making the independent clauses into two sentences, or by separating the two independent clauses with a semicolon.

Example:

There were many reasons why the first colonists went to the New World, some were running away from punishment and persecution while others were simply looking for adventure.

either:

> There were many reasons why the first colonists went to the New World. Some were running away from punishment and persecution while others were simply looking for adventure.

or:

> There were many reasons why the first colonists went to the New World; some were running away from punishment and persecution while others were simply looking for adventure.

1. The new city library has opened therefore yesterday I went there to do some research for my American history paper.

2. A fire nearly destroyed the old building, it took three years for the new library to be built.

3. Many books were lost in the fire, nevertheless the new library has the third largest collection in the country.

4. I feel very fortunate to live nearby otherwise I'd have to take a train or bus into the city.

5. The new building has six levels, the history department is on the first floor.

6. I was the first person to walk in when the doors opened, consequently I didn't have to wait for a computer.

7. Now that the catalogues are computerized, it's much easier to do my research, it takes much less time to find the books I need.

8. I had decided to write my paper on how the first permanent English settlements were established, I found four books on the subject.

9. I had everything I needed however as I read the books, I began to realize that the settlers themselves were much more interesting than the settlement process.

10. I then decided to switch the subject of my paper, I would write about the reasons why people came to the New World.

Connect the two independent clauses with a comma and one of the following connecting words: **and, for, yet, so.**

Example:

People once thought that conditions on Mars might be suitable for some forms of life; now we know that the Martian climate is too harsh for any form of life as we know it.

People once thought that conditions on Mars might be suitable for some forms of life, but now we know that the Martian climate is too harsh for any form of life as we know it.

1. Mars is one of the easiest planets to spot in the night sky; Venus is the planet that comes closest to Earth.

2. We can only make out a few dark markings when we look at Mars through a telescope; pictures taken by space probes show the surface in great detail.

3. Orange-red rocks and soil cover the surface of Mars; it is called the Red Planet.

4. Much of the soil on Mars is very fine; when the Martian winds blow, they cause huge dust storms.

5. No water flows on Mars today; markings show us that at some time in the past it almost certainly did.

6. The Martian climate is too harsh for humans; the atmosphere is frigid and without oxygen.

7. Much of the surface of Mars consists of flat plains; there are also volcanic ridges.

8. In some ways Mars is similar to Earth; it has seasons, polar ice caps, and an atmosphere.

9. Space probes on Mars have tested the soil for signs of life; no traces of life have been found.

10. Some people have suggested that a curious rock formation on Mars could be a huge sculpture of a Martian face; it could be a natural phenomenon created by the winds.

C. Avoid Faulty Shift in Person

When you start writing either in the first person (**I, we**), the second person (**you**), or the third person (**he, she, one, anyone, a person, they**), you must keep to the same person. You must not shift from one group to another. You may shift from *she* to *one* because they are in the same group, but you cannot shift from *you* to *one*.

Faulty Shift in Person:

> In America *one* is taught to place the unused hand under the table when eating. On the other hand, in many European countries *you* are taught to place both hands on or above the table.

Correct Shift in Person:

> In America *one* is taught to place the unused hand under the table when eating. On the other hand, in many European countries *one* is taught to place both hands on or above the table.

or:

> In America *you* are taught to place the unused hand under the table when eating. On the other hand, in many European countries *you* are taught to place both hands on or above the table.

Faulty Shift in Person:

> *People* who exercise reduce their tension, anxiety, and depression. However, a *person* who exercises in order to avoid his or her problems is not necessarily reducing his or her stress, especially if *you* have to go back to the same old problem the next day.

Correct Shift in Person:

> *People* who exercise reduce their tension, anxiety, and depression. However, a *person* who exercises in order to avoid his or her problems is not necessarily reducing his or her stress, especially if *he or she* (or *the person*) has to go back to the same old problem the next day.

Using too many *one's* in a piece of writing looks unnatural. If you begin with *one* you can continue with he or she since both *one* and *he* or *she* are in the same group.

Example:

> If one follows all the rules in this book, one should be able to write well.

This sentence would sound more natural if you were to write:
> If *one* follows all the rules in this book, *he or she* should be able to write well.

Exercise 1

Correct any faulty shifts in person in the following sentences.

1. I think of tigers as African animals although we know they're native to Asia.
2. If one wants to succeed, they have to study hard.
3. People should know that if you speed you'll eventually get a ticket.
4. I like being in the play because you have fun at rehearsals.
5. In the days before television, people used to get together more often and you would play board games.
6. Alice's Restaurant gives you free cups when you buy extra large soft drinks.
7. All those team members who want to play next semester have to keep your grades above 2.0.
8. If you want to lose weight, one is going to have to eat less and exercise more.
9. As we looked out on the horizon, you could see the storm clouds gathering.
10. If a person reads the newspaper every day, they will stay informed on current events.

Exercise 2

Correct any faulty shifts in person in the following sentences.

1. Students may bring your books and notes into the exam room because this will be an open-book test.
2. One should go hiking if they really want to see the Grand Canyon and its flora and fauna.
3. I used to be afraid to talk in front of a group, but I've discovered that the more you give presentations, the more you get accustomed to it.
4. You should see a doctor about that cough because one could get pneumonia and then one would really be in trouble.
5. Anyone can learn to play an instrument if they have patience and a little talent.

6. As we drove through areas of the West that were once dry and uncultivated, one could see that dams and irrigation have transformed them into prosperous communities.

7. You don't feel good when you know you haven't been kind to a friend.

8. We got caught in a thunderstorm and you could tell we weren't going to get home in dry clothes.

9. I'm discovering that you must have a lot of patience if you want to care for sick children.

10. After seeing *Death of a Salesman*, one has to agree with Arthur Miller that Willy Loman was a modern tragic hero.

Exercise 3

Correct any faulty shifts in person in the following paragraph.

As I joined my fellow climbers on Mount Everest, you knew my dream was finally coming true. We set off on our climb to the final summit at 6:15 a.m. on June 18, after the weather had cleared. One could see for miles and we were all so exhilarated. However, our good mood didn't last long. A clear day also meant a cold day and on the way up our oxygen cylinders froze. Anyone knew we were in trouble. There was a danger we wouldn't have enough oxygen. The going was extremely slow and they could cover only one foot a minute. The final obstacle was a solid wall of rock forty feet high and covered with ice. We thought our route was blocked. One had to think quickly, as our oxygen was getting low. We tried one way, then another, and you knew our time was running out. Eventually we found a way over it and edged ourselves to the top. There we stood, at the top of the world, and you thought it was the most spectacular sight we'd ever seen. I, myself, knew it was the most incredible feeling you had ever had. Nevertheless, one may have conquered the highest mountain, but to a person one felt that many challenges remained for us. No sooner were we down than one was planning the next expedition.

D. Avoid Faulty Subject and Verb Agreement

Subject and verb agreement often presents problems for some learners of English since there are some subjects that take singular verbs and others that take plural verbs. Remember that the subject and verb must agree in person and number. The following are some rules to keep in mind:

▶ **Subjects Taking a Singular Verb**

1. Subjects with the following prepositional phrases take a singular verb:

together with	as well as
along with	in addition to
accompanied by	among

Example:

Among William Saroyan's works is *The Human Comedy*.

2. When *it* introduces a sentence, *it* takes a singular verb.

Example:

It was her voice that astonished everyone.

3. When the words below are used as subjects they take a singular verb:

one	any + singular noun	some + singular noun
nobody	either	each
anybody	somebody	no one
neither	every	anyone
someone	nothing	everybody
anything	something	everyone
	everything	

Example:

Everyone *was* amazed by her voice.

▶ Subjects Taking a Plural Verb

1. When subjects are joined by *and* or *both . . . and*, the verb is plural.

Example:
> Both her mother and her father *were* present.

2. The words *several, both, many*, and *few* always take a plural verb.

Example:
> Many *were* shocked by the decision.

▶ Subjects Taking Either a Singular or a Plural Verb

1. *A number of* takes a plural verb, but *the number of* takes a singular verb.

Example:
> A number of notable people *were* at the reception.
> The number of people at the reception *was* amazing.

2. The words below take a singular or plural verb depending on the noun that follows them:

none	no	all
some	most	half
any	majority	percent

Example:
> Sixty percent of the women *are* employed.
> Sixty percent of the money *is* hers.

3. When subjects are joined by *either . . . or, neither . . . nor*, or *not only . . . but also*, the verb is singular or plural depending on the subject nearest to it.

Example:
> Not only her parents but also her teacher *was* proud of her.
> Not only her parents but also her school friends *were* proud of her.

4. Some words look plural but are singular; some words look singular but are plural.

Example:
> Physics *is* her favorite subject.
> No news *is* good news.
> The phenomena *are* being investigated by scientists.
> The data *are* processed.

Exercises: Subject/Verb Agreement

Exercise 1

Choose the correct form of the verb in parentheses.

1. Specialized training and licensing (is/are) required for the job.
2. Nothing (appeals/appeal) to us more than becoming marine biologists.
3. Somebody (has/have) got to do something about that broken air conditioner.
4. Few taxpayers (was/were) happy with the rise in payroll taxes.
5. A trust fund in addition to her salary (was/were) the income she lived on.
6. Many (was/were) happy to see a new shopping center constructed in town.
7. No one (was/were) smiling, however, when the new shopping center caused major traffic problems.
8. Several (was/were) tempted to move out of town.
9. Neither director (ignores/ignore) the reviews after opening night.
10. More than fifty percent of the voters (was/were) satisfied with the president's mastery of foreign policy.

Exercise 2

Choose the correct form of the verb in parentheses.

1. A lower wage accompanied by higher prices (is/are) the formula for inflation.
2. The largest public works project in history (was/were) set in motion by the Interstate Highway Act of 1956.
3. Statistics (is/are) difficult for many students.
4. Any living organism (performs/perform) certain activities basic to the life process.
5. Everyone (was/were) in a panic when the room shook and the lights went out.

6. It (was/were) Kennedy who ordered his science advisers to increase their efforts on the space program.
7. Among the amphibians (is/are) the frog.
8. Neither the senators nor the president (pretends/pretend) to be able to easily make government more efficient.
9. The heart as well as the blood vessels (is/are) part of the circulatory system.
10. Not only radicals but also the average American (was/were) alienated from the political system in 1968.

Exercise 3

Choose the correct form of the verb in parentheses.

1. Most American Indians (was/were) not prepared for urban life.
2. Along with windmills, solar power (is/are) the best alternative energy source.
3. The ruggedness of the mountain together with its great height (makes/make) it one of the most dangerous for climbers.
4. His complete collection (remains/remain) on exhibit at the art museum.
5. None of the legislators (was/were) completely happy with the Clean Water Act.
6. Exercising regularly as well as avoiding smoking (helps/help) prevent heart disease.
7. The number of accidents occurring at that intersection (is/are) frightening.
8. Fully two-thirds of the population (is/are) at risk of getting the highly contagious disease.
9. A number of protesters (was/were) trying to stop the oil pipeline project in Alaska.
10. Half of us (was/were) trying to study while the others were listening to music.

E. Avoid Faulty Parallel Construction

Correct parallel construction adds clarity and impact to your writing. Parallel construction is used in a sentence to express two or more ideas in a series in the same grammatical form.

Faulty Parallel Construction:
> Her favorite sports are swimming, skiing, and to skate.
> (items do not have all the same form)

Correct Parallel Construction:
> Her favorite sports are *swimming, skiing,* and *skating.*
> (all items have the same form: gerund)

Words such as *by, in, to, a, the,* and *that* usually are repeated when applied to both items.

Faulty Parallel Construction:
> By working hard and making the right decisions he made a name for himself.

Correct Parallel Construction:
> *By* working hard and *by* making the right decisions he made a name for himself.
> (*By* should be repeated after *and* to make both parts parallel.)

Here are some more examples:

Lacking Parallel Construction	Having Parallel Construction
When he ran for the presidency, he promised to cut taxes, to clean up the environment, and he was for eliminating corruption.	When he ran for the presidency he promised to cut taxes, to clean up the environment, and to eliminate corruption. (All items start with *to* and a verb.)
Thomas Hardy was an English novelist, a short-story writer, and he wrote poetry.	Thomas Hardy was an English novelist, a short-story writer, and a poet. (All items are nouns.)
Peter helps his sick friend by taking notes for her and he helps her with homework assignments.	Peter helps his sick friend by taking notes for her and by helping her with homework assignments. (Both items start with by + gerund.)
June wanted her traveling companion to have similar interests, to be independent, and who liked the outdoors.	June wanted her traveling companion to have similar interests, to be independent, and to like the outdoors.
Of all the moons in our solar system, Io is the most colorful, fascinating, and its volcanos are active.	Of all the moons in our solar system, Io is the most colorful, fascinating, and volcanically active. (All items are adjectives.)

Here are examples of thesis statements which should always use parallel construction:

Lacking Parallel Construction	Having Parallel Construction
Students can get good grades if they 1. do the required reading. 2. carefully taking notes. 3. do their studying for tests.	Students can get good grades if they 1. *do* the required reading. 2. *take* careful notes. 3. *study* for tests.
In my opinion, the best kind of vacation includes 1. an exotic location. 2. I like resting and relaxing. 3. actively doing sports.	In my opinion, the best kind of vacation includes 1. *an exotic location.* 2. *rest and relaxation.* 3. *sports activities.*
Anyone can write well if they learn to 1. logical thought. 2. organizing ideas coherently. 3. clear expression of ideas.	Anyone can write well if they learn to 1. *think* logically. 2. *organize* ideas coherently. 3. *express* ideas clearly.

Many of the sentences lack parallel construction. Cross out the part that is not parallel and write the correction above.

Exercise 1

1. Jennifer is tall, green-eyed, and has a witty way about her.
2. Not only is Roland a brilliant scientist, but he plays baseball excellently and plays the saxophone well.
3. Before I make a dress for you I have to take your measurements, then finding a pattern and selecting the cloth.
4. Only after having the muffler fixed and the brakes checked will I be able to drive my car again.
5. The teacher insisted that everyone attend the labs and that all assignments be handed in on time.
6. My job consists of stocking all the shelves, take inventory once a week, write up orders, and supervision of the cashiers.
7. She likes to work on her computer and playing softball.
8. The traffic officer was stopping cars from entering the parade route, but he was letting pedestrians through.
9. Our living room is 12 feet wide and 15 feet in length.
10. Between watching television and he played baseball, Ron managed to get his homework done.

Exercise 2

1. Santa Barbara is a beautiful area with a lovely coastline, there are mountains, and a city having Spanish-influenced architecture.
2. Before committing time and material to a finished painting, an artist will often sketch and experiment until the form seems exactly right.
3. Regina was undecided whether she should take a train down to Florida or a flying in her friend's small plane.
4. Tom is an excellent dancer and who is also a talented soccer player.
5. The movie was interesting and emotional but could not easily be understood.

6. It was only by luck and because of the time that I saved my luggage from being placed on the wrong ferry.

7. A college education frequently leads to increased earning power and to a better quality of life.

8. Mark just bought a new refrigerator with two freezer compartments, a water dispenser, and it's capable of making ice.

9. Photosynthesis is the process by which plants trap solar energy, converting it to chemical energy, and storing it in organic molecules such as sugar.

10. Humans learned first to speak and only much later were writing an alphabet representing speech.

Exercise 3

1. The lens of the eye bends the light rays that come from an object, forms an image of the object on the retina of the eyes, and this image is changed to nerve impulses which travel to the brain.

2. The effects of acid rain have been to increase the acidity of thousands of northern and mountain lakes, it has stripped the leaves and needles from millions of acres of trees, and is etching away the surfaces of buildings and monuments.

3. As we approached the park entrance, a forest ranger stopped our car and told us not to feed the bears because they were wild, fierce, and a danger to humans, particularly at that time, which was just after their winter hibernation.

4. The witness was unwilling to testify because he was afraid of the accused man's ties to the criminal world, his dislike of the publicity the trial was getting, and his feeling that it wasn't his duty to testify since he was a foreigner in the country.

5. I was overwhelmed by the choice of cars on the lot, which included sportcars with their clean lines and bright colors, family sedans with their practical styles and features, luxury cars having rich interiors, and trucks that had big tires and were capable of four-wheel drive.

Make the parts of these thesis statements parallel.

1. I haven't decided which college to attend, but I know I want a school with
   a. the instructors have to be good.
   b. a nice campus.
   c. it has to have a theatrical arts program.

2. Strikes, though sometimes necessary, also mean
   a. loss of wages for workers.
   b. they interfere with production in the company.
   c. they disrupt the flow of goods and services to consumers.

3. The world-wide problem of providing fresh water for a growing population can be solved by
   a. converting salt water from the oceans.
   b. more lakes can be made into reservoirs.
   c. conservation measures.

4. I think national holidays are important because they
   a. people are given time for rest and recreation.
   b. community activities bring people together.
   c. encourage patriotism.

F. Avoid Shifts in Time

When writing your essay, avoid shifting in time from present to past or from past to present. If you start in the past do not shift to the present. Keep to the same time throughout your essay. In the following few sentences, the writer starts with the past tense, shifts to the present for a while, and then goes back to the past.

> In 1482 Leonardo da Vinci left Florence for Milan, where he became the official artist to the duke of Milan. While he was there, he embarked upon many projects, one of which was his famous painting of the *Last Supper*. For this painting he uses an experimental mural technique which causes the painting to deteriorate soon after it is completed. Leonardo stayed with the duke until his fall from power in 1499.

The sentences should all be in the past tense:

In 1482 Leonardo da Vinci left Florence for Milan, where he became the official artist to the duke of Milan. While he was there, he embarked upon many projects, one of which was his famous painting of the *Last Supper*. For this painting he used an experimental mural technique which caused the painting to deteriorate soon after it was completed. Leonardo stayed with the duke until his fall from power in 1499.

Exercise 1

Correct the shifts in time in this reading.

I had the greatest adventure of my life last summer when I went to South Africa. I visit the great game parks and stay a week in the Drakensberg Mountains. As I drive into Main Camp at Giant's Castle Game Reserve, the air is chilly and misty, the sky a deep gray. My hut was the last in a row of straw-roofed cottages set on the edge of the hillside with an eagle's view of the river valley. Rising above it are the edges of red sandstone cliffs, their peaks so high as to be lost in haze. It is a very peaceful scene as eland, very large African antelopes, grazed on the red slopes above the rushing waters of the river.

In spite of distant thunder I am too curious to wait, so I explored a path that wound down a ledge to the river bank. Muddy soil makes the descent dangerous, as I slip and slide through the brush and the grass as high as my head. Nevertheless, I got safely down to the river and jump on rocks to the other side and up the hillside to where I'd seen the eland. But they'd vanished, and for good reason. In an instant, the sky opens, rain pours down and in ten seconds I was drenched. Thunder, lightning, and wind roar through the pass.

I turn and ran back for camp. I pushed aside brush, skidded on rocks, and suddenly run right into an eland, big as a horse. Talk about startled. He goes one way and I go the other. I scramble up the slippery, rocky slope as quickly as my feet could carry me.

What a relief it is to finally reach the cottage, light a fire, and get into dry clothes. I stood in front of the large window with a hot cup of tea as a torrent of rain forms a silver veil over the valley and mountains. I know right then that a true adventure had begun.

Correct the shifts in time in this reading.

Sailing can be fun but last summer I learned a lesson I'll never forget.

I was in New Hampshire visiting my cousins when I come up with the bright idea to go sailing on the lake. I had sailed a couple of times in Southern California where I was raised, so I feel confident that I can captain my inexperienced but enthusiastic crew. We make picnic lunches and put on our bathing suits, and talked at length about the wonderful day ahead of us.

The sky is blue and the sun shines brightly the morning of our excursion. I was accustomed to days like this in Southern California where two or three summer months go by without so much as a drop of rain. What I didn't know was that in New Hampshire, a glorious morning had nothing to do with how the day would end, or even what it will be like by noon.

With only our beach towels and a picnic basket, we go down to the boathouse and rented a 15-foot sailboat. I quickly show my sailing skills as I raise the sail, catch a gentle breeze, and we glided across the calm, sparkling water. An hour goes by. I give my cousins a sailing lesson and we headed for a distant island to have our picnic lunch.

About halfway to the island, I noticed that the gently breeze is now a brisk wind tugging at the sail. The water is getting rough, too, and the wind was making the boat heel—that is, tip on one side—and at times the sail was almost touching the water. We have to use our weight to keep the boat from going over. Our pleasant sail is quickly turning into quite a challenge.

The once sunny sky was now gray and threatening. Where had the clouds come from, I wonder? If I had known anything about New England weather I would have been aware that storms came up in the blink of an eye. I was worried, but I don't want to frighten my cousins any more than they already are. Thunder roared across the lake and a flash of lightning lights the sky toward the opposite shore.

We had to get off the water fast, or risk being struck by lightning. The shore is too far away by then, however, so I head toward the island. We nearly overturned several times and manage to lose our picnic basket. It is as dark as night and a heavy rain makes it almost impossible to see. The storm was quickly bearing down on us and the lightning getting closer. Suddenly we were caught in a small whirlwind and I briefly lose control of the boat. But just when I thought we'd be swimming to shore, the wind shifts and comes from behind us, pushing us toward the island. In a few moments we are on shore, cold and hungry, but safe. We stayed there all night, but are able to safely make it home the next morning.

7. PUNCTUATION

A. Capital Letters

1. Capitalize the first word of every sentence.

2. Capitalize the first, last, and every important word in a title. Do not capitalize short connecting words, articles, and prepositions of fewer than five letters unless they begin or end a title.
   The Woman of Mystery
   Where Are We Going To?

3. Capitalize the first word in a direct quotation.
   He said, "This is the place where I stayed."
   "This is the place where I stayed," he said "and this is the place where I hid the money."

Note: Do not capitalize the first word after an interruption between parts of a sentence.

4. Capitalize the names of people, places, languages, races, nationalities, and religions.

John Newman	France	English	Hinduism	Utah
Christianity	The Grand Canyon		The Atlantic Ocean	

5. Capitalize months, days of the week, and special days, but do not capitalize the seasons.

August	Friday	Fourth of July	winter

6. Capitalize the names of specific people or things.

Dr. Peters	Professor Brown	Fifth Avenue
Mississippi River	Freud	the *Los Angeles Times*

7. Capitalize historic events, periods, movements, and documents.

the Civil War	the Bill of Rights	the Roaring Twenties

Note: Do not capitalize centuries, as in eighteenth century.

8. Capitalize the names of educational institutions, departments, courses, and degrees.

Glendale College English 101
Department of History Bachelor of Arts

9. Capitalize organizations, government departments, political parties.

Postal Service Republican Party Democrats
Metropolitan Museum of Art Medical Board of California

10. Capitalize abbreviations that show time, national and international organizations, divisions of government, and radio and television station names.

B.C. U.N. NBC KLOS IBM NATO

Exercises: Capitalization

Exercise 1

Add the necessary capital letters.

1. He has always wanted to write a book about the south and the history of the creoles.

2. "let out the sail!" Martha yelled, as a sudden gust of strong wind rushed across chesapeake bay.

3. I was pleasantly surprised to see professor Rogers back from his archaeological dig in the middle east and back in the classroom teaching ancient history 101.

4. An article in last thursday's *los angeles times* reported that the elephant population in kenya has tripled in the last ten years due to the government's conservation measures.

5. *My fair lady* has had one of the longest runs in broadway history and has been translated into french, german, italian, japanese, and many other languages.

6. I'm fond of thanksgiving, and even memorial day, but there's nothing like the fourth of july for fun and excitement.

7. As we turned east on sierra highway, we could clearly see the san gabriel mountains ahead of us.

8. since professor white has become the new head of the philosophy department at bloomfield college, more students are signing up for philosophy courses than ever before.

9. I went to see the new animated dinosaur exhibit at the boston natural history museum and it was really thrilling.

10. When the mississippi river rose to flood stage, many people fled to higher ground, where the red cross had set up shelters.

Exercise 2

Add the necessary capital letters.

1. while I was working at the library last night, I helped senator todd find a book on the constitution, an american ship active in the war of 1812.

2. Samantha's dream of going to harvard university to study medicine was finally realized last september.

3. for my world cultures class, I'm going to write about my visit to an indian reservation in arizona last summer.

4. In many parts of the world, christians and muslims have lived peacefully side by side for generations.

5. our state representative always says, "good government begins at the local level."

6. In the years following world war ll, there was much discussion in the united states on the question of lowering the minimum voting age to eighteen.

7. In *reflections on Gandhi*, George Orwell wrote: "of late years, it has been the fashion to talk about Gandhi as though he were not only sympathetic to the western left-wing movement but were integrally part of it."

8. I can't say that I had a very nice labor day weekend because my best friend was sick with the flu, my car broke down, and it rained from friday through sunday.

9. "Please," we begged our biology professor, "postpone our midterm exam until next monday so we'll have the weekend to study."

10. The kern county women's club is planning to have a rummage sale next autumn on the grounds of the presbyterian church.

Exercise 3

Add the necessary capital letters.

1. my dentist, dr. Robert Nathan, jr., has an office on waterford street, but he's looking for new office space in the cooper building near the bank of america on fifth avenue.

2. ramses II was one of egypt's longest-reigning monarchs, ruling the ancient kingdom for sixty-six years until he died in 1213 b.c. at about ninety years of age, when his body was placed in a tomb alongside many other great rulers in a place called valley of the kings.

3. Peter, an art student from england, is working with me during july and august on the new "origins of man" research program at the smithsonian institute.

4. democrats and republicans in the u.s. senate temporarily put aside their differences to vote for an important budget bill that a group called citizens for a responsible government has been urging for two years.

5. according to the audubon society, the everglades and other important wetland areas in the south and west are in grave danger of disappearing forever.

6. Noel wanted to trade in his old pontiac for a new ford mustang, but when he went shopping at the anderson ford dealership last saturday he quickly changed his mind after seeing the new sticker prices.

7. In december, I'm going on my first trip to the south pacific, where I hope to visit the places in tahiti where the french artist Gauguin lived and worked.

8. "would you like to go to a play tonight at the doolittle theater?" Joel asked. "it's a wonderful comedy called 'it's a great life,' and I'm sure you'll enjoy it.

9. I went to the martha graham memorial library last monday to do research for my paper on antarctica, but I was surprised to find it closed; that is, until I remembered it was president's day, a federal holiday in america.

10. "All your reservations have been made, reverend Graham, including your flight on british airways to london, your room at the dorchester hotel, your tour of buckingham palace, your personal visit to lord north, and your ferry trip across the english channel."

B. Quotation Marks

Use quotation marks around a direct quotation, or the exact words of a speaker, that is shorter than three lines.

1. Put periods and commas inside quotation marks.
"I'm so surprised," she said, "that I'm doing so well in physics."

2. Put colons and semicolons outside quotation marks.
"You're welcome to come here and visit anytime": those were her very words.

3. Put exclamation points and question marks inside quotation marks if they are part of the quotation. If they are not part of the quotation, they go outside.
"Are you ready to go?" he asked.
"Did you call and say, "Hold the tickets for us at ticket counter number one"?

4. When a quoted sentence is in two parts, the second part begins with a small letter unless it is a new sentence.
"I'm sure I told you to be ready by six o'clock," she complained. "I can't believe you're not even dressed yet."

5. Put single quotation marks around a quotation within another quotation.
"I was hiking down the path," she explained, "when I heard someone crying, 'Help me, please.'"

6. Put quotation marks around foreign words or words that are used in a special way.
Honeybees communicate the source of nectar to one another by doing a little "dance" in a figure-eight pattern.

7. Put quotation marks around the titles of articles from periodicals, magazines, and newspapers; chapters of books; short stories; poems; and songs.
"Researching Your Subject" is a chapter in *Scientific Report Writing*, a required textbook for biology students.

In the article, "Plants for All Seasons," published in the May 1995 issue of *Southern California Gardening*, the writer tells how a garden can bloom all year, regardless of the weather or time of year.

Note: The titles of books, magazines, journals, newspapers, and movies must be underlined or italicized.

Exercise 1

Add the necessary quotation marks.

1. I'll meet you at 3 o'clock, she promised, and then I'll help you with your science project.

2. Run! he shouted. There's a snake under that rock.

3. You're not going to believe what Professor Walsh just told me, Brian announced. He said, I believe yours was the best term paper I've ever read.

4. Do you believe he said, John, you made the team?

5. In his article, Deep Cover in Belize, in the summer issue of *Escape* magazine, Tony Perrottet discusses his recent experiences in the still-undeveloped island country of Belize.

6. Don't panic: that's Perrottet's number one rule of jungle survival, as written in his article.

7. When I asked what the second rule of jungle survival was, his words were: Find the river; that's what I did and why I survived.

8. As he crawled along the ledge in a near panic, he asked, What do I do next?

9. People who like to read travel books but rarely leave their home-towns are called *armchair travelers*.

10. In Johnny Clegg's album, *In My African Dream*, the song Scatterlings of Africa is a blend of Zulu chants and Western folk-rock.

Add the necessary quotation marks.

1. He said, Be sure to vote for my candidate; however I voted for the person I liked the best.

2. In the article Ramses the Great, published in the May 29, 1995, issue of *U.S. News & World Report*, the author discusses the significance of the recent discovery of the tomb of the Egyptian king, Ramses II.

3. The author writes, Could Ramses II have been the pharaoh of the Exodus?

4. Go on, go on, urged the guide to the reluctant tourists waiting at the edge of the rope bridge. This is what you came here for.

5. Coronary artery disease is relatively uncommon in people with very low cholesterol levels: these are the words of leading U.S. heart disease researchers.

6. A computer adds to our experiences, he said, but it doesn't replace them.

7. Waving her grades in front of him, she shouted, I can't believe you said, Oh, that professor is easy; you should sign up for his class!

8. *Stunning* was the word the designers used to describe their creation.

9. T. S. Eliot's The Love Song of J. Alfred Prufrock is the first poem in my book *Collected Poems 1909-1935*.

10. I hate having to do library research on a beautiful day like this, she grumbled, when I could be running on the beach instead.

Exercise 3

Add the necessary quotation marks.

1. I can't wait to go to the Computer Expo in New York! she declared. It's going to be so exciting.

2. The last time we talked, you said, I'm not going. What happened since then? Robert asked in surprise.

3. Well, Natalie replied, I read all about it in an article called The Computer Revolution, which appeared in last week's *Time* magazine, and that's what influenced me to go.

4. Did I hear you say, This is my favorite class?

5. In bats, the *arm* bones are light and strong, and the *finger* bones are very long.

6. I know I've always said I wanted to be a biologist, he admitted, but I've decided to study anthropology instead.

7. This is what I read: The koala can meet all its needs for shelter, food, and water in a eucalyptus tree; nevertheless, it's hard to believe.

8. I can't believe we're lost. You said, I know the way to the Humanities Building! Ralph cried excitedly. Now I'll be late for class.

9. Order, adaptation, metabolism, movement, responsiveness: these are the five characteristics of life, as written by Hopson and Veres in the chapter, What is Life? in their book *Biology! Bringing Science to Life.*

10. Spanish settlement in New Mexico, writes Davidson, was dominated by ranchero families who grazed large herds of sheep along the upper Rio Grande valley.

Exercise 4

Add the necessary quotation marks.

Watch out there! Nick warned me as I slipped on a loose step. This house is old enough to crumble beneath our feet.

I'll be careful, I assured him, but thanks for the warning.

It was almost midnight and my friends and I were determined to stay in what everyone in the neighborhood considered a *haunted* house. You must have a tape recorder, mirror, flashlight, and a camera with infrared film: this was our ghost-hunting book's list of required items, and we had them all.

Is it midnight yet? Eliot asked.

Yes, now everyone be quiet, said Maureen. The book says, There must be absolute silence or the spirits will not show themselves.

Everyone silently seated themselves on the floor of the attic. Maureen used her flashlight to scan Chapter 3, How to Catch a Ghost, in her book *The Art of Ghost Hunting.*

Nick whispered, None of us really believes in this, you know; nevertheless he was trembling. He looked in the direction of a creaking sound we'd all heard. Turn off that flashlight! he said excitedly. This could be it!

Didn't I just hear you say, None of us really believes in this? I asked.

Be quiet, Maureen whispered, or we'll never see a ghost tonight.

Suddenly, cold air rushed past us. Did you feel that? asked Eliot. We all nodded silently. According to our book, this was the first sign of a ghostly presence.

C. Commas: Rules 1, 2, and 3

There are six important rules governing the use of the comma. First we'll look at three of them.

1. Use a comma before *and, but, for, or, nor, yet,* and *so,* when they connect two independent clauses.
   They believe that you have a good chance of winning, but you must continue to train vigorously.
   We can start work on Monday, or we can wait until the following week.
   She wanted to take a vacation but couldn't get time off.
   (The two clauses are not independent, and therefore no comma is required.)

2. Use a comma between items in a series.
   He is intelligent, charming, and rich.
   We flew to Paris, rented a car, and drove to Lyon.

Items in an address or date or place names are separated by commas like items in a series.
   We went to UCLA, Los Angeles, California, for her graduation.
   On August 31, 1991, he joined the group.
   She has been living at 3590 Observatory Avenue, Salisbury, North Carolina, for nearly twenty years.

3. Use a comma following an introductory word, or group of words, or a dependent clause that does not flow smoothly.
   No, I can't be there at that time.
   Oh, I didn't mean to do that.
   Working until the early hours, he finished writing his paper.
   After class was over, the teacher talked to two of the students.
   (A dependent clause at the beginning requires a comma after it.)

Punctuate these sentences with commas where necessary.

Example:

Learning to use a computer can be frustrating yet it is rewarding.
Learning to use a computer can be frustrating, yet it is rewarding.

1. We have a variety of services to help you with your new computer program and this section summarizes these services.

2. If you have a question about your new program contact our product support representative.

3. Outside the United States contact Support Services at the office that serves your area.

4. Within the United States you can obtain product support in several ways: telephone fax machine mail or in person.

5. You can call to hear recorded responses to common questions or you can order notes to be sent on your fax machine.

6. Every Monday Wednesday and Friday our help lines are open between 6 a.m. and 6 p.m.

7. Our offices are located at 2020 Madison Avenue Computer Town Ohio and they are open five days a week.

8. Our service representatives are knowledgeable and efficient yet they are also friendly and helpful.

9. Our representatives are very busy so you must be prepared to give the following information: type of hardware how the problem occurred and how you tried to solve it.

10. We are always eager to solve your problems but if you prefer to become an expert yourself we also offer training classes.

Exercise 2

Punctuate these sentences with commas where necessary.

1. For our school holiday we had a choice of going to the beach the mountains or the desert.
2. It wasn't an easy choice nor was it a very democratic one.
3. Only Carl had a car so we went where he wanted to go.
4. Well his decision was to go skiing.
5. Even though I didn't know how to ski I went along to be with my friends.
6. Besides it was December and it seemed right to be in the snow at Christmas time.
7. On the morning of December 20 we all met at Carl's house had breakfast and then got on the road.
8. Everyone was very happy and excited about being on vacation for we'd all had a grueling semester of lectures studying and tests.
9. Halfway up the mountain we got caught in a snowstorm.
10. Carl had snow tires but the road conditions were so bad that we had to turn around and go back home.

Exercise 3

Add the necessary commas.

1. Believe it or not the world's most advanced scientists are taking lessons from insects. In a new area of research called biomimitis they are studying how insects turn nature's simple building blocks into materials superior to man-made products. For example spiders can spin protein into silk threads that are tougher than the material used to make bulletproof vests and the abalone has a shell twice as strong as most advanced ceramics. Natural materials have many advantages so scientists are trying hard to unlock the secrets of nature.

2. In 1994 Norwegian explorer Boerge Ousland became the first person to walk the North Pole alone and he was unaided. He had a sled on which he carried his tent sleeping bag skis and medical supplies. After his trip he said that the steep icy ridges were nearly impossible to get the sled across yet he made the trek in 52 days.

3. About 65 million years ago a large percentage of the animal life on the planet perished. For scientists this has always been a mystery. However most scientists now believe that a huge meteorite was the cause of the devastation. They believe it was as large as five miles across that it struck the earth near the coast of the Yucatan Peninsula in Mexico and that it caused tidal waves earthquakes and even volcanic eruptions.

4. I've started shopping for my first new car but I haven't had much luck so far. At first I knew what model I wanted or at least I thought I did. Now I'm not so sure. What I do know is that it has to have an automatic transmission a V6 engine good suspension and good fuel economy. I'd like it to be comfortable but I'd also like it to be sporty. Well I'm sure that if I look hard enough I'll soon find the car of my dreams.

Exercise 4

Add the necessary commas.

Natural history museums are interesting exciting places to visit. For students of earth science biology anthropology and archaeology they are good places to conduct research. In addition the museums often employ students and for some young researchers they are an excellent training ground. Like all museums natural history museums rely on the generosity of donors. The more patrons a museum has the easier it is for the museum to acquire new exhibits and artifacts conduct special educational programs employ researchers and curators and maintain their buildings. Natural history museums are popular with adults but children love them too. There are exhibits on everything from outer space to inner earth and it is that variety that makes it so interesting and fun for visitors of all ages. In other words a visitor can learn what the surface of Mars looks like today or what the habits of a wooly mammoth were 500 years ago. Naturally the dinosaur exhibits are the most popular with children. Seeing these huge ancient animals in natural settings is fascinating for them yet it can also be frightening if the exhibit has movement and sound effects.

C. Commas: Rules 4, 5, and 6

4. Use commas to set off an expression that interrupts the flow of the sentence such as *I think, for example, in fact, however, nevertheless, besides, by the way, indeed,* and *likewise.*
   > Driving on the freeway, I think, is much more dangerous than flying.
   > I hope, of course, he'll be there.
   > We believed, however, it was not the right thing to do.
   > We are very busy now; therefore, it will have to wait.

A word is more likely to be an interrupter if it is in the middle of the sentence rather than the beginning or the end. The words that are interrupters in the above sentences are not interrupters in the sentences below, and, therefore, do not need to be set off by commas.
   > I think driving on the freeway is more dangerous than flying.
   > Of course I'll be there on time.
   > However good your reasons, they won't accept it.
   > Therefore we left the country and came here.

In the above sentence *however* is used with the meaning "no matter how" and does not require a comma. Remember that when *however* is used between two independent clauses, it requires a semicolon before it. The three uses of *however* are shown below:
   > There is an important meeting tomorrow; *however,* I will be out of town.
   > (connector between two independent clauses: semicolon before it)
   > We believe, *however,* it is not the right thing to do. (interrupter in the middle of the sentence: set off with commas)
   > *However* good your reasons, they won't accept it.
   > (meaning "no matter how": no commas.)

5. Use commas to set off the name of a person spoken to.
   > George, are you coming tomorrow?
   > I have just faxed the letter, Jan.
   > I know, Tony, you are telling the truth.

6. Use commas to set off nonessential elements. Nonessential elements may add important information to the sentence but are not essential to the meaning of the sentence. Look at the following example:
   > Billie Holiday, who was also known as Lady Day, was famous for her unique singing style.

The clause *who was also known as Lady Day* is not essential to the meaning of the sentence. If we take the clause out we still know who the subject was and what she was famous for. We can, therefore, set off the nonessential elements by the use of commas showing that the clause can be left out.

Look at the sentence below:

The woman who was also known as Lady Day was famous for her unique singing style.

The clause *who was also known as Lady Day* is essential to the meaning of the sentence. If we take it out, the sentence would read: The woman was famous for her unique singing style. We would not know who the woman was. Since this clause is essential to the meaning of the sentence, no commas are used to set it off.

Dow Jones and Company, a financial publishing firm, computes averages for each trading hour of every business day.

In the sentence above, the words *a financial publishing company* can be omitted without changing the meaning of the sentence. Since this is a nonessential element it is set off by commas indicating that it could be left out. However, read the following:

A financial publishing firm computes averages for each trading hour of every business day.

A financial publishing is essential to the meaning of the sentence or else we would not know who computes the averages for each hour. Since this element is essential to the meaning of the sentence, no commas are used to set it off.

Exercise 1

Punctuate these sentences with commas where necessary.

Example:

There's no place like the West however when it comes to searching for ghost towns.
There's no place like the West, however, when it comes to searching for ghost towns.

1. I hope of course that you'll forgive me for not having written sooner.

2. I've been very busy; nevertheless that's no excuse for waiting a whole month to write to you.

3. I'm enjoying my summer in California naturally and have lots to tell you.

4. Have you ever visited a ghost town Charlie?

5. Yesterday I went to three ghost towns places that vanished over the past 100 years and found it very interesting.

6. The ghost town Las Cruces was our first stop.

7. Charlie would you believe that a few signs crumbling shacks and a broken fence are all that's left of this town?

8. Alice Walker a local historian told me that a family was brutally murdered there in 1864 all over the rights to a stagecoach station.

9. However hard the town tried to overcome its past no one could forget what had happened.

10. The town remained a stage stop although the population gradually dwindled and finally the railroad put an end to its usefulness.

Exercise 2

Add the necessary commas.

1. Margaret Benson who recently wrote a book on aging is going to lecture our sociology class today.

2. She will I'm sure talk about the diet exercise and other lifestyle habits she believes can prolong our lives.

3. Benson's book *Growing Older: Facts and Myths* is a best seller among young and old alike.

4. I'm still in my twenties; of course but I realize that it's never too early to start living a healthy life.

5. I'll be very interested Eleanor in what you have to say after listening to Benson's lecture.

6. You are after all the oldest person I know.

7. Anyone who lives into his or her nineties as you have must know something about aging gracefully.

8. Senior citizenship after all is something we all must face.

9. Anyone who is honest will admit that growing old is not something he or she looks forward to although it can be a very rewarding time of life.

10. Knowing you though makes me feel better about it all.

Add the necessary commas.

1. Archaeologists scientists who search for and study the remains of human life and culture have much to tell us about art and humanity. Art it seems comes naturally to humans. In the Ice Age about 35,000 years ago Cro Magnon people in Europe painted the walls of their caves. They in addition carved figurines and decorated their everyday implements weapons and tools. The finest examples of prehistoric art by the way have been found in France.

2. I was wondering Martin if you'd like to go to Fiji with me in September. I'm going to Vanua Levu Fiji's biggest island to see a friend of mine who is doing some research there. Vanua Levu is located in the far north of the Fiji chain an hour's flight from the main island and it has one of the most lovely dramatic coastlines in the South Pacific. I'm sure you'd enjoy yourself; however I'll understand if you can't make it. It is after all just before the new semester begins.

3. The endoscope in my opinion is the most important of all the fiber optic devices. An endoscope a narrow tube containing fiber optic cables allows a doctor to see inside a body without cutting it open. The tube is inserted into an opening in the body such as the throat and strands of pure glass transmit light along the fibers to light up the interior. I know a doctor who has used this wonderful device. The endoscope he declares has revolutionized his practice of medicine.

4. I have just believe it or not bought a musical recording for my plants. I'm not certain frankly if this will help them grow; however there have been many experiments on the consciousness of plants. I know of one biology professor who took identical plants and put them in three rooms. He cared for them of course exactly the same. There was one difference however and that was in the recordings he played during the day. The results which are very interesting were published in his book *Plantasia*. It seems the plants thrived with classical and rock music; however the plant exposed to daily news broadcasts abruptly died!

Add the necessary commas.

Rain which has always been considered a source of life has taken a different turn in some places. Rain in the northeastern United States for example is four times more acidic than it was in 1900. This increased acidity has consequently damaged the environment. It has caused among other things fish to die in lakes whole forests to be stripped of leaves and needles and buildings and statues to corrode. Scientists who have studied the effects of acid rain are quite certain of its causes. The burning of oil and coal for electricity they are sure is the biggest cause. It throws massive clouds of sulfur dioxide and nitrogen oxides which are acid-producing substances into the atmosphere. Knowing what causes acid rain and doing something about it however are two different things. Until people throughout the world therefore are ready willing and able to use alternative forms of energy the destructive effects of acid rain will continue.

D. Other Punctuation

Period

1. Use a period at the end of a statement or command. In informal writing, a period can be used after a single word.
    Vitamins are essential to your health.
    Take two capsules a day.
    Thanks. That'll help me.

2. Use a period after an abbreviation.

Question Mark

Dr.	Wed.	Jan.	A.M.

Use a question mark after a direct question. Do not use a question mark after an indirect question. In informal writing, a question mark can be used after a single word.
    Are you going to New York?
    She asked if I was going to New York.
    Really? I thought you were joking.

▶ Exclamation Mark

Use an exclamation mark after interjections, strong commands, and emphatic statements.

Amazing! I knew you could do it. (Interjection)
Quick! Quick! We're going to be late. (Strong command)
It's not true! (Emphatic statement)

Note: A period is not used at the end of a title of a work. A question mark or an exclamation mark can be used where appropriate.
The Tale of Two Cities
Who's Afraid of Virginia Woolf?
Shape Up!

▶ Semicolon

1. Use a semicolon between two independent clauses not joined by one of these connecting words: *and, but, for, or, nor, yet, so.*
   Estimates of the size of seas vary greatly; seas do not have clearly defined boundaries.

2. Use a semicolon to separate phrases or clauses in a series if they contain commas.
   Some of the world's principal seas include the South China Sea, the Caribbean Sea, and the Mediterranean Sea; the Gulf of Mexico and Hudson Bay are also in this category.

▶ Colon

1. Use a colon to introduce a series after a complete sentence.
   Franklin was known for the following inventions: bifocal glasses, the lightning rod, the Franklin stove, and a glass harmonica.

2. Use a colon to introduce a quotation. Note that we often use a comma to introduce a quotation too.
   In *Poor Richard's Almanac* Franklin recommended moderation: "Early to bed and early to rise makes a man healthy, wealthy, and wise."

▶ Dash

Use a dash to show a break in thought or tone.
I can fix it—at least, I think I can.
He lost all my computer files—that's when he got a new job—and it took me a long time to forgive him.

Add the necessary punctuation (period, question mark, exclamation mark, semicolon, colon, or dash).

Example:

I have two goals one is to invent something useful to humankind the other is to visit another planet.
I have two goals: one is to invent something useful to humankind; the other is to visit another planet.

1. Have you ever thought about becoming an astronaut

2. Gosh I think it would be fascinating

3. Future space travel will include the following space stations, laboratories on the moon, and the exploration of Mars all the experiences I'd like to have

4. Shuttles will carry parts into orbit for a space station then astronaut-engineers will put the parts together

5. Shuttle craft will visit the station on a regular basis they'll bring new crews and fresh supplies

6. Would you like to stay on a space station

7. What an exciting way to live

8. Of course, a person could also experience these emotions loneliness boredom anxiety and even fear

9. I have a lot of enthusiasm for space travel therefore I don't think I'd have any problems

10. I'd like to pilot lunar ferries well any interplanetary craft would be fine

Exercise 2

Add the necessary punctuation.

1. A large section of northeastern Alaska has been set aside for preservation it is called the Arctic National Wildlife Range

2. At 13,000 square miles, it's huge the scenery is breathtaking

3. It's the largest wildlife refuge in the US that only adds to its unique status as the nation's only arctic preserve

4. There are many reasons for setting aside this land preserving the Arctic vegetation protecting its animals and controlling the exploitation of its natural resources

5. What would we do without protected lands

6. Would anything still be in its natural state fifty years from now

7. The arctic preserve incorporates a portion of the North Slope that's the vast plain that falls gently from the foothills to the Beaufort Sea and all the eastern part of the Brooks Range

8. It's home to a variety of animals caribou grizzlies sheep foxes and many kinds of birds

9. The area provides the kind of wilderness experience people dream of well at least I do

10. On a recent trip I had some wonderful experiences I recorded them on film and in a daily diary

Exercise 3

Add the necessary punctuation.

1. A black bear eats all these things berries ants honey roots fish frogs and mice What a healthy appetite The bear is getting ready for a long, winter hibernation Would you like to do that Many people believe that all bears sleep in caves however, that's not really true Caves aren't always available, so sometimes bears lie in hollow trees or holes in the ground or among some rocks

2. How has American music developed over the years Our music teacher, Ms. Rogers by the way, she's an excellent pianist explained it all to us American music has always been influenced by many ethnic and cultural traditions Much can be said about the contributions made by immigrant German and Greek conductors French composers Austrian musicians Of great importance were the African immigrants they of course created the music of jazz

3. Acupuncture is an ancient Chinese healing art it dates back to 3,000 B C that is based on the belief that there's a connection between the body's organs and its surface What does this have to do with medicine Acupuncture works on the principle that in all diseases, mental or physical, there are tender areas at certain points on the body these disappear when the disease is cured They are called acupuncture points Acupuncture involves the stimulation of these points with fine needles What a way to treat a patient

4. Do you like sprouts in your salads If you do you might consider growing your own My Is it easy First you soak the seeds in water overnight then you cover the bottom of a jar with the soaked seeds Rinse the seeds daily Remember to keep them in a dark place until they are almost ready to eat

| Exercise 4 |

Add the necessary punctuation.

What is a laser Most people have heard of lasers however, many don't actually know what a laser is and how it works Did you know that laser light is a pure beam of light It is also very powerful As a matter of fact, it can burn a hole in a coin in a matter of seconds Now, that's something The laser it was invented in 1960 is a device that can produce a pure and powerful beam of light The light from a laser is different from ordinary light in three main ways power concentration and purity Laser light contains light of only one color ordinary light is a mixture of many colors Since its invention, many uses have been found for lasers in a variety of areas medicine physics earth science astronomy engineering and manufacturing Lasers now have thousands of uses, including these treating cancer, measuring the speed of light, and finding the distance from the planets to the earth Imagine All this from an invention that was first thought to be useless

8. SPELLING

If you have problems with spelling, the improvement of your writing must begin with the improvement of your spelling. However, the problem of spelling will not improve by itself or with time; it must be worked on.

To begin with, use a dictionary to check the spelling of words that you are unsure about. Make a list of words that you have looked up and practice their spelling by visualizing them and by writing them over and over again.

This section starts with some commonly confused words. Add other words to this list that you get confused with. Look them up in the dictionary and write two sentences using each word. Also in this section are some useful rules which will help you to remember the spellings of words.

A. Confusing Word Pairs

Read the definitions and choose the correct word for each sentence.

1. **advice** / *noun*, an opinion given as to what to do
   advise / *verb*, to give advice to, counsel

   (a) My guidance counselor gave me some excellent _____ on

   how to choose a career.

   (b) Whether you want it or not, there's always someone ready to give

   you some _____ .

   (c) Imagine my surprise when the company president asked me to

   _____ him regarding our next advertising campaign.

   (d) I wouldn't _____ anyone to visit India during the

   rainy season.

2. **counsel** / *verb*, to advise; *noun*, advice; a lawyer in court
   council / *noun*, a group of people called together for discussion, an
   administrative or legislative body

   (a) Changing the school colors was discussed at our last student

   _____ meeting.

   (b) Everyone thinks I should become a psychiatrist because

   people are always asking me to _____ them when they have

   problems.

   (c) _____ for the defense successfully blocked the introduction

   of evidence concerning a past lawsuit.

   (d) Elections for the city _____ are next week and so far it looks

   like voter turnout will be low.

3. **affect** / *verb*, to influence
   effect / *noun*, result, impression

    (a) The sun's rays have a damaging _____ on the skin, which

    can cause premature aging and cancer.

    (b) Earthquakes _____ animals in ways that are still not

    completely understood.

    (c) The movie had an emotional _____ on the audience, which

    was clearly visible on their faces.

    (d) I am very grateful that fame does not _____ my best friend's

    kind and friendly personality.

4. **allusion** / an indirect reference
   illusion / a false impression

    (a) The speaker made an _____ to the protesters in the audience.

    (b) Krista made an _____ to her accident once but has never dis-

    cussed it with me.

    (c) On a hot day, the heat waves on the road will produce an

    _____ of a pool of water.

    (d) After reading the reviews, the director realized that his dream of

    receiving the Oscar for best director was only an _____ .

5. **illegible** / physically hard or impossible to read because of bad
                    writing or printing
   unreadable / too complicated, badly written, or uninteresting to read

    (a) My teacher's handwriting is so _____ that I can't read her

    comments on my compositions.

    (b) I took one look at the theories and formulas in my physics book

    and declared it _____ .

(c) When the Egyptian tomb was discovered, archaeologists were disappointed to find that most of the writing on the walls had deteriorated so much as to be _____ .

(d) Although this novel started out to be interesting, the plot became so confusing that it made the rest of the book _____ .

6. **certainly** / definitely, truly
   surely / expresses surprise, doubt

   (a) It is _____ a magnificent day for the beach.

   (b) _____ you're not thinking of missing the concert tomorrow night.

   (c) She is most _____ the right person for this job.

   (d) You wouldn't consider cancelling your trip, _____.

7. **compliment** / something said in praise
   complement / makes complete or perfects

   (a) I'll consider this raise a _____ on my work.

   (b) The colors in your blouse _____ the rest of your outfit.

   (c) Everyone was surprised when the candidate gave his rival a _____ on his speech.

   (d) The dessert is a _____ to the meal.

8. **infamous** / having a bad reputation, notorious
   unknown / not known

   (a) Although she had previously published three books, the author was _____ until her fourth book was a bestseller.

   (b) The crimes of mass murderers are so shocking that the criminals inevitably become _____ and can remain so for centuries.

(c) Paul was _____ among his friends for borrowing money and never paying it back.

(d) It's amazing that a year ago this popular presidential candidate was an _____ senator from a small eastern state.

9. **first** / before all others in a series of things or actions
at first / initial attitude or belief before a change

(a) _____ it was believed that the earth was at the center of the universe.

(b) She was considered, _____ , one of the suspects.

(c) I couldn't see the star _____ , but then I adjusted my telescope.

(d) _____ , sprinkle the seeds on top of the soil; then cover the seeds with about $1/2$ inch of soil and water thoroughly.

10. **disinterested** / impartial, indifferent
uninterested / not interested, bored

(a) Joel must have been _____ in the movie because he slept through most of it.

(b) Thanks for asking me to go to the game with you tomorrow, but the truth is that I'm totally _____ in football.

(c) It's been very difficult to find _____ people to serve on our panel of judges.

(d) An investigation of the congressman revealed that his work on the bill pertaining to offshore oil leases was not entirely _____ because he had substantial oil company stocks.

11. **principal** / first in rank, importance; the head of a school
    principle / a fundamental truth or law, a rule of conduct

    (a) He gave his _____ reason for being here as the desire to

    improve himself.

    (b) I met the _____ of the local high school and he appears very

    dedicated to improving the curriculum.

    (c) She explained the underlying _____ for her actions but it

    wasn't enough to avoid a reprimand.

    (d) My _____ place of residence is New York City, but I have a

    second home in Cape Cod.

12. **emigration** / leaving a country or region to settle in another
    immigration / coming into a new country to settle

    (a) Whenever the economy is unstable, people begin to call for limits

    on _____ into the country.

    (b) _____ from Ireland to America was at its height during the

    years of the Potato Famine.

    (c) The _____ of large numbers of professionals from Third

    World nations makes it difficult to maintain institutions in the

    countries they leave.

    (d) The _____ of farm workers to this area has been crucial to

    the success of our farming industry.

13. **exhausting** / very tiring
    exhaustive / thorough, leaving nothing out

    (a) An _____ investigation was concluded when the criminal

    was finally captured.

(b) Participation in the expedition was an _____ but rewarding experience.

(c) _____ tests and research were conducted to find the cause of the disease.

(d) After an _____ week at work, everyone is looking forward to the three-day holiday weekend.

14. **unsatisfied** / unfulfilled, not satisfied with the amount or quantity
dissatisfied / displeased, not satisfied

(a) The manager was so _____ with the rate of production that he called an early morning meeting with all the workers.

(b) In spite of a dozen new television shows this season, the viewing audience's need for stimulating entertainment remains _____

(c) I've eaten two candy bars and a bag of potato chips but my appetite for junk food is still _____ .

(d) If you're so _____ with the way Andre cuts your hair, why don't you go to another salon?

15. **moral** / good in conduct or character, having to do with right and wrong, lesson
morale / group spirit

(a) Everyone's _____ was lifted when the sun finally came out on the third day of our vacation.

(b) The _____ of the story is: Don't depend on others for your success.

(c) There's nothing worse than working in an office in which

_____ is bad, so our boss does everything she can to keep

the atmosphere pleasant.

(d) Many people want to do what is _____, but find it difficult to

resist the temptation to place their own needs first.

16. **historical** / concerned with history
historic / important in history

(a) The first flight of the space shuttle was an _____ event in the

U.S. space program.

(b) I like _____ books because I feel I'm learning something

while I'm being entertained.

(c) The president is planning a summit of world leaders that is

certain to be a _____ meeting.

(d) Shakespeare's _____ plays include *Julius Caesar* and

Henry V.

17. **device** / *noun*, something planned or constructed for a particular purpose
devise / *verb*, to plan, invent, arrange

(a) I'll try to _____ a way to get out of work early so we can

start out on our trip before dark.

(b) I need a _____ that will hold my books securely on the

shelves in the event of an earthquake.

(c) He was rewarded by the company for making a _____ that

reduced the machine's breakdown rate by more than half.

(d) Margaret must _____ a schedule that allows her to meet her

family's needs and still get her work done.

18. **misused** / improperly, incorrectly used
    disused / no longer used

    (a) An Apollo rocket engine, _____ since its last space mission, will be placed on exhibit at the Smithsonian Institute.

    (b) His recommendations for improvement of the program were _____ to shut the program down, causing the loss of many jobs.

    (c) New products, in particular, must come with clear directions so they will not be _____ by consumers.

    (d) My father's dream came true when he was able to buy a small, _____ ranch at a very low price.

19. **prophesy** / *verb*, predict
    prophecy / *noun*, a prediction

    (a) Jill has an amazing ability to _____ when we'll be given a surprise quiz.

    (b) It's starting to rain, so I guess your _____ about the weather was correct.

    (c) If I had only believed in your _____ , I wouldn't be in so much trouble right now.

    (d) I wish I could _____ the outcome of next week's election.

20. **ingenious** / clever
    ingenuous / frank, naïve

    (a) He was too _____ to suspect that his friends were taking advantage of him.

    (b) What I liked about her was that although she'd had some devastating experiences, she still maintained a certain _____ quality.

(c) Inventors rely on their _____ minds to come up with

new ideas.

(d) That was an _____ plan you had to keep Martha's birthday

party a surprise.

B. Useful Spelling Rules

▶ **The final _y_**

Rule 1: The final _y_ of a word changes to _i_ if it is preceded by a consonant
before any ending except -_ing:_

happy–happiness	copy–copies	try–tried
worry–worrying	try–trying	lady–ladies

Rule 2: The final _y_ is unchanged before any ending if it is preceded by
a vowel:

stay–staying	pay–paying	portray–portrayed

Exercise 1

Write the present and past participle of the following verbs:

1. reply   _____   _____
2. play   _____   _____
3. deny   _____   _____
4. annoy   _____   _____
5. qualify   _____   _____
6. bury   _____   _____
7. marry   _____   _____
8. destroy   _____   _____
9. supply   _____   _____
10. convey   _____   _____
11. fry   _____   _____
12. terrify   _____   _____

Add the endings given to the following words.

1. salty + ness   _____
2. glory + ous   _____
3. seventy + eth   _____
4. pay + able   _____
5. body + ly   _____
6. copy + er   _____
7. rely + able   _____
8. study + ous   _____
9. vary + ous   _____
10. enjoy + ment   _____
11. funny + est   _____
12. carry + er   _____

Rule 3: When adding the ending of the third person singular of the simple present tense or when making it plural

a. if the *y* is preceded by a consonant, change to *i* and add -*es*.

pay–pays	cry-cries	copy–copies

b. if the *y* is preceded by a vowel, it does not change. Just add *s*.

turkey–turkeys	body–bodies	baby–babies

Exercise 3

Give the third person singular of the simple present tense for the following verbs:

1. hurry _____   7. fly _____
2. play _____   8. worry _____
3. supply _____   9. study _____
4. dry _____   10. carry _____
5. employ_____   11. qualify _____
6. convey_____   12. display _____

Make the following words plural:

1. way _____ 7. monkey _____

2. victory _____ 8. laboratory _____

3. sympathy _____ 9. sky _____

4. valley _____ 10. folly _____

5. story _____ 11. story _____

6. supply _____ 12. toy _____

▶ The *i* before *e*

Rule 4: Write *i* before *e* except after *c* or when it is sounded as *a*.

brief	piece	receive	belief	ceiling

Exceptions:

either, neither, leisure, weird, seize

▶ Doubling Consonants

Rule 5: Words of one syllable ending in a consonant preceded by a single vowel, double the consonant before a suffix beginning with a vowel.

omit–omitted	rub–rubbed	ship–shipping

Exercise 5

Add the endings given to the following words:

1. trip + ed _____ 7. bet + ing _____

2. win + ing _____ 8. slam + ing _____

3. hot + er _____ 9. stop + ed _____

4. hum + ing _____ 10. wet + er _____

5. drop + ing _____ 11. rob + er _____

6. beg + ar _____ 12. big + est _____

Rule 6: Words of more than one syllable follow Rule 5, if the word is accented on the last syllable. Do not double the final consonant if the accent is not on the last syllable.

occur–occurred	begin–beginning (accent on last syllable)
profit–profited	benefit–benefited (accent not on last syllable)

Exercise 6

Add the endings given to the following words:

1. enter + ed _____
2. water + ed _____
3. offer + ed _____
4. murder + er _____
5. confer + ing _____
6. consider + ed _____

7. happen + ed _____
8. regret + ed _____
9. admit + ed _____
10. compel + ing _____
11. consider + ed _____
12. upset + ing _____

Rule 7: When a word ends in two consonants or a consonant preceded by two vowels, the consonant does not double before any suffix.

beat–beaten	fast–faster	long–longer

Exercise 7

Add the endings given to the following words:

1. wood + en _____
2. set + ing _____
3. root + ed _____
4. rot + ing _____
5. sweat + ing _____
6. bud + ing _____

7. slim + er _____
8. slip + ed _____
9. lean + est _____
10. harvest + ing _____
11. feed + ing _____
12. slam + ed _____

Rule 8: Words with one syllable and one vowel cannot end in *-c* alone, but must have *-ck*.

| music | panic | luck | sick | neck |

Words of one syllable with two vowels must have *k* only, not *ck*.

| beak | look | freak | seek |

Exercise 8

Add -c, -ck, or k to the following words:

1. toni + _____
2. sti + _____
3. tri + _____
4. ba + _____
5. too + _____
6. wre + _____
7. brea + _____
8. ro + _____
9. lo + _____
10. picni + _____
11. publi + _____
12. emphati + _____

Rule 9: Words with one syllable and one vowel end with the double consonants *-s, -f, -c, -l, -z*.

| bell | buzz | miss | fill |

Exceptions:

| bus | this | us | has | if |

Add the extra consonants where necessary to the following words:

1. stuf-	_____	7. bal-	_____
2. buz-	_____	8. peril-	_____
3. pil-	_____	9. stif-	_____
4. whiz-	_____	10. clif-	_____
5. rebel-	_____	11. jaz-	_____
6. mos-	_____	12. pul-	_____

Rule 10: Words with one syllable and one vowel do not end in a single -*l*. Words of one syllable and two vowels do not end in -*ll*.

well	travel	vowel	peel	pill

Add an extra -l where necessary to the following words:

1. seal-	_____	7. disposal-	_____
2. sil-	_____	8. appal-	_____
3. parallel-	_____	9. fulfil-	_____
4. formal	_____	10. repel-	_____
5. appeal-	_____	11. until	_____
6. casual-	_____	12. duel-	_____

Words with a Silent e

Rule 11: Words ending with a silent *e* drop the *e* when they add a suffix beginning with a vowel.

live–living	smile–smiling

Exceptions:

agreeing	seeing	guaranteeing	saleable

Add the endings indicated to the following words:

1. care + ing _____
2. arrive + al _____
3. rhyme + ing _____
4. continue + ing _____
5. tire + ing _____
6. dine + ing _____

7. noise + less _____
8. use + ful _____
9. hygiene + ic _____
10. love + ly _____
11. vote + ing _____
12. hope + less _____

Rule 12: Words that end in *-ce* and *-ge* keep the silent *e* when suffixes are added, except for suffixes beginning with *-e* or *-i*.

age–aging	ageless	change–changing	changeable

Exercise 12

Add the endings to the following words:

1. spice + y _____
2. replace + able _____
3. judge + ing _____
4. arrange + ment _____
5. manage + able _____
6. advantage + ous _____
7. engage + ing _____
8. peace + ful _____
9. service + able _____
10. trace + able _____
11. grace + ious _____
12. encourage + ment _____

Plurals

Rule 13: Most nouns form the plural by adding -*s*.

book–books	pen–pens

Words ending in -*s*, -*sh*, -*ch*, -*x*, or -*z* form the plural by adding -*es*. When the word does not end in the letter *e*, the plural -*es* is added.

dress–dresses	box–boxes	watch–watches

Words ending in -*y* and preceded by a consonant form the plural by changing the *y* to *i* and adding -*es*.

fly–flies	sky–skies

Words ending in -*f* or -*fe* form the plural by adding -*s*, or by changing the -*f* to -*ve* before the plural ending.

thief–thieves	roof–roofs

There is no rule and both types of endings are common.

The plural of words ending in -*o* preceded by a vowel is formed by adding -*s*. The plural of words ending in -*o* preceded by a consonant is formed by adding -*s* or -*es*.

-*o* preceded by a vowel:	ratio–ratios	studio–studios
-*o* preceded by a consonant:	potato–potatoes	cargo–cargos

Exceptions:

Musical terms ending in -*o* form the plural by adding -*s*: piano-pianos, solo-solos

Some words have irregular plurals:

child–children	goose–geese	mouse–mice
tooth–teeth	woman–women	man–men
	foot–feet	

Some words have the same form in the singular and plural form.

deer	trout	sheep	Chinese species

Words borrowed from Greek, Latin, and French keep the plural form of the original language.

basis–bases	datum–data	medium–media
phenomenon–phenomena	alumnus–alumni	analysis–analyses

Exercise 13

Make the following words plural:

1. hero   _____   7. fox   _____

2. self   _____   8. company   _____

3. success   _____   9. eighty   _____

4. photo   _____   10. tornado   _____

5. index   _____   11. gulf   _____

6. reef   _____   12. approach   _____